AUSTIN FRIARS

N.V. VAN DE GARDE & CO'S DRUKKERIJ, ZALTBOMMEL

AUSTIN FRIARS

History of the
Dutch Reformed Church
in London
1550 — 1950

BY

J. LINDEBOOM

Theol. Dr., Professor of Church History in the University of Groningen

Translation from the Dutch

by

D. DE IONGH

Deacon of Austin Friars

WITH 6 PLATES

THE HAGUE
MARTINUS NIJHOFF
1950

PRINTED IN THE NETHERLANDS

CONTENTS

INTRODUCTION . . . .   IX–XII

Chapter I

FOUNDING AND SUBSEQUENT DIFFICULTIES. THE
FIRST YEARS OF THE COMMUNITY   1–28

Dutch refugees in England: 1–3; Joh. à Lasco and
Utenhove: 3–7; the Charter of King Edward VI: 7–10;
Austin Friars: 11–14; the books of instruction and the
service books of the Community: 15–17; Utenhove's
rhymed version of the Psalms: 17–18; First difficulties,
Queen Mary: 19–20; wanderings by the Community:
21–22; Emden: 23–24; church officials and liturgy:
24–28.

Chapter II

INTERNAL AND EXTERNAL STRENGTH. SAFEGUARD-
ING OF DOCTRINE   29–60

Return and restoration of the Community: 29–31; changed position: 31–33; support to the Church in the home
country: 33–37; maintenance of doctrine: 37–39; the
affair Velsius: 39–41; the affair Van Haemstede: 41–45;
the affair Van Winghen: 46–51; action against unsound
doctrines: 51–53; diminishing insistence on doctrine:
53-57; opposition against the putting to death of heretics:
57–58; training of ministers: 59–60.

Chapter III

MAINTENANCE OF MORAL DISCIPLINE. PHILANTHROP-
IC AND SOCIAL ACTIVITIES   61–87

Need for moral discipline: 61–63; extensive measures
towards this end: 64–68; the moral condition of the
Community: 69–71; social-pastoral care of the Community: 72–77; help for persecuted Protestants on the Continent: 78–81; changing needs: 82–83; care of the poor
by the deacons: 83–85; measures for assisting theological
students: 85–87.

Chapter IV

THE RELATIONS WITH OTHER REFORMED CHURCHES
IN THE LOW COUNTRIES AND IN ENGLAND   88–116
Initial great importance, subsequently diminishing for
the Churches in the Netherlands: 88–91; difficulties in the
domain of organization, opposition on the part of England: 91–93; the Synod of Dordrecht: 94–96; lasting personal contacts:96–97;relations with the French Community, claims by them on the church building: 98–101; all
the same good relations: 101–103; other Dutch Reformed
Communities in England; 104–108; later settlements,
Hatfield Chase: 108–111; the Colloquia, initial thriving,
subsequent decay: 111–116.

Chapter V

THE RELATION TO CHURCH AND STATE. THE STRUG-
GLE WITH ARCHBISHOP LAUD 117–149
Political relations, opposition on the part of population
and guilds, protection by the government: 117–120;
unaccommodating attitude of James I, imposition of
fine: 121–125; involved in the struggle between King and
Parliament, favourable conditions during the Commonwealth: 125–127; relations with the ecclesiastical authorities, judicious attitude towards the State Church: 127–
130; the relations with the superintendents: 130–133;
anti-puritanical tendencies: 133–136; Archbishop Laud:
136–141; opposition by the Dutch-French synod: 141–
145; Laud's stubborness, his fall, relief for the Community: 145–149.

Chapter VI

THE COMMUNITY IN THE 17TH AND 18TH CENTURIES 150–173
Dangers from Puritanism and Independentism during
the Commonwealth: 150–153; the Restoration and the
Glorious Revolution: 153–154; internal difficulties: the
Rev. Van Cuilemborgh, the Rev. Ten Harmsen: 154–159;
harmonious relations within the Consistory: 160–161;
the Rev. Ruytinck, relations with Duraeus: 162–165;
increasing liberty in religious teaching, process of
secularization: 165–166; the Community languishes:
167–168; tale of woe of the organ: 168–169; the library
and the archives, Hessels's Archivum: 169–173.

Chapter VII

THE VICISSITUDES OF THE CHURCH BUILDING. THE
COMMUNITY IN THE 19TH AND 20TH CENTURIES . . 174–197

Description of the church and its interior, difficulties
in connection with the tower: 174–176; acquisition of
the churchyard: 176–178; difficulties with tenants and
neighbours: 178–179; the fire of 1862: 180–181; the
Community's properties and their management: 181–
183; growing prestige, relation to the Netherlands Royal
House: 183–184; the Rev. Adama van Scheltema,
unorthodox orientation of the Community: 186–187; the
Rev. Baart de la Faille, social activities; 187–189; the
Rev. Van Dorp, the second world war: 189–191; the
destruction of the church building: 191–193; possibilities
for the future, relations with South Africa: 193–197.

APPENDICES

    I. The Charter of King Edward VI 198–200
       Translation of the same 200–203
    II. List of the ministers of the Church 204–205
INDEX 206–208

LIST OF THE PICTURES

    I. Facsimile of the Charter.   7
    II. Austin Friars and its surroundings in the
       16th century.   11
    III. Western front and entrance of the old church.   14
    IV. The interior of the old church about the mid-
       dle of the 19th century.   104
    V. The interior of the restored old church.. . .   181
    VI. The interior of the church of St. Mary.. . .   191

INTRODUCTION

To anyone at all acquainted with the place which the Dutch Reformed Church in London has occupied during the centuries, it will not cause surprise to hear that I hesitated for a moment before accepting the invitation from its Council to relate the history of the Church on the occasion of its four hundredth anniversary. Not much time was left, and the material was voluminous. Only few church communities possess such a wealth of written documents bearing on their past history, or have been the centre to the same extent of so many varied activities. However, there were considerations on the other side, which made me decide to undertake the work. The extensive archives of the Church are well arranged and well preserved. The most important part, the voluminous correspondence, consisting mainly of letters addressed to the Church Council, has been made available, in a highly meritorious manner, by J. H. Hessels' publication: "Ecclesiae LondinoBatavae Archivum". Only a small part of the — often very detailed — minutes of the Council meetings has been published, but these publications by Dr. A. Kuyper and Dr. A. A. van Schelven cover two very important periods in the history of the Church. In addition, there are the publications of the Marnix Society, viz. Ruytinck's "Gheschiedenissen" (History) and its sequels, and the Acta of the Colloquia of the Dutch church communities in England. Finally, there are the monographs on the initial years of the Community and its most prominent figures, of which we will only recall here the excellent works by Pijper with his "Jan Utenhove" and by Van Schelven with his "De Nederlandsche Vluchtelingenkerken" (the Dutch Refugee churches). It is unnecessary for me to acknowledge how all this material has facilitated my task and the grateful use I have made of it.

Meanwhile I remained faced with the difficulty inherent in the extensive volume of the material. The three heavy quarto tomes of the "Archivum" with their more than 4400 letters and documents, contain almost inexhaustible material. The contents of Ruytinck's history and of the acts of the Colloquia are important. So are the 10 minute books (Acts), of which the first three have been published, though it should be observed that the seven later books are of less importance than those published. I should mention that I have in no way exhausted all available sources, nor have I drawn on all the available material such as Acts of the Coetus, accounts, registers of members, property records, etc. Neither have I included in my examination the numerous files with accounts and statements of receipts and expenditure. Time was lacking; moreover, such labour would have led me astray from the aim which both the Church Council and I had in view.

The method of treatment and arrangement of the material presented another difficulty. I have abstained from adopting a strictly chronological method. It would have resulted in a rather incoherent summary which could only have been made moderately acceptable by continuous repetitions, in themselves unnecessary. Instead of such a horizontal method of treatment I could have chosen a vertical method, proceeding systematically according to particular subjects, each one treated in chronological order. However, this might have spoilt the historical continuity of the whole. I therefore decided on a combination of the two methods. The first chapter: foundation, the first years, called inevitably for chronological treatment. In the second chapter I passed to a more systematic treatment of doctrine, differences on doctrinal questions, and church discipline, especially during the first decades of the life of the Church. The third chapter which treats of moral discipline leading to Poor Relief, social and philanthropic activities, links up with the second. The fourth chapter deals with the relations with other Reformed churches, first of all with those in the home country and then with those in England: the French and the Dutch. The relations with the political and ecclesiastical powers in England form the subject of the next chapter in which the difficulties experienced during the reigns of James I and Charles I called for rather more extensive treatment. In a sixth and a seventh chapter, covering respectively the 17th/18th and 19th/20th centuries, I have returned to the more chronological treatment followed in the beginning.

In the notes I have accounted for my facts and statements.

The notes are fairly numerous, but I have guarded against transferring part of the text to the notes. They do not contribute to the account of the events, nor do they contain any special information. They can be left unread by anyone not specially interested. I have not wished to follow the bad habit of relegating the documentation of the facts in a work intended as a historical study, to an appendix. The titles of works quoted are only given in full the first time. I have made an exception in the case of sources to which repeated reference is made. In these cases the titles have been very much abbreviated. They are:

Ecclesiae Londino-Batavae Archivum. Tomus secundus. Epistulae et tractatus cum Reformationis tum Ecclesiae Londino-Batavae Historiam illustrantes (1544–1622). Edidit Joannes Henricus Hessels, Cantabrigiae 1889.

Id. Tomus tertii Pars prima [without the dates], Cantabrigiae 1897.

Id. Tomus tertii Pars secunda, Cantabrigiae 1897. These are referred to subsequently as: *Archivum*, II, III[I] and III[II].

Acten van de Colloquia der Nederlandsche gemeenten in England, 1575–1609 (Acts, i.e. minutes, of the Colloquia of the Dutch church communities in England, 1575–1609), edited by J. J. van Toorenenbergen, with appendix: Uittreksels uit de Acten der volgende Colloquia (Extracts from the Acts of the following Colloquia); in the publications of the Marnix Society, Series II, Part I, Utrecht 1872 — referred to as *Colloquia*.

Gheschiedenissen ende Handelingen die voornemelick aengaen De Nederduytsche Natie ende gemeynten wonende in Engelant ende int bijzonder tot Londen, vergadert door Symeon Ruytinck, Caesar Calandrinus ende Aemilius van Culenborgh, Dienaren des Godlicken Woords (Histories and Acts concerning mainly the Dutch settlements and Church communities in England, more especially the one in London, compiled by Symeon Ruytinck, Caesar Calandrinus and Aemilius van Culenborgh, Ministers of the Word of God), edited by J. J. van Toorenenbergen; in the publications of the Marnix Society, Series III, Part I, Utrecht 1873 — referred to as: Ruytinck, *Gheschiedenissen*.

Kerkeraads-protocollen der Hollandsche Gemeente te Londen, 1569–1571 (Resolutions of the Council of the Dutch Church in London, 1569–1571), edited by Dr. A. Kuyper; in the publications of the Marnix Society, Series I, Part I, Utrecht 1870 — referred to as: *Kerkeraads-protocollen 1569–1571*.

Kerkeraads-protocollen der Nederlandsche Vluchtelingen-Kerk te Londen, 1560–1563 (Resolutions of the Council of the Dutch Refugee Church in London, 1560–1563), edited by Dr. A. A. van Schelven; in the publications of the Historisch Genootschap (Historical Society), established in Utrecht; third series, No. 43, Amsterdam 1921 — referred to as: *Kerkeraads-protocollen 1560–1563*.

The other Acta (minutes) volumes have been indicated by me with the number under which they appear (partly) in the archives of the Church, i.e. *Acta* with the numbers IV–X, being part IV: Nov. 11, 1571 — Aug. 31, 1572; V: Sept. 4, 1572 — July 16, 1573, and June 26, 1578—Sept. 20, 1585; VI: July 16, 1573—June 5, 1575; VII: 1609—1632; VIII: 1632—1670; IX: 1671—1814; X: 1815—1901 (continued by the Trustees — 1923).

The consultation by me of these and other sources would not have been possible if the Church Council, following in this an old tradition (see page 172), had not enabled me to have access to them in Groningen, for which purpose the University Library extended its hospitality. I am greatly indebted to the Library for this and for the ready help received from its staff. I express my thanks to the Church Council and not least to its Chairman, the Reverend R. H. van Apeldoorn, for their unstinted co-operation and for the way in which they have given me a free hand in the writing of this work. Further, I thank the sexton of the Church, Mr. J. Rus, who has now filled this post for nearly 50 years, for his help in enabling me to consult the archives — a most essential help, because the present conditions of storage (fortunately only temporary) of the valuable records constitute a considerable handicap. A few of the records, actually not of very great importance, I have not been able to consult.

This work has been rendered into English by Mr. D. de Iongh, Deacon of Austin Friars, to whom I here tender my gratitude; in particular for the painstaking care he bestowed on the translation as well as for the pleasant way in which the translator has collaborated with the author.

No one can be more conscious than I am of the fact that the historical treasures in the possession of the Dutch Church in London, equally important to the history of the Netherlands as to its own history, are not exhausted by the History here offered. But I do think that what follows gives in a harmonious and balanced whole a picture of this Church Community which in the past was honoured as "Mother of all Reformed Dutch churches" and which is borne to-day by the interest, the grateful memory and the piety of many.

Groningen, December, 1949.   L.

CHAPTER I

FOUNDING AND SUBSEQUENT DIFFICULTIES
THE FIRST YEARS OF THE COMMUNITY

Land surfaces divide, seas unite — this paradoxical truth, borne out by history at so many points, also finds its substantiation in the relations between England and the Continent. The sea pre-eminently creates opportunities for large scale intercourse and transport. Presently, the particular occasions, which lead to the realization of these possibilities, arise, the mutual economic needs, the commercial spirit of adjacent peoples, their more or less aggressive imperialism, the striving after religious liberty, furthered — be it unintentionally — as well as thwarted, by intolerant governments. All these factors have contributed, now separately, now combined, towards the establishment, during the centuries, of active relations between England and the near part of the Continent, France and the Low Countries. They also led to settlement in the country overseas, the generally higher cultural standards on the Continent making for a larger influx of pioneers into England than in the reverse direction. We may pass over the developments in this respect in the Middle Ages [1]. That they were already significant at the beginning of the period with which this history deals, may be gathered from the preamble of a law of 1540: "the King, our most dread Sovereign Lord, calling unto his blessed remembrance the infinite number of strangers and aliens of foreign countries and nations which daily do increase and multiply, etc." [2]

---

[1] A short survey in W. J. C. Moens, *The marriage, baptismal and burial Registers, 1571–1874, and Monumental Inscriptions of the Dutch Reformed Church, Austin Friars, London,* Lymington 1884, p. IX fl.

[2] John Southerden Burn, *The history of the French, Walloon, Dutch and other Foreign Protestant Refugees, settled in England, from the reign of Henry VIII to the Revocation of the Edict of Nantes, etc.,* London 1846, p. 2. — An account of the commercial relations between England and the Low Countries in Ruytinck, *Gheschiedenissen,* pp. 1–7.

Lindeboom   1

The emigration from the Low Countries must have received a powerful stimulus round about 1544 as a result of the intensified and more and more systematized religious persecutions, coupled with an ever more threatening encroachment upon civil rights and liberties. Charles V, the Habsburg emperor, king and lord, had got his hands free, and he applied himself with determination to the rooting out of heresy in the lands over which he ruled, even if it had to be at the cost of abolishing existing privileges. We must not imagine, however, that the England of those days gave the impression of being an asylum which offered unlimited freedom of faith and conscience, as we understand it today. King Henry VIII might have broken with Rome, yet his Anglican Church in no way offered a free shelter for Reformation doctrines. The supremacy of the Pope was no longer acknowledged, the dissolution of the monasteries had yielded considerable gains, the aspirations of his private life had been satisfied, but the King did not wish for further radical changes, especially not in the domain of church doctrine. The "Bloody Statute" of the six articles of 1539 was anything but Protestant, The remark by Luther to the effect that the King was quite prepared to kill the Pope's body, but that he preserved his soul — his doctrine — was well founded. With the King it was more especially motives of an economic character, which moved him to make use of the craftmanship and trade of the foreigners, by admitting them as residents into his country, just as in the political sphere he sought, from purely opportunist motives, to join the Protestant Schmalcaldic Union in Germany. What the refugees hoped to find in England was, therefore, probably more conditions of life which did not encroach too much on their liberties. Yet we may take it that the Protestant currents in England — obstructed but never entirely suppressed — which lived in its people, did lend a certain attraction to the prospect of settling there. We should bear in mind in this connection the growing volume, at that time, of the imports of English translations of Reformation literature, printed in Antwerp and elsewhere. It is by these channels that the translation of the Bible by William Tyndale reached England [1].

The somewhat unstable course in religious matters and church affairs, which had been pursued under Henry VIII, was replaced

---

[1] See M. E. Kronenberg, *Verboden boeken en opstandige drukkers in de Hervormingstijd*, Amsterdam 1948, p. 97–110.

by one having greater stability, when his ten-year old son, Edward VI, succeeded him in 1547. The regent, the King's uncle the Duke of Somerset, and Cranmer, Archbishop of Canterbury (only little persuasion was needed to make him change his course), took the further development of the Reformation in hand in a definitely evangelical sense, a Reformation bearing in an increasing manner the Swiss-Calvinistic stamp, even though in the liturgy of the Book of Common Prayer, an Anglican-Catholic element remained for ever preserved. Foreign theologians were invited to give the lead to the revision of doctrine and church order. Petrus Martyr Vermiglio and Martin Bucer became professors of divinity in Oxford and Cambridge respectively (at a salary of not less than £ 100), Bernardino Ochino became a canon of Canterbury, with dispensation of residence. Also the Polish nobleman Johannes à Lasco came over from East Friesland. It was not for nothing that the English reformer and subsequent martyr, Hugh Latimer, had said in a sermon delivered before Edward VI: "I could wish that we could collect together such valuable persons in this kingdom; it would be the means of ensuring its prosperity" [1]. For even in this matter we may not close our eyes to the matter of fact considerations which contributed to the favourable reception, which the foreigners found in England. The industries which they established in the country — which in this respect was still very backward — made for prosperity. Southerden Burn mentions amongst the industries which were brought over by the immigrants from the Low Countries, the manufacture of gloves, leather goods, hats, pins and textiles, the growing of vegetables, dyeing and land drainage. After 1567, when the foreigners settled in Norwich, production there rose immediately to a value of £ 100.000 [2].

There is abundant reason for looking more closely at à Lasco, because of his significance for the happenings to be related here [3]. Born about 1499, and originally destined for the priesthood, he came, during his study travels through Western Europe, in touch with humanistic and reformatory personalities, especially Erasmus has meant much to him. Yet it was not until 1540 that

---

[1]) Burn, *History of the Refugees*, p. 2.
[2]) *Ibid.*, p. 253–263.
[3]) See for a description of à Lasco's life the article à Lasco in *Biographisch Woordenbork van Protestantsche Godgeleerden in Nederland*, Volume V, The Hague 1943, p. 592–615, with extensive references to sources.

he abandoned the intended career of a statesman and prince of the church, and identified himself with the Reformation. He found an asylum in East Friesland, where the widowed countess Anna readily made use of his learning and organizational talents by appointing him in 1543 Superintendent of all churches in her country. Apart from his acting as Superintendent — the office being an embodiment of the Lutheran principle that the supreme leadership and supervision in church matters should be vested in the temporal authorities — he organized the church in a Protestant spirit, be it only to a moderate degree. His activities in this sphere lasted until 1548, when the countess, for political reasons, joined the peace movement of the Leipzig Interim, which aimed at an accord between the Roman and the non-Roman elements, however with such a preponderance of the Roman element, that it was wholly unacceptable to a man of his views. He accepted an invitation from Cranmer to assist him in the organization of the English State Church. Passing through Holland, Brabant and Calais, à Lasco journeyed to London where he stayed from 1548 until 1549 with Cranmer at Lambeth Palace. That the services which he rendered were appreciated, may be gathered from a gift of £ 50 awarded him by the Privy Council. No longer finding a sphere of action in East Friesland, à Lasco gave ear in 1550 to repeated invitations from England to settle there. He arrived on the 13th May of that year, and wrote a week later to Maarten Micron, who later became minister of the Dutch Church, and to Heinz Bullinger in Zürich, that there were plans for establishing a German Church, "ecclesia germana", with himself as Superintendent [1]. Shortly afterwards he was naturalized, with his wife and children [2]. He lived in Bow Lane where later his wife died. He married again shortly afterwards. The building of a house for him in the grounds of Austin Friars was in preparation.

In 1550 à Lasco became the recognized leader of all the foreigners, that is of those originating from the Low Countries, France, Italy and Spain. How it came about that from this medley of foreigners a Dutch congregation emerged, is a development

---

[1] German was a term which was applied to the inhabitants of the Northern Netherlands, Brabant and Flanders, and to all Low German speaking peoples.

[2] We must not attach to this transition to the state of "denison" the significance attached to our term "naturalization".

which it is extremely difficult to envisage with any degree of accuracy [1]. It may be taken for granted that the Dutch in London, possibly as early as 1547, held services in an Anglican parish, the church building having been placed at their disposal. In 1549 the "Germani" had their own congregation with preachers. They met in a church belonging to the French. An estimate of that year puts their number at from four to five thousand, no doubt too high a figure, considering that the population of London was below 100,000. Six to eight hundred is probably nearer the mark [2]. In any case they acted in close contract with the French speaking foreigners, the latter probably preferring to keep somewhat in the background on account of the state of war which existed between England and France. As regards the origin of the refugees we may safely assume that the majority were South Netherlanders. As late as 1575, the "Classis" of Walcheren wrote: "we do know that the greater part of your members do not originate from Holland (i.e. the provinces of South & North Holland) and Zeeland" [3]. In the early years this will have been the case to an even greater extent. We must not picture this Dutch Church Community to ourselves as being in any way highly organized. Certainly, the Community had tried to get a permanent minister, but it was not until a report dated June 29th, 1550, that it transpires that the Fleming Maarten Micron "inter privatos parietes" acted as preacher [4] — from which description, "within the walls of a private house", we may conclude that these gatherings were not as yet formal church services. It is not to be wondered at that efforts were being made, with the aid of those in authority, to find a proper place in which to hold these meetings.

Pijper has expressed the opinion that à Lasco may not have participated in the initial efforts to obtain a church building, seeing that neither he nor Utenhove are mentioned in the account which Ruytinck has subsequently given of the royal

---

[1] What follows has mainly been based on the very plausible reconstruction by Dr A. A. van Schelven, *De Nederduitsche vluchtelingenkerken der XVIe eeuw in Engeland en Duitschland en hunne beteekenis voor de Reformatie in de Nederlanden,* 's Gravenhage, 1909, pp. 59–64.

[2] On the subject of these figures see F. Pijper, *Jan Utenhove, His life and works,* Leiden 1883, page 57 et seq. The figure 600–800 given there appears to me to be more acceptable than van Schelven's estimate of over 500 (p. 69).

[3] *Archivum,* II, p. 514.

[4] Pijper, *Utenhove,* Appendix, p. LXVIII (letter from Utenhove to Bullinger).

favour [1]. We read there how a certain Francisco Berti with the Duchess of Suffolk, "a diligent and God-fearing woman", had been discussing the difficult circumstances of the foreigners, how she mentioned the matter to "doctor Cooke and Mr. Cheeke, the King's tutors", and how further, through their intervention, "Mr. Armigall Wayd and Mr. Hunnings, the one being Clerk of the Council, the other of the Privy Seal", acting on behalf of the King, placed the former church of the Augustine Friars at the disposal of the pastors Maarten Micron and Wouter Delenus [2]. Van Schelven has placed this transfer in the early spring of 1550. We already saw that à Lasco arrived a few months later. According to Ruytinck he made a statement to the effect that the transfer, which bore as yet a somewhat provisional character, would be confirmed and officially ratified. This was done by the famous Charter, dated July 24th, 1550. On the preceding 29th June the young King had noted in his diary: "It was appointed that the Germans should have the Austin Friars for their church to have their service and for avoiding of all sects of Anabaptists and such like" [3].

Before we occupy ourselves more closely with the Charter it may be useful to call attention to Jan Utenhove [4], the man, who is referred to by Ruytinck as à Lasco's principal co-worker in this matter and whose name is connected in the closest way with the coming into being of the London Community. He was born in Ghent, of a well established family, and had studied at Louvain University. His family was one of those which, on account of the religious persecutions, fled in 1544 to Aachen where they founded a Walloon community. From his contact with prominent figures of the Reformation he acquired a theological background. In 1548 he crossed to England where he associated

---

[1] *Ibid.*, p. 62.

[2] Ruytinck, *Gheschiedenissen*, p. 12.

[3] Burn, *History of the Refugees*, p. 186. There is in the possession of the English Presbyterian Church a large painting representing King Edward VI handing over the Charter. The King is surrounded by a number of contemporary figures of the Reformation. According to an article in *The Journal of the Presbyterian Historical Society of England*, May 1914, this painting dates, according to the unanimous and independent judgment of a number of experts, from the first half of the 17th century. The portrait of the King appears to have been copied from an older painting by Will. Stretes, a Dutch painter in the service of Edward VI which represented the bestowal of a similar royal favour. The likenesses of à Lasco and Knox (his inclusion in the picture is not correct) are taken from *Icones* by Theod. Baza.

[4] See the work already mentioned, by F. Pijper, *Jan Utenhove, etc.*

Plate I

Facsimile of the Charter

with Cranmer. In Canterbury he assisted in the founding of a
Walloon community. His first stay in England only lasted a
short time. Having returned to the Continent, he again met
prominent personalities connected with the Reformation, i.e.
in Zürich Bullinger, in Geneva Calvin, in Strassburg à Lasco,
who was then staying there. In the autumn of 1549 he returned
to England, but he deemed it advisable to make Canterbury no
longer his place of residence. The restive state of the country at
that time may well have influenced his decision. There was
much opposition among the people to the course pursued by
Somerset and Cranmer, the nobility and the higher clergy.
Somerset even fell into disgrace at Court. Utenhove went to
London and there he has helped from the start to bring the
foreign Church Community into being, more particularly the
Community consisting of "Nether Germans" or "Netherlanders",
he himself acting as one of the first elders. We will often meet
him in this capacity and in his labours in drawing up a form of
public worship. Perhaps we should, at this stage, give an indication of the theological standpoint of Jan Utenhove. It was
pronouncedly Reformed, not Lutheran, and as regards the doctrine of Communion — an important shibboleth in those days —
orientated more towards the Zwinglian-symbolic than towards
the Calvinistic-realistic conception.

Let us now consider the Charter, the pivot on which the
existence of the Dutch congregation in London revolves [1]. We
cannot convey better what constituted the principal features of
the Charter, to the foreigners who were its recipients, than by
quoting the words of the same Utenhove in the letter which he
wrote about it to Calvin [2]: "We have been granted certain things
which we had not expected, yes, we have actually been given
more than we had asked for. In the first place we have the joint
use of the church of the Augustine friars, to which the King has
given the name of Temple of Jesus [3]. It has been presented to
both nations [4]. It is being repaired at the King's personal expense.

---

[1] It has often been reproduced in print, in the original Latin, and in translation.
In Latin, amongst other publications in *Archivum*, III[1], pages 4–7, in a translation
in Ruytinck, *Gheschiedenissen*, pp. 12–16.

[2] In Calvini *Opera*, Vol. XIII (*Corp. Reform.*, Vol. XLI), Brunsv. 1875, col. 628
et seq.

[3] In the stained glass window in what became the deacons' room, the name
"templum Jesu" remained preserved up to the time of the destruction in 1940.

[4] That is the French-Walloon and the Dutch.

The unadulterated Word may be proclaimed in it and the sacraments administered as instituted by Christ the Lord without any 'superstitie'. We are also permitted to exercise church discipline in accordance with God's Word. Further, and for this we had not asked, we have nothing to do with the Bishops, not even with the Bishop of London. They have taken this in very bad part. Yes, the Bishop of London and the other Bishops and the Archbishops of the realm, the Mayor, the sheriffs and alder-men of London, are enjoined and strictly commanded not in any way to interfere with our churches, but to leave it to us to act and organize matters in our way, even if we deviate in our ceremonies and church customs from the Anglican. The King has appointed four ministers of the Word: two in the Walloon Church, namely Richardus Vauvilius and Franciscus Rivius [1] and two in the Dutch, Martinus Micronius and someone else [2]. Super-intendent, as it is called here, or supervisor on behalf of the King, will be Mr. à Lasco, who is the head of both churches. The election of ministers, elders and deacons rests entirely with the congregations, but the elected minister, as also the superinten-dent, must be submitted to the King for confirmation. This is the main substance of the royal, really authentic letter which we possess. It is certainly no small thing that we are free from the yoke of the Bishops and for that may the Lord be praised eternally. Amen''.

It is not without good reason that his letter, which undoubtedly reflects the standpoint of the foreigners, stresses with such emphasis the autonomy of the congregations with regard to the State Church and its Bishops. For, contrasted with the episcopal system of the Anglican Church, the foreign church communities with their presbyterian organization of minister, elders (presby-ters) and deacons, designated (more or less) by the members themselves, constituted an exceptional case. If the Church of England was, so to say, ruled from above downward, with the royal authority at the top, in hierarchical relationship, the new communities, just as the Reformed churches on the Continent, were administered from below upwards, and the authority of the dignitaries and the higher councils rested really on the will and on the expressed views of the bulk of the believers. One might

---

[1] They had both been monks.
[2] Viz. Gualterus Delenus (Wouter Delen).

call this form of government democratic, in contrast to the aristocratic mode of government of the State Church with its bishops, provided one bears in mind that this relative democracy was a very different thing from what we understand today by the word. This, the most important difference between the two forms of church organization, both for those days and for subsequent periods, deserves special consideration. The one feature in which the self-governing aspect was somewhat restricted was the function of the superintendent, which may be regarded as a small Anglican reservation, in this form an entirely acceptable one. Another reservation might be found in the phrase: "super-intendens et ministri (i.e. superintendent and ministers) sint et erunt unum corpus corporatum et politicum". The closing words point sufficiently clearly, and in an entirely satisfactory manner, to the autonomous character of the organization, but it is certainly striking that it is not the Community, with all the church dignitaries, but only the superintendent with the ministers (therefore from the top), which constitute and will continue to constitute that one "corpus corporatum et politicum". There has been much to do subsequently on this question of complete or partial autonomy.

There is another reason why the Charter is remarkable. The opening words speak of the motives which have moved the King to grant it. In his capacity as "Christian ruler", "defender of the faith", he considers it his duty to succour those who, on account of their religion, are oppressed, expelled and banished. But, in fact, there was a second motive. One side of it transpires clearly from the words taken from the King's diary quoted above: "for avoiding of all sects of Anabaptists and such like". Evangelical refugees, Calvinists and Lutherans, could be appreciated as broth-ers and sisters in the Faith. But amongst those who had severed their ties with the Roman Church were also to be found the spiritual sectarians, the "Täufer", those who in their opposition to an organization imposed from above, rejected all authority and restraint in church and sometimes even in state matters, revolutionary spirits whose extreme individualism was as yet completely unacceptable in the closed, static church- and state structures of those days. And even though the actual Anabap-tists had dispersed after the collapse of their holy Sion in Mün-ster, the name continued to inspire a holy fear of subversive efforts towards a complete revolution of church, political, and social life. Such things could be expected of refugees from the Continent (Anabaptists had actually come to England) but a dependable, well regulated body such as the French and Dutch communities, actually constituted a counterweight against such tendencies. In addition — and this touches the other side of the King's intention — Edward VI, under the influence of his counsellors, was by no means disinclined to continue along the road of the Reformation in the spirit of the Reformed foreigners. This did not mean that he wanted to become completely unfaithful to the Anglican spirit. A well-ordered religious Church Community, which was founded on a biblical, apostolic basis, could serve as an example and assist in expelling the last remnants of papal influence.

The gift and its confirmation did not yet mean that the communities immediately had the unrestricted use of the church. To begin with, there were a lot of repairs to be done, and the Lord Treasurer did not consider it commensurate with the dignity of the King to hand over the building in an unworthy condition [1]. There was more behind this zeal, namely the attitude of opposition on the part of the Bishops, especially of Ridley, the Bishop of London, so that the Lord Treasurer even went so far as to insist, in a communication to à Lasco, that the foreigners should adopt the English ceremonial or that, otherwise, they should demonstrate from God's Word that this ceremonial was wrong. It was not until the 17th December of that year, 1550, that this wrecking opposition was overcome [2]. Actually there was at first considerable doubt as to whether the matter would ever be righted. Meanwhile the congregation had recourse to another place of worship. So numerous were the people who attended these services that the authorities placed a second church at the disposal of the refugees. In future the French would worship in the chapel of the St. Anthony Hospital in Threadneedle Street, the use of which had been granted them by the Chapter of Windsor, whereas the Temple of Jesus remained reserved for the exclusive use of the Dutch. The latter contributed towards the restoration of the French chapel. We need not

---

[1]) See Van Schelven, *De Vluchtelingenkerken*, p. 69 et seq.
[2]) M. Woudstra. *De Hollandsche Vreemdelingengemeente te Londen gedurende de eerste jaren van haar bestaan*, Groningen 1908, p. 20.

Plate II

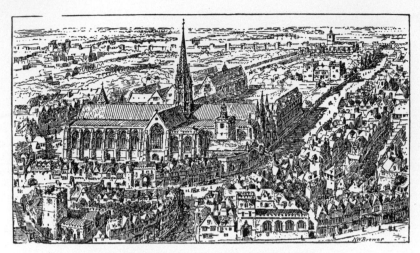

OLD BROAD STREET AND AUSTIN FRIARS, LONDON

Austin Friars and its surroundings in the 16th century

occupy ourselves further with the fate of the French congregation [1].

The time has arrived for looking more closely at the valuable gift of the church in Austin Friars which the Boy-King had intended for use by the foreigners, actually only the nave and the aisles, therefore excluding the choir and the transepts [2]. The Augustine (mendicant) Friars, Friar Hermits of the Order of St. Augustine — not to be confused with the Augustine Canons, who had their monastery in Aldgate — had come to Britain in 1252, settling at first in Wales. Their London settlement was founded in 1253 by Humphrey de Bohun, earl of Hertford and Essex, Constable of England, after his return from his crusade, "to the honour of God and His blessed Mother, ever Virgin, and for the health of the souls of himself, his ancestors and his descendants". His descendant, Humphrey de Bohun, reconstructed the church in 1354. The spire was blown down in a storm. It was replaced eight years later. It was this new spire of which Stow, as late as about 1600, said: "I have not seen the like" [3]. The new church was large and beautiful, the largest friars' church in England. The friars, who moved about a great deal amongst the people, had their establishments in the towns. They drew large numbers by their preaching and had need of big churches. The church was built in the decorated style. The east wall of the choir stood in what is now Broad Street, the west entrance was at what later became Austin Friars. But the entire complex of the monastery buildings occupied a much greater area. It was bordered on the west by Copthall Avenue, in the south by Throgmorton Street, whereas in the north it reached as far as the London Wall. The London priory was actually the head quarters of the Friar Hermits in England. The foundation grew to be rich and the church was embellished as a result of numerous gifts. Prominent persons attached value to finding their last resting place in the church. Cater mentions from the "Calendar

---

[1] See Burn, *History of the refugees*, pp. 24 et seq. The church in Threadneedle Street was destroyed in the Great Fire of 1666. For a picture of the rebuilt church see p. 24. Since then the French Community has moved twice, in 1841 to St. Martin-le-Grand, E.C., and in 1893 to Soho Square, W.

[2] For what follows see W. A. Cater, *The priory of Austin Friars, London, 1253– 1538. Reprint from the Journal of the British Archaeological Association*, March and June, 1912.

[3] John Stow, *Survey of London*, edition Clarendon Press, London 1908, Vol. I, p. 177.

of Patent Rolls" amongst others, Edward, the eldest son of the
Black Prince and Richard, earl of Arundel, who was beheaded
on Tower Hill in 1397. It was said of him that his head had
become rejoined to the body. The King caused the case to be
investigated and ordered the Friars to put an end to the devotional practices which had grown up around the miracle [1]. Also
the barons who fell at the battle of Barnet (1471) were interned
in the church. For the rest not many events of outstanding
importance can be reported in connection with the mediaeval
church, unless one likes to recall the first contact of the edifice
with the subsequent owners, when in 1381, during the rising led
by Wat Tyler, thirteen "Flemings", who had taken sanctuary
in the church, were dragged from the church and beheaded [2]. It
has been held on the strength of a passage in one of Erasmus'
letters, that he stayed in the priory of the Austin Friars, but it
is much more probable that the "Augustinienses" which he
mentions in this letter were the Austin Canons, to which order
he himself belonged [3]. What is very probable is that Myles
Coverdale, himself a monk, worked about 1529 in Austin Friars
at his translation of the Bible.

The secularization and the forcible expropriation of the
monasteries, naturally also affected the Augustins. In 1538 the
Priory was dissolved and its possessions confiscated. Actually,
before this event, a divine connected with the Protestant Embassy
of the Count of Hessen and the Duke of Saxony had preached in
the church. At the dissolution the monks were ejected. There
were many debts, few unburdened assets. Thomas Cromwell,
who was for a time the compliant favourite of the King, Master
of the Rolls, later Lord Privy Seal, had himself a large house
built in the churchyard on the strength of a contract with the
Friars — the King's favourites were not slow in securing for
themselves substantial portions of the booty. Sir Richard Riche,
the Solicitor General, was presented with the larger part of
the monastery buildings to the north of the nave of the church.

---

[1] The legend in connection with this figure of ghostly apparitions, was still connected with the Church in the beginning of the 20 th century.

[2] See Burn, *History of the Refugees*, p. 186 (based on Stow, *Annals*, ed. 1615, p.
288).

[3] Erasmus to Andreas Ammonius, 11 Nov. 1511, from Cambridge, enquiring after
a place where he could stay in London: "Fortassis apud Augustinienses aliquod est?"
Compare P. S. Allen, *Opus Epistolarum Des. Erasmi Rotterod.*, Tom. I, Oxoniae 1906,
p. 483.

Sir William Poulett, Lord St. John, later marquis of Winchester, got another part of the grounds and buildings, and a short time afterwards he also entered into possession of Sir Richard's properties. In 1551 he obtained, in addition, part of the church building, viz. the choir and the transepts, as well as the tower above the crossing. He used this space for storing corn, coal and such like. His son went one worse. He sold the tombstones and the monuments in this part for £ 100, replaced the lead of the roof by tiles, and converted the space into a stable for horses. At the dissolution the nave of the church remained provisionally in the hands of the King. In 1545 it served as a store for wine from captured French vessels. A year later a cargo of alum was stored there. This was the condition of the building when it was assigned to the foreigners in 1550.

We can gather from all this that when the foreigners obtained possession of their part of the church, the nave and the aisles which constituted the part allocated to them, were already separated by a wall from the transepts. Yet the dimensions were still considerable, nine bays deep. Those who have known the church before 1940, will remember the spacious nave, flanked by the two aisles. The self-evident ownership of the walls, moreover, brought with it — in consequence of the "totam terram, fundum et solum" of the Charter — the ownership of the massive buttresses which extended about 5 feet beyond the wall, and the broad footings of the foundations and of the ground between the buttresses. This circumstance has later played an important role when differences of opinion arose as to the extent of the property rights. There were no buttresses along the eastern half of the north wall, as the cloister here adjoined the church, thereby providing sufficient counter pressure.

The church of the former Austin Friars, henceforth the property of the refugee community, was situated in the heart of the City. The City at that time constituted most of London. The gates: Moorgate, Bishopsgate, Aldgate, etc. fulfilled their original function in the wall enclosing the town, which extended eastwards to the Tower, westwards to Temple Bar. The river formed the boundary on the south. Yet, in the 16th century, building development had already taken place beyond the City walls. Suburbs had come into existence, but Islington in the north was still an isolated village, and where now the British

Museum stands, falconry was practised. Across the Thames there
was the important development of Southwark, and it was
especially here that many of the foreigners resided. London
Bridge, with its shops on both sides, formed the connection
between the two parts of the town. The beautiful church spire
of Austin Friars was one of the one hundred and twenty which
rose above the town, because we must remember that the City
of London was densely populated, although there was no lack
of open spaces. Many of the principal streets were still unpaved.
The Strand was actually not paved until the reign of Queen
Elizabeth. The streets were on the whole narrow and dirty. The
refuse accumulated to such an extent that an order was issued
during plague epidemics under which the citizens had to burn
the refuse in front of their houses three times a week. As late as
1630 we meet with complaints about the heaps of refuse which
were deposited in front of the entrance of the Dutch Church, and
in 1647 it was found necessary to caution those living close to the
Church, not to leave their refuse lying about in the street [1].
Street lighting was very primitive. Crime flourished and it was
definitely unsafe to venture out in the dark. A busy port and
centre of commerce, such as London was, attracted all kinds of
foreign elements. Among these were to be found the enterprising
and the energetic, who brought prosperity, but also adventurers
and persons of doubtful character, who became parasites on the
population. So it was also with the strangers who found their
religious and social fulcrum in the refugee churches. The greater
part consisted of persons of principle and conviction, who had
had the courage to leave their country for the sake of their civil
and religious liberty, but inevitably there was an admixture of
unruly elements, to whom all social restraint was irksome [2].
The great need was for bringing the people together into an
ordered community, and as moral discipline was then held to
stand in the closest possible relation to conformity in religious
belief, as laid down in a well defined church doctrine, the foreign
religious communities were in duty bound to further the spiritual welfare of their members by the teaching of dogma, as well

---

[1] *Acta* VII, f° 206 r°, VIII, f° 185 v°.

[2] See for this description and for a picture of contemporary life, amongst other
works: M. St. Clare Byrne, *Elizabethan life in town and country*, London 1925; L. F.
Salzman, *England in Tudor Times*, London 1926; Erich Marcks, *Königin Elizabeth
und ihre Zeit*, Leipzig 1897 (*Monographieën zur Weltgeschichte*, II).

Plate III

Western front and entrance of the old church

as by strict religious instruction generally, and thus to create orderly conditions. They had, as it were, to start from scratch. As the newly arrived refugees had outgrown the teaching and discipline of the Roman Catholic Church, they had to be brought together into a Christian and social community, and united by strict conformity of creed and obedience to church discipline. This was done by means of books of religious instruction and by church order and liturgy.

In the Dutch Community this was the task of the governing body, which consisted of the Superintendent, à Lasco, the ministers Wouter Delenus and Maarten Micron, the elders and the deacons, each four in number, they having been appointed immediately in 1550 by vote in accordance with apostolic injunction. Amongst them elder Jan Utenhove, by virtue of his social background and theological training, was especially prominent. We have already met him and à Lasco. It remains to devote a few words to the two ministers. Wouter Delen (or Delenus), who was born in Alkmaar, had already been won for the Reformation in 1552, since when he had laboured in various places for its propagation. Since 1539 he had been living in London, where at a later date he occupied the post of "biblioscopus regis" (royal librarian ? censor ?). Of the two ministers he was the more learned, Maarten Micron ("the small one") being more of a preacher for the people, although he too was a scholar [1]. Micron was a Fleming, born in Ghent and originally a physician by profession. Having fled to Germany on account of his faith, he had there come into contact with Utenhove and also with the English Reformer, John Hoper, who had left England for the Continent on account of the persecution by Henry VIII, and who inclined towards the Puritans. When he returned to England in 1549, Micron, who had married the maid servant of Hoper's wife, accompanied him. In all probability Wouter Delenus' son, Peter, also officiated from the start as an assistant-preacher.

These men, in addition to carrying out their pastoral duties, devoted themselves to theological and liturgical subjects and produced a number of written works. These were of the highest importance, not only to the London Community for which they were intended, but also to the development of the Reformation in the Low Countries. Among these works is à Lasco's book on

---

[1] See concerning him Dr J. H. Gerretsen, *Micronius*, Nijmegen 1895.

church doctrine, "Compendium Doctrinae in qua Peregrinorum
Ecclesia Londini constituta est" [1], which appeared in 1551 and
was intended for the instruction of those, who were no longer
Roman Catholics, in their new faith. There is an element of
doubt as to whether this book is exclusively the work of à Lasco
or whether the ministers have contributed to it. The true position
probably is that both subject and framework were supplied by
à Lasco, and that the ministers, having accepted them in the
main, worked them out in detail [2]. The work has been unjustly
called the London Confession of Faith. It is more in the nature
of a tract on the true Church and of an apologia aimed at demon-
strating that this London church, based as it was on an apostolic
foundation, could be regarded as being a true church, than a
confession on all the points of the Faith. The Sacraments, for
instance, are hardly referred to [3]. It did in so far fulfil the part
of a confession of faith, in that everyone who joined the Community, had to sign it [4]. This makes it the more easily understood,
why already in 1551 Utenhove supplied a translation of the work:
"Een Cort Begrijp der Leeringhen, van die waerachtighe ende
eender Ghemeynten, dewelcke door de Ghemeynten der Wyt-
landischen te London ingestelt is enz." [5] In addition, à Lasco,
during his stay in East Friesland, had drawn up the so-called
Emden Catechism, written in the dialect of East Friesland.
This was translated into Dutch by Utenhove, also in 1551, as
"De Catechismus oft Kinderleere enz." It consisted of 250
questions and answers and was intended to be learned by heart
by the older children. Every Sunday, in the afternoon service,
a part of it was recited and then explained by the minister [6]. In
addition, Micron wrote in 1552 a "Small Catechism", more
concise, but yet containing 134 questions and answers. It was
intended for children from 5 to 11 years of age, who had to

---

[1] It has been printed in the edition published by Dr. A. Kuyper of Johannis à
Lasco *Opera tam edita quam inedita*, Amstelod. 1866, Tom. II, p. 285–339.

[2] Compare the writer's article: *Daniël Gerdes en zijn onderwijs in de Kerkgeschie-
denis aan de Groninger Hoogeschool*, in *Historische Avonden*, III, Groningen 1916,
pp. 109–112, 118.

[3] Van Schelven, *De Vluchtelingenkerken*, p. 73.

[4] Pijper, *Utenhove*, p. 75, with the references.

[5] The title (old Dutch) has been arrived at by reconstruction, as there is no copy
extent of the 1551 edition. Later editions are from 1553 and 1565; compare Pijper,
Utenhove, pp. 73 et seq.

[6] *Ibid.*, pp. 76 et seq. Included in à Lasco, *Opera*, ed. Kuyper, Tom. II, pp. 341–475.

demonstrate their proficiency in the matter twice a year before the congregation. à Lasco wrote an introduction to it [1]. The book was also to a certain extent intended for the parents, so that they might instruct their children. There also appeared in 1553 a book of instruction, "A short inquiry into the Faith, etc." [2], intended for those who wished to join the Community, we should say a little book for use in the preparation for confirmation. It is uncertain whether à Lasco or Micron was the author, as also whether the book was originally written in Latin or in Dutch. The latter is the more likely. It probably replaced the "Cort Begrijp" as a form for signature on joining the Church. However, the "Cort Begrijp" has not disappeared without leaving a trace. It found a place in Datheen's Book of Psalms to which further reference will be made.

A modern person may well be astonished at the extreme care which was devoted to the teaching of doctrine to the old, the young and the very young, as if it had been the intention to turn all the members of the congregation into theologians. But we repeat: these people had to be taught everything, suitable books of instruction did not exist, and the excessive concentration on the teaching of doctrine happened to be an expression of the spirit of the age, which revolved around the "true teaching". It saw nothing incongruous in young children being brought up on hair-splitting and abstract theological problems.

It was not only the "true teaching" which was the special concern of the Church's leaders. The form of the services for public worship had equally to be built up from the ground, so to say. In 1551 Utenhove presented the Community with a rhymed version of 25 psalms, to which a few hymns had been added, all of them provided with original musical settings, more stately and more suitable for use in church than the wordly tunes to which up to now the rhymed psalm versions of Van Zuylen van Nyevelt had been sung. This collection was gradually enlarged, and in 1565 a complete collection of the Psalms made its appearance. Utenhove had died in the previous year. Within a comparatively short time Utenhove's psalms had to give way to those of Datheen. Although the fact is to be regretted, seeing that the

---

[1] M. Woudstra, *De Hollandsche Vreemdelingengemeente te Londen*, etc., pp. 74 et seq.
[2] Included in à Lasco, *Opera*, ed. Kuyper, Vol. II, pp. 477–492.

poetic value of Datheen's version was, in general, inferior to that
of Utenhove's, the change-over can be understood. The French
example must have been infectious, seeing that the French used
the beautiful Geneva tunes to which also Datheen's psalms had
been set. Ruytinck said later that Datheen's psalms "were
better versified and corresponded with the tunes of the French
psalms" [1]. A contributory cause was the use which was made of
Datheen's version in the Low Countries. The change-over was
made in 1571. The final decision may well have been influenced
by the circumstance that the Community at that time included
many, who had escaped from the thick of the struggle and from
the most deadly perils and with whom the battle songs still lay,
so to say, on their lips. It was especially those people, who longed
for the moment when the Lord would provide "an opening", who
were loth to sacrifice the continuity of their devotional songs.
The initial impulse came from the sister Community in Norwich,
where many of these fugitives resided. On Easter Day 1571 the
London congregation made a start with the singing of Datheen's
psalms after it had been announced to the Community "that
the ministers had permitted the change not lightly, nor from
bias against the memory of the late honoured Jan Utenhove" [2].
Utenhove's poetic *oeuvre* has however not gone out of use entirely.
Datheen had taken over two of Utenhove's hymns in his collection of psalms and these continued to be sung in the London
Church. One of them "a short prayer preceding the sermon",
remained included, though slightly altered, amongst the "Eenige
Gezangen" at the back of the collection of psalms of the Netherlands Reformed Church, and in this way has also found its place
in the new hymnal of that Church, dating from 1938.

Less haste was made with the drafting of the church order
and of a fixed liturgy, than had been applied to the compilation
of the book of instruction. An explanation can be found for this.
It was just in this sphere, apparently more so than in the sphere
of religious instruction, that differences with the English State
Church, with its episcopalism and ritualism, were bound to show
themselves. There are indications of provisional rules relative to

---

[1] Ruytinck, *Gheschiedenissen*, p. 85.
[2] *Kerkeraads-protocollen 1569–1571*, pp. 277, 302, 306, 311. For extensive references to this procedure see Pijper, *Utenhove*, pp. 251–254; for the preceding tale of
woe, pp. 213–234.

the liturgy having been drawn up, such as certain set prayers and a liturgy for the Communion Service. No complete systematic whole was arrived at, however, during the first three years of the Community's existence, even though the Reformed path along which matters would ultimately develop, was indicated with sufficient clarity.

In this way the Dutch Church Community, by a system of trial and error, but not without firmness of purpose, carved out its way from the beginning. Naturally, difficulties presented themselves. However, the esteem in which the Community was held increased so greatly that the Government in 1553 made a ruling that a Dutch person must be a member before he could be granted citizenship of London [1]. Reports of a few of these difficulties have survived. One concerns an internal question of dogma [2]. Seven questions and answers relating to the dogma of the descent into hell, had been added to the second edition of the Emden Catechism. The object of this was to take up a position opposing that of Delenus, who wanted to see the article concerning the "descensus ad inferos" deleted from the articles of faith of the Community, a standpoint, of which he had up till now not given any evidence. It became a point of dispute. In the end Delenus was brought to admit that he had erred. In passing, mention may be made of another objection which had been advanced against this minister, namely that he had objected to the bending of the knee at the Communion Service as being an expression of a (Roman) superstition. We may conclude from this that everything was done to avoid departing in too great a measure from English custom. For the bishops had by no means abandoned their opposition to the Dutch Church. This is proved by the other difficulty [3]. The bishops had succeeded in persuading the Privy Council that the Church would have to conform to the English ritual. In vain did à Lasco strive to ward off the danger. Utenhove tried to get Calvin to remind the King cautiously in his dedication to the English King of his "Interpretation of Isaiah", of the interests of the Dutch Community. How, or by what means, is not known, but before the untimely death of the King, the Dutch Church succeeded in securing the right to use

1) Van Schelven, *De Vluchtelingenkerken*, p. 104.
2) *Ibid.*, pp. 74 et seq.
3) Pijper, *Utenhove*, p. 67.

its own form of baptism and Communion. We may also gather from this what caution had to be exercised in the matter of church order and liturgy [1].

But the greatest catastrophe which could befall the young community, had still to come. On July 6th, 1553, the young King, Edward VI, died, only sixteen years old. Against the wishes of the dead King and mainly through the machinations of the nobility, his half-sister Mary, the Roman Catholic daughter of Henry VIII from his first marriage, came to the throne. This brought a change in the course followed by the Government, and not least in the attitude of the authorities towards the Dutch Church. The papacy was restored, with a harshness and cruelty which have earned Mary Tudor the sobriquet "bloody". The refugees no longer felt safe. Two Danish ships, "the Moor" and "the Small Crow", which were lying at anchor in the Thames, seemed to offer them an opportunity of escaping from persecution. On the 17th September they set sail from Gravesend and thus began a long and anxious peregrination for the full account of which we are mainly indebted to Utenhove's report, written largely as an apologia against the opposition which they were later to experience [2]: "Simplex et fidelis narratio" [3]. Also Micron and L. Harboe have written on the wanderings which were to follow. There were about 175 persons on board, among them à Lasco, Micron and Utenhove. Those who stayed behind saw them off and gave them a touching farewell at which the psalms which were sung told of a consolation and an encouragement which are not of this world. After a short religious service on the

---

[1] The extent to wich the question of ceremonial occupied the minds of those inside the State Church, is evident from the so-called Garment Struggle. When in 1550 John Hoper, who inclined towards the Puritans, was appointed to the see of Gloucester, he objected to being installed wearing the vestments of an English bishop, which he held to be reminiscent of Rome. He thought that this was superstitious and this regulation, imposed by the State, to be an encroachment upon the liberty of the Church, which should be guided only by apostolic precept. This notorious struggle ended by Hoper giving in, after he had allowed the case to go to the length of his being incarcerated for opposing established authority. It is probable that the first manifestation of a fundamental difference, which would disturb the English State Church for centuries to come, contributed to the decision to debar the foreigners from the free exercise of their liturgy. Compare Pijper, *Utenhove*, p. 93–99.

[2] Amongst other sources, the attack on their Communion teaching by the opponent Joachim Westphal, whom we will meet later.

[3] The work has been republished, with an extensive introduction, by Dr. F. Pijper in *Bibliotheca Reformatoria Neerlandica*, Vol. IX, the Hague 1912, pp. 1–186. — Dr. Kuyper's thesis that the "Narratio" was largely the work of à Lasco, is refuted by Pijper, *Utenhove*, pp. 175 et seq.

spot — it happened to be a Sunday — those remaining behind
returned to London. The vessels were soon separated by a storm.
There were further heavy storms, the smaller ship only reaching
Elsinore after having been a month at sea. The larger vessel,
on which were the three leaders, did not arrive until the beginning
of November, after touching two deserted Norwegian ports.
Great privations were suffered on this voyage. Worse was still
to come. The three leaders journeyed to Coldingen in Jutland,
where the King, Christian II, was staying at the time. A sermon
by the Court preacher, to which they had to listen before being
granted audience of the King for which they had asked, and in
which sermon this Lutheran inveighed in violent terms against
the false prophets who did not subscribe to the Lutheran teaching
on the Communion, did not hold out prospects of a favourable
reception. The King, though not disliking the visitors personally,
did, after certain preliminary discussions which, in the initial
stages, seemed to proceed favourably, cause a command to be
sent to them to leave the country immediately. They were not
even permitted to communicate with the others, who had found
a provisional shelter in Copenhagen. à Lasco and Utenhove,
therefore, travelled by land through Holstein to Emden, Micron
following somewhat later. If the others had hoped for a moment,
on the strength of the not unsympathetic attitude of the Copenhagen magistrate, that they would be allowed to stay for the
time being, their hopes were soon dashed, because the Government, incited by the Lutheran Church leaders, and afraid of
revolutionary disturbances — they looked upon the Reformed
as a kind of Anabaptist — were adamant. The fugitives were
told that they must leave by the 15th December. They split up
into four groups in order not to arouse suspicion. In this way they
embarked in midwinter on their grim voyage across the sea. The
destination was Rostock, Wismar and Lübeck. Leaving the
quay they intoned the 2nd Psalm (in the rhymed version by
Utenhove):

> Why do the nations so furiously rage together,
> and why do the people imagine a vain thing?
> The kings of the earth stand up and
> the rulers take councel together,
> Against the Lord and against his anointed
> Whom he has sent to succour all mankind.

The sea voyage, in midwinter, was once again very trying. At an early stage, because of adverse winds, the fugitives had to lie at anchor for days on end, as they had been forbidden, on pain of death, to set foot again on Danish territory. After suffering much cold and privation, two of the groups at last reached Rostock. Driven also from there, on account of their religious convictions, by the Lutheran authorities, they proceeded to Wismar, where the third group joined them. Micron attached himself to the wanderers, as they were beginning to feel the need of theological guidance. For they were now being attacked from two sides, namely from the side of the Lutherans and from that of the Baptists. Their leader, Menno Simonsz, who propagated his cause in the coastal districts from Friesland to Pomerania, wanted to argue with them. A debate between him and Micron, which lasted for days, ended as usual in that neither party yielded to the other [1]. It is illustrative of the tragic aspect of all dogmatic quarrels, that the Lutheran pastors managed in the end to cause an order of expulsion to be made against the exiles, based on suspected Anabaptism to which the Mennonites had tried in vain to convert them! The journey now led to Lübeck, where all the groups became united again. But also here they came face to face with Lutheran bigotry. Once more the points of difference between the Lutheran and the Reformed conceptions, more particularly in the matter of the Communion Service, caused the wanderers to be refused shelter. Hamburg now became their destination. The Lutheran zealot, Joachim Westphal, at first seemed to be not unkindly disposed towards them, but also here the dogmatic antithesis proved to be stronger than Christian brotherhood. Once more driven out, the exiles at long last reached Emden, and this town proved to be a safe refuge. The widowed countess, Anna, though in general she advanced the Lutheran cause, allowed the exiles to stay in her town, and here they could now look forward to better times. A memorial tablet in the principal church records their gratitude. It embodies a representation of a small ship — symbolically the church and also emblem of their wanderings — and bears the following legend in the Dutch language:

---

[1] See J. H. Wessel, *De leerstellige strijd tusschen Nederlandsche Gereformeerden en Doopsgezinden in de zestiende eeuw*, Assen 1945, p. 169 et pass.

God's church, prosecuted, expelled,
God has here given consolation.

Also other groups from the London Community had gradually
come to Emden, either directly or indirectly. The last of them
left London in the early spring of 1554, led by Wouter and
Peter Delenus. The French refugees had also left London. They
found a refuge in Wezel.

The story of these events is as unedifying as it is moving. It is
a deeply disappointing spectacle to see men, who themselves
have revolted against religious coercion, and who have suffered
persecution, act with intolerance against victims of intolerance
who happen to hold views different from their own. The occasions seem to us today to be largely trivial points of difference.
For instance: to what extent does the Lutheran conception of
Communion do greater justice to the presence of Christ at the
Service than does the Reformed conception? Must we conceive
of this presence as a consequence of the omnipresence of Christ
(Luther) or not (Calvin)? And so forth. We should realize,
however, that to the people of those days, who lived in the thick
of theological and religious controversies, which affected them
deeply, these were burning and vital questions, which determined
their conception of life and of the world, and forced them, for
the sake of their conscience, to make a definite choice. The least
attractive role in this drama was undoubtedly played by the
Lutheran zealots, just as in most cases of friction between
Lutheran and Reformed interests the Lutheran zealots constituted the aggressive and intolerant party. But also for them it was
a matter of principle. Are we thoroughly convinced that Micron
and his followers never gave occasion, by a certain challenging
violence in their confession, to intolerant reactions? There is
evidence of hypersensitiveness and of uncalled-for offensive-
ness in the attitude of à Lasco and his followers [1]. In any case
it is striking that discussions which began with a certain amount
of goodwill, often ended in a clash. These observations are not
intended to cast the blame on the persecuted, but in order that
we may judge the regrettable events as objectively as possible.

---

[1] Pijper in *Bibl. Ref. Neerl.*, IX, pp. 21 et seq. — Moreover: the *Narratio* is surely
not only intended as a report on the happenings, but also as a piece of polemics.

The members of the London refugee Community remain examples, to the bitter end, of fidelity to principle, courage and readiness to make sacrifices.

We may pass by the events of the years spent in Emden, of which moreover little is known. Yet these years were not without significance for the London Community, because in them the fruits were gathered, which careful tending had brought gradually to maturity during the early London period, namely a detailed systematic church order and liturgy. Actually there were two works. In the years 1554 and 1555 there appeared in Emden Micron's "Christian Ordinances of the Netherlands Communities of Christ, those of the Christian Prince, King Edward VI, instituted in London in the year 1550 etc." [1], and à Lasco's "Forma ac Ratio tota ecclesiastici ministerii in peregrinorum, potissimum vero Germanorum Ecclesia instituta Londini etc." [2] As the titles are similar, so are the contents of these works, partly running parallel, partly supplementing each other. Yet there are differences. Micron's work is concise and to the point, à Lasco's circumstantial. Strictly speaking they are not a church order and liturgy in the true sense (Micron's work comes nearest) but they are more in the nature of ideal formulations of what the London Community had had in mind prior to 1553 and had only succeeded in realizing in part. In how far these ideas had been realized, how exactly the life of the Church had been ordered, will probably never be known, because, with the exception of the Charter, which, under the care of Micron, got to Emden and continued to be preserved there, the archives for the years 1550–1553 have vanished without leaving a trace. That it was Micron's intention to offer a treatise on liturgy and church order is also evident from his introduction: "As we, as servants of the Community, had to listen daily to these and similar calumnies" (by which he means untrue accusations concerning the character and the methods of the London Community) "we have been obliged in London to put in writing the ordinances of our Community in an orderly and faithful fashion". He mentions also the help which he had got from à Lasco's

---

[1] Full title in Woudstra, *De Holl. Vreemdelingengemeente*, pp. 38 et seq. Compare pp. 90 et seq. The library of the Amsterdam University possesses a copy of the first edition; Van Schelven, *De Vluchtelingenkerken*, p. 81.

[2] In à Lasco, *Opera*, ed. Kuyper, Vol. II, pp. 1–283.

work, which at that time was still in manuscript. After all the notice which the two works have received, it remains a problem to determine what exactly is the relationship between them [1]. Also Utenhove appears to have had a hand in it, as translator of à Lasco's work, a translation of which nothing further is known [2]. We can only say with certainty that à Lasco's" Forma ac Ratio" is a detailed and elaborate study and that Micron in his "Christian Ordinances" adapted it for practical use.

We have only space for a short summary of this, the first Netherlands church order and liturgy. There is no need to go into the theological background [3]. The general spirit is most definitely Reformed, not Lutheran. à Lasco himself says that he had in mind in particular the example of the churches in Geneva and Strassburg [4], which, therefore, presupposes considerable Calvinistic influence, even though the influence of Zwinglian Zürich is plainly discernible. Indeed, this is not to be wondered at. Micron, as also Utenhove, had leanings towards the Zwinglian, not the Calvinistic school of thought [5], and also à Lasco could not be labelled without qualification as a Calvinist. For instance, the share which he grants to the congregation in matters of church governance, is greater than with Calvin. In the first place let us look at the offices of the Church. Strictly regarded they are two in number, the elders and the deacons, which certainly is not unscriptural. The former are more closely defined and distinction is made between the Minister of the Word and the elders. Reasoning along scriptural lines, the office of superintendent presented something of a problem. He was a figure who did not fit in with Reformed church law and whom the Church owed (though he had been accepted without dislike), to the principle of supervision by the Civil authority, which had been imposed on the Church in conformity with English practice. The embarrassment is reflected in the effort which is made to make the function of superintendent acceptable. In one place he is represented as minister of the Word, in another as having been appointed to his very special function, as "named superintendent

---

1) Also the exposition by Woudstra, *De Holl. Vreemdelingengemeente*, pp. 85–89, offers no solution.
2) Pijper, *Utenhove*, p. 84.
3) Van Schelven, *De Vluchtelingenkerken*, pp. 81–101, deals with this extensively.
4) à Lasco, *Opera*, Vol. II, p. 50.
5) Indicated by Pijper, *Utenhove*, pp. 39–42.

by His Royal Majesty in his letter of privilege, that is Overseer".
And in order to gloss over the departure from Scripture, an
appeal is actually made to the figure of Peter, whose special
position was determined by Christ when he was commanded to
stablish the other brethren in the faith (S. Luke 22 : 32). It is
an argument that savours of Rome, in any case a first step on
a dangerous road, and one which would certainly not have been
accepted some decades later by the Reformed puritanism in the
English State Church. The Superintendent has regulative and
executive powers, and this is certainly not nullified by the
circumstance that he is "In the service of the Word and of the
Sacraments and of the use of Christian penalties", "of equal
authority as the others". We should be clear on the point that
it was only in strictly ecclesiastical matters that the competence
of the superintendent did not exceed that of the elders and
deacons. In matters of church governance his powers did exceed
those of the elders and deacons. In the matter of the election
of the dignitaries an entirely individual way was followed,
diverging from that of Geneva and Strassburg and having more
an old-apostolical character: the members of the Community
nominated candidates, after fasting and prayer, and those who
had received most votes were thereupon discussed in the Church
Council, whereupon further voting determined the final choice.
It then lay with the congregation as a whole to bring forward
possible objections against those elected.

Three services were held during the week, two on Sunday and
one on Thursday [1]. All three services had certain features in
common, viz. prayer (concluded with the Lord's Prayer),singing
of psalms, consideration of a passage from Scripture, announcements, closing prayer. On Sunday mornings there was added:
reading of the Law, confession of sin (from the pulpit), pronouncement of forgiveness or of judgment, reciting of the Apostles'
Creed, baptism, solemnization of marriage, as the case might be,
singing of psalms, appeal on behalf of the poor, and the pronouncement of the Blessing. There was no organ accompaniment to
the singing. On Sunday afternoons this second part of the
service consisted mainly of a discussion of the Catechism, when
the children from 11 to 14 years had to answer the questions, and
on Thursdays the "prophesy". This "prophesy" was a remarkable

---

[1] Compare Woudstra, *De Holl. Vreemdelingengemeente*, pp. 47 et seq.

institution. Calvin would have nothing to do with it, but à Lasco
attached great value to it. It originated from Zürich — indication
of the Zwinglian orientation — and its nature is best indicated
by the present-day word "discussion". For it was an exchange of
thought between congregation and ministers, whereby the former
raised questions and objections relating to the doctrine taught.
It therefore bears a pronounced "communal" character. In order
somewhat to restrict the scope of this communal practice, which
in its excessive manifestation was such a typical characteristic
of Anabaptism, Zwingli, who certainly was no friend of Anabaptism, designated certain persons, who by virtue of study were
better qualified for the task, to speak and render testimony.
Such persons were called prophets. On the one hand a position
was thus taken up in direct opposition to that of the Anabaptists,
who rejected the idea of having trained ministers. On the other
hand the right of the congregation to speak and "prophesy"
from their midst was not curtailed, because, was not the prophet
a scripturally recognized dignitary and the "prophesy" a function in the communal life of the old Church? One need only read
such passages as I Cor. 12 : 28, 14 : 29, Eph. 4 : 11. In this way,
in the Thursday services "those who have been ordained to put
the questions" were invited to bring forward, be it on their own
initiative, or at the suggestion of a member of the congregation,
those matters which "in the sermons of the preceding weeks
appear to have been presented either incorrectly, obscurely,
or inadequately" by the ministers of the Word.

Baptism and Communion were the sacraments, also the marriage contract was confirmed as a sacred act within the body of
the congregation. At the Communion Service, which was held
every two months, the congregation was seated around a table.
At the age of fourteen one could be admitted to the Communion
table. Communion was preceded by "censura morum" by ministers and elders and the refusal of admission to the Communion
table was used as a measure of discipline. In order to preserve
purity of doctrine and of morals (these were considered to be
entirely on one and the same level), among the congregation,
an obstinate transgressor, after admonition and punishment by
the Consistory, was debarred from taking part in the Communion
Service, after which expulsion from the Community could follow.
Re-instatement on repentance and confession of guilt always

remained possible, however. Actually, it is questionable whether this use of the Communion as a means of exercising discipline is scriptural. Would it not be more correct to let the exclusion from Communion coincide with the expulsion? However this may be, the custom spread via Emden to Geneva and to the religious communities in the Palatinate, and further to the Reformed churches of France and the Netherlands. Actually the custom seems to have reached Strassburg already a decade after it had been introduced in the London Church [1]. These are about the principal points of the church order and liturgy of the young London Community, which deserve special notice. There remain to be mentioned the weekly meetings of the Consistory, the observation of days of fasting and days of prayer — not at settled times but as the need arose —, internment in the Church (with a ritual which was more Anglican than Calvinistic in character).

Before we take leave of this first period in the history of the Dutch Church in London, it behoves us to mention a labour which was completed during the exile, but which yet had its origin in the earliest life of the Church, namely the translation of the New Testament by Jan Utenhove, published in Emden in 1556. This translation was not a success. There were too many objections, especially to the language and to the spelling. It was never accepted to any appreciable degree. The Liesvelt Bible, based on Luther's translation, was the one which was used. In 1559 a revised edition by Johannes Dyrkinus of Utenhove's New Testament was published in Emden. Godfried van Winghen made a new translation of the Old Testament, also based on the translation by Luther. Through a combination with the New Testament translation of 1559 there came into existence the so-called Deux-Aes Bible, which for decades has remained the accepted translation in those countries where Dutch was spoken. It was also used in London until it was replaced here by the translation made by order of the States General in the years 1618–1619 [2].

---

[1] See T. J. van Griethuysen, *De ontzegging van het Avondmaal, aan de afsnijding voorafgaande, bij de Gereformeerde Kerken niet van den aanvang af in gebruik, maar eerst later in hare tucht-oefening opgenomen*, in *Studiën en Bijdragen*, T. III (1876), pp. 294–340. — The refutation by Van Schelven, *De Vluchtelingenkerken*, pp. 100 seq. is not convincing in my opinion.

[2] See for Utenhove's translation of the New Testament the extensive account by Pijper, *Utenhove*, pp. 114–142.

CHAPTER II

INTERNAL AND EXTERNAL STRENGTH
— SAFEGUARDING OF DOCTRINE

On November 17th, 1558, Queen Mary died. It was laid down in the testament of Henry VIII that his second daughter, Elizabeth, should be her successor, and, in fact, Parliament recognized her as such. Not so Pope Paul IV, however. On the contrary, he declared her to be unfit for the throne on account of her birth. If Elizabeth had ever had any inclination towards the Roman Church, this attitude made her choose the side of Protestantism without reservation. Hers was not a strongly marked religious spirit, but she was deeply conscious of the significance of the English Church which had been the national church of old, and she wanted, from conviction, to give her support to its independence of papal authority in the spirit of her father, or perhaps, even more in that of her late brother. The Church presented itself to her in its unbroken apostolic and episcopal tradition, but cleansed in the spirit of the Reformation in accordance with scriptural theology. For the rest she had no wish to exercise authority over the Church's teaching, but only over Church government and hierarchy as "Supreme Governor," not as "Supreme Head". She saw no objection, within certain limitations, to a growth in strength of the Reformed elements in her realm, particularly if this would further the material well-being of her people. Sagacious, almost to the point of being cunning, she was averse to extremes, as also to that extreme Puritan Calvinism voiced by the Scottish Reformer, John Knox, who, in his "First Blast of the Trumpet against the Monstrous Regiment of Women", of 1558, claimed for the people (the Reformed people) the unrestricted right to insurrection, and who rejected government by women.

By 1559, when the Queen had freed herself unequivocally

from the papacy, the fugitives began to return in large numbers, amongst them the Dutch and French London communities [1]. In March prior to their return, the fugitives in Emden had already appointed two men, Antonius Asche and Dr. Dumasius, to proceed to London and to inquire there into the condition of the members who had stayed behind. They reported that the position was still uncertain — the publication by John Knox, already referred to, had not made the Queen any more favourably inclined towards any who called themselves Reformed — but that the London brethren were particularly anxious to see Peter Delenus. In May, however, Adriaan van Haemstede, of whom more presently, came to London, entirely on his own initiative (the Emden Church Council had actually asked him to go to Holland) and began to preach to the members, first in a private house and later in a church. Asche and Dumasius now adressed themselves to the Court and submitted a copy of the Charter, but they solicited, in particular, the support of William Cecil, Lord Burghley, the influential favourite and Secretary of Elizabeth. Some time elapsed before the decision was received. Meanwhile, the Dutch Community had, in addition to Van Haemstede, found unofficial leaders in Utenhove and Peter Delenus, who had returned in the meantime, the former with the original Charter which had accompanied the fugitives to Emden. The petition for recognition and re-instatement was repeated, and at last, on February 24th, 1560, the Queen returned a favourable reply, though under conditions of much greater restraint than those which had obtained before. Whereas sympathy for the oppressed had contributed to the Queen's decision, the motive of Edward VI c.s.: to have a model Reformed community in his realm, no longer held for her with her pronounced Anglican High Church standpoint. What did tell was the consideration that the foreigners might possibly advance the prosperity of her realm. The foreigners were again permitted to constitute themselves as a church; the Jesus Temple was returned to the Dutch in a suitable condition (it had been used during Mary Tudor's reign as a kind of storage place for the Navy [2]). However, the Community would not again

---

[1] Van Schelven, *De Vluchtelingenkerken*, pp. 131–135, has thrown light on this.
[2] Ruytinck, *Gheschiedenissen*, p. 32. Em. van Meteren, in the reminiscences on his youth, mentions that only "the Dutche pulpit" remained standing; *Archivum* III[1], p. 1213.

be an independent "corpus corporatum et politicum". Although a request for this had been made, à Lasco was not re-instated as Superintendent. On the contrary, the Community had to accept supervision by the Bishop of London. The effect of this was that the Dutch Community, though still retaining a certain measure of autonomy, was absorbed into the body of the English State Church. For all practical purposes, the Bishop — then Edmund Grindal — became superintendent [1]. à Lasco did not return to England. He had found a new field of religious activity in Poland where he died on January 8th, 1560,

The supervision by the Bishop of London has from time to time made itself felt in more or less radical ways. We shall repeatedly come across instances. One which occurred soon after the re-instatement, may be cited here. In 1571 there was held in Emden a synod (having a limited national character) of Dutch churches. This synod has been of fundamental importance for the establishment of the Reformed Church in the Netherlands. Foreign church communities in England (even then London was not the only one) had been invited to attend this gathering of "Churches under the Cross," but they were unable to send their representatives in time. It is doubtful, however, whether they would have received the necessary permission. For, in connection with a letter written on behalf of the synod, inviting the churches to organize themselves into "Classes" and to arrange for representation at future synods, Ruytinck mentions that in reply to a request to the Queen on this matter, a letter prohibiting them from so doing was received from the "commissarissen", by whom he means the bishops of the various dioceses — "commissarii in religionis causis" [2]. All the same, a little later, gatherings of the "Classes" were instituted, the so-called "Colloquia", to which further reference will be made. In addition, there were meetings within the "Coetus" which comprised the foreign congregations in London, viz. the Dutch, French, Italian and Spanish, the last-named as and when they existed, which was not always the case. Even over this

---

[1] Compare Pijper, *Utenhove*, pp. 194–198, where can also be found the refutation of the supposition that Utenhove was superintendent for a short while. The opinion expressed by Van Schelven in *De Vluchtelingenkerken*, p. 138, that Grindal did not exercise his function as superintendent in his capacity as Bishop of London, appears to the author to be incorrect; it is contradicted by the events.

[2] Ruytinck, *Gheschiedenissen*, p. 85. Cf. *Archivum*, II, pp. 391 et seq.

Coetus the Bishop of London exercised a certain measure of supreme authority. There was a right of appeal against the decisions of the Coetus, and the final decision rested with the Bishop who could exercise a veto by the issue of a so-called letter of inhibition [1].

The restoration of 1560 also brought changes in the internal structure and in the customs of the Community. The congregation lost the right to nominate persons for election as members of the Consistory. Henceforth nominations were made by the Consistory. It appears that appointments to vacant seats on the Consistory were made from a certain number by the drawing of lots [2]. The number of ministers was increased to four (in 1588 there were even five ministers [3]), the elders now numbered 12, the deacons 14. These high numbers were maintained for a long time, even if in later years the seats were not always occupied. The stipend of a minister, £ 30 plus £ 6 for rent in the very early days, was not inconsiderable for those days. It is understandable that the institute of the "prophesy" could not maintain itself. It was first reduced and altogether abolished in 1571 [4]. Ruytinck reported of it that it gave offence, and we have no difficulty in understanding this, because the institute gave bigoted elements in the congregation an opportunity to air their views and because it could easily create suspicion as to the true character of the Community. However, the character and composition of the Community also underwent a gradual change. After insurrection and armed revolt had broken out in the Low Countries in the 'sixties, there was an increase in the numbers of militant individuals prepared to wage a violent struggle rather than compromise their principles. The outcome was at first a certain contrast in type between the old and the new foreigners, though as time went on these differences gradually disappeared, partly because emigration for the sake of the Faith decreased after the 'seventies. It is once more difficult to form an estimate of the size of the Community which would be approximately correct. From the nature of the case the numbers fluctuated. The increase in the number of minis-

---

1) Dr. A. Kuyper, *De Hollandsche Gemeente te Londen in 1570–71*, in *Voor Driehonderd Jaren*, Utrecht (1870), pp. 137–168.
2) *Acta V, f° 19 v°*.
3) Ruytinck, *Gheschiedenissen*, p. 148.
4) *Acta 1569–71*, p. 276.

ters points to a mounting membership. Careful calculation has shown [1] that in 1561 there were 500–600 members (over 14 years of age). This number soon rose to approximately 1000. Towards the end of the 'sixties it approached 2000, to go down again afterwards. Southerden Burn gives for 1567, as a result of a count of the foreigners according to the Wards, 2993 Dutch persons out of a total of 3760. If we take into account the fact that these 2993 were not all members of the Church, we may conclude that the figure of 2000 mentioned above is more or less correct [2].

The substitution in 1571 of Datheen's rhymed version of the Psalms for that of Utenhove's has received mention (see page 18). Five years later the catechism of Micron was replaced by the Heidelberg catechism. This was not done on dogmatic grounds, but for the sake of uniformity. At that time the Heidelberg catechism had been introduced in all the Dutch communities in England and the Colloquium of that year decided to press London to follow this example [3].

In yet another respect did the position of the London Community undergo a change during this period, especially in the 'seventies, namely in its relations with the Low Countries. Up till now these had been the centre of gravity, whilst London was the central point where many fugitives had found a safe shelter. But at home the country was getting into a state of utter confusion. The revolt brought distress and situations crammed with dangerous possibilities, in which those engaged in the struggle, i.e. the revolting towns, the Prince of Orange and his counsellors, sometimes looked around in desperation for financial and material help and for moral support. It is then that the London Community — and with it the other communities which had gradually come into being — becomes the centre to which hopeful glances are cast, to which requests and supplications for help as well as impatient demands for money and cannon are addressed; also for preachers who, with their

---

[1] Van Schelven, *De Vluchtelingenkerken*, pp. 138 et seq.
[2] Burn, *History of the Refugees*, pp. 5 et seq.
[3] The opinion expressed by Van Schelven, *De Vluchtelingenkerken*, p. 142, that the delivery of burial sermons had been discontinued is based, in the author's opinion, on a misreading of Ruytinck, *Gheschiedenissen*, pp. 97 et seq., where it is stated that, in order not to offend the English ecclesiastical standpoint, the delivery of burial sermons by Dutchmen in English churches was being discontinued.

word, could encourage and comfort and who, with their knowledge of organization, could give guidance to those church councils which took a prominent part in the struggle. Very enlight-
ening in this connection are the words in which Ruytinck paints
the great change of 1572, the year of the liberation of Brille,
Flushing, Enkhuyzen, Delft, Dordrecht, Rotterdam: "The Prince
with the object of following all this up to the full, has begun
to introduce good order and discipline, both on water and on
land, to which end he has instituted a Provincial Council in
Holland [1]; yes, he has given evidence of his diligence in the
founding of God's Community, for he has written to the community here, kindly requesting it (because of the abundance
of the harvest) to send over reliable ministers for the spreading
of the Gospel over there". The Dutch Community complied with
this request; many ministers were "prepared". This was done by
and within the Community and subsequently also on the Continent. The Rev. Bart. Wilhelmi and the Rev. Godfried van
Winghen crossed the sea, their places being taken by Johannes
Cubus, who had previously served the Community as a school
teacher, and Jacobus Regius [2]. In June, 1574, Taffin appealed
to the Church in London because of the shortage of ministers
in the provinces of Holland and Zeeland [3]. In 1578 the Consistory indicated certain candidates to be trained especially for
the ministry in the Low Countries [4]. The following year the
Church Council at Bruges enquired after students whom the
London Community had sent to Geneva to study there. The
London Council replied that it was as yet uncertain when these
students would have completed their studies and that in any
case the Council would not commit itself [5]. Ghent also asked
for additional ministers. London replied that the matter of training was well in hand and that three ministers of the Word would
be sent, provided they were willing to go. London would pay
their expenses [6].

Material assistance was also needed. In July of the great

---

1) i.e. the Provinces of North and South Holland.
2) Ruytinck, *Gheschiedenissen*, pp. 86 et seq.
3) *Acta* VI, f° 35 v°.
4) *Acta* V, for Sept. 1578.
5) *Acta* V, for April 1579.
6) *Acta* V, for May 1579.

year 1572 Enkhuyzen asked for cannon and victuals [1], and the menaced town of Dordrecht appealed for grain "as the whole of Holland depends on Dordrecht" [2]. Gifts of money were also forthcoming in good measure. The money gifts from London in 1572 totalled £ 156, to which must be added £ 25 from the communities outside London. In view of the confused times and the distances involved, it was, of course, difficult to obtain convincing evidence that good and proper use was made of the help sent. On February 15th, 1573, the elder Van der Beke, who was then in Delft, wrote that he could thoroughly recommend a continuation of the assistance. It appears that complaints had been made in the Consistory that the money did not always get into the right hands. There seems to have been also a certain distrust of the Prince [3]. The Prince himself did not tire in his appeals to the London Community. Yet London achieved much in the giving of help. For instance, in 1572 it sent to Flushing a contingent of soldiers "in the service of Her Majesty and of the Prince" [4]. The other communities did not lag behind. Norwich wrote to London on June 27th, 1573, that they had collected £ 95 in the space of two months; how much had London collected? A joint remittance might be made. Moreover, in the coming months they would equip a number of soldiers. Let London act likewise. Norwich added that these soldiers came from its own community, some having volunteered on account of declining business, whilst in the case of others the sole motive was a spontaneous desire to help — a guarantee that the cause was close to their hearts and that there would be fewer cases of plunder and other excesses [5].

Occasions for misunderstandings and for the display of impatience were, of course, not lacking. On August 19th, 1575, the "Classis" Walcheren of the Home Church, wrote a violently worded letter to the Consistory in London: "You continue to live in peace and quiet, yet we will not assume that you have lost your love for your country. It is the Prince himself who keeps pressing us and who considers that you are in default, presupposing not ignorance but love of money. And though

---

1) *Archivum*, II, pp. 420, 423.
2) *Archivum*, III[1], pp. 177 et seq. 'Holland': the province of (N. and S.) Holland.
3) *Archivum*, III[1], pp. 200–204.
4) *Archivum*, III[1], p. 215.
5) *Archivum*, III[1], p. 232.

this is purely a political question, we churches did not want to decline to give suit to the request of Governor Boisot, and that is why we are writing you this letter" [1]. A few weeks later the Prince himself wrote again to the Consistory, asking them to send cannon [2]. In England, too, with the steadily growing political tie between the two countries, pressure was being exerted. In 1584 Sir Francis Walsingham asked the London Consistory to assist the menaced city of Ostend with troops, money or ammunition. This call was answered and help was sent. The Communities of Norwich and Colchester did likewise, sending respectively 88 and 34 men [3]. On July 24th, 1586, Walsingham asked for £ 800 towards the equipment of a regiment of soldiers to be sent to the Low Countries, but this time a refusal was sent by the French and the Dutch in a letter pointing to the assistance which had already been given, and claiming that they were just then engaged in collecting money for fitting out another contingent of soldiers [4]. In 1587 the Queen sent an appeal because of the threat of the Armada [5]. On April 3rd, 1588, the Privy Council asked for a contribution towards a draft of 10,000 soldiers [6]. It gradually became too burdensome for the Community. "Do not lay too heavy a burden on us", they wrote on September 9th, 1588, to Walsingham; "our numbers are small. We maintain four ministers, three students, sixty poor families, and, in addition, many poor displaced persons" [7]. To which Walsingham replied: "Let the foreign churches then raise £ 100". The object was the relief of Bergen op Zoom [8]. In 1589 money was raised for a Dutch company under the command of Sir John Norris and Sir Francis Drake [9],

How difficult the times still were for the people of the Low Countries transpired from a letter which the young minister,

---

1) *Archivum*, II, pp. 513 et seq.
2) *Archivum*, II, pp. 520 et seq.
3) *Archivum*, II, pp. 785 et seq., 809.
4) *Archivum*, III[1], pp. 834 et seq.
5) Ruytinck, *Gheschiedenissen*, pp. 144 et seq.; cf. Moens, *The Dutch Church Registers*, p. XXVI.
6) *Archivum*, II, p. 826. In this year the Rev. Jac. Regius distributed amongst members of the congregation a number of commemorative medals, which had been struck on the occasion of the victory over the Armada; Moens, *The Dutch Church Registers*, p. XXVI.
7) *Archivum*, III[1], pp. 881 et seq.
8) *Archivum*, II, p. 832.
9) *Archivum*, III[1], pp. 888 et seq.

Johannes Lamotius, who had been sent by London, wrote from Dordrecht on August 31st, 1592. The letter read: "I am going as a minister to Nieuw Gieskerk, but conditions there are very unsettled because of the proximity of the Spanish garrison in Geertruidenberg. Last year they massacred the population round about Geertruidenberg and burned down the villages. True, Nieuw Gieskerk is situated rather more inland, but when the waters are frozen and the nights are long, they can easily put in an appearance". The Consistory took up the cudgels on behalf of its ward and wrote to Dordrecht, asking if they could not have sent this young and inexperienced man to a less dangerous post [1]. And as late as 1603, when Ostend was besieged, the ministers of Middelburg and Flushing wrote, asking for the recruiting officers to be assisted in their task, so that these might be able to recruit reliable and religious persons for the Zeeland regiments; beggars and vagabonds were no earthly use [2]. The London Community certainly stood for much in the national cause during those initial years. It was more than an outpost, being rather a centre of organization, of moral and material support. Mention should also be made of the continuous opposition to trading with the enemy — a national failing, not confined to those times — as in 1575, according to Ruytinck, and in 1584, when the Colloquium as well as the London Coetus issued a warning against supplying victuals and ammunition to "les tyrans ou persecuteurs de leglise," "de vianden der waerheit" (the enemies of truth) [3]. Besides, if the Dutch Community ever failed to exercise vigilance, the English authorities saw to it that the Dutch commercial spirit was suitably curbed. As early as 1569 we meet with a letter from the Privy Council on behalf of the Queen, containing a warning that all persons who, on account of their religion, had found asylum and freedom, should abstain from transactions with the countries belonging to the Kingdom of Spain [4].

The Community in London could never have been such a tower of strength if it had not been a strongly united body. The dis-

1) *Archivum*, III^{I}, pp. 944, 947.
2) *Archivum*, III^{I}, pp. 1093 et seq.
3) Ruytinck, *Gheschiedenissen*, p. 99; *Archivum*, III^{II}, p. 2885; *Colloquia*, p. 79.
4) *Acta 1569–71*, p. 51.

ciplinary teaching and the moral discipline exercised by its spiritual leaders in the congregation served to bring about and
promote this unity. In the midst of a raging sea of disorder and
licentiousness, it had to be the firm basis of an orderly and moral
mode of life, in accordance with the infallible teaching of Holy
Scripture. The fact of having found this safe harbour of refuge
was looked upon as a special blessing from God. In return, those
who had been thus blessed must show themselves worthy by
faithful observation of the rules which God, in His Holy Word,
had given to His chosen people, to whom the Community felt
itself to belong. In a subsequent chapter this question of the
maintenance of moral discipline will be fully dealt with. At this
juncture we can limit ourselves to a general reference. This same
Word of God, so it was argued, bore unequivocal witness to,
and supplied practical indications of the way in which the unity of the Church could be kept alive by means of a uniform religious conviction and confession of faith. It was for this that
the books of religious instruction of the Church existed. Having
been compiled by the Church's own ministers, they were free
from papal errors and contained in unequivocal terms what was
necessary for individual salvation and for uniting all members
in conformity of religious conviction. But this made it necessary for an anxious watch to be kept lest any unorthodox ideas
should creep in. No erroneous views on the part of individual
members should be allowed to disturb this unity. A stand had
to be made against heterodoxy. Heterodoxy had to be met by
admonition and punishment, if necessary by expulsion, so that
the Community might stand before God as an entity which confessed the True Faith. Persons who had been transferred from
any of the other communities, had to submit to an examination
in the faith if any time had elapsed since their departure. The
minute books of the first years are largely filled with reports
of the individual consideration given to all persons already connected with the Community or who wanted to enter into relationship with it [1]. It is only natural that just in those early days,
when the hard-won unity was threatened most, and when individual convictions on matters connected with the Reformation still manifested themselves in so many and varied ways
above the din of the spiritual battle, maintenance of doctrinal

---

[1] *Acta* V, f° 25 r°; VI, f° 39 r°.

discipline was at its most severe. It was especially the Baptist and other sectarian elements which again and again opposed the process of the gradual consolidation of the Church's unity. On the other hand, it was only natural that the Church suspected the presence of Baptist and other unorthodox tendencies, even in cases of slight deviation from its doctrine. A few of these persons with their followers caused rumours and commotion in those early years. We will look at them, both for the sake of their own significance and for the light which they throw on the Community, in this early period of its existence.

In the early part of 1563 a certain Justus Velsius made his appearance in the Community, "a strange muddle-headed individual, holding sundry erroneous views, which he thought to impart to others, both secretly and in public". He influenced the minds of many persons to the extent of their beginning to accept some of his teachings. One of his tenets was that man did not become justified before God by belief in the righteousness of Christ, but because man, when he is born anew, attains that perfection which was in Adam [1]. An individualistic enthusiast, therefore, who, in the matter of those born anew, assumed perfectibility, the possibility of man's attaining perfection by his own efforts. Justus Velsius [2], a man of great gifts, but of a restless, turbulent spirit, was born at The Hague about 1505. He was a typical figure of the Renaissance, and his religious individualism cannot be accommodated in any of the confessional movements of his time. He had studied in Bologna, and taught medicine and Latin in Louvain and philosophy in Strasburg. He inclined towards the Reformation, but was also in sympathy with the idea of a Catholic Church cleansed of its abuses, and this led him to exchange his chair at Strasburg for one in Roman Catholic Cologne. His published writings, however, reflected too many heresies for him to be able, in the long run, to maintain his position there or in the Reformed foreign community in Frankfort, where he settled subsequently. His spiritual and Anabaptist principles led to his adopting an entirely individual standpoint, and this caused him to be looked upon as a heretic practically everywhere. After staying at Heidelberg and Mar-

---

[1] Ruytinck, *Gheschiedenissen*, pp. 57 et seq.
[2] For extensive references to him, see C. Sepp, *Kerkhistorische Studiën*, Leiden 1885, pp. 91–179.

burg, he came to London in 1562. The institute of the "prophesy" was for such a figure the perfect medium for propagating his ideas. On March 18th, 1563, he opposed in the "prophesy" the minister Nicolaas Carineus, saying that "man can be without sin" if in consequence of rebirth the old man was drowned "like Pharaoh in the sea" and he thus became "godly through renewal like glowing iron and shining suns"; inwardly, man could then be perfect as Adam was before his fall [1]. But this was not all. He submitted a written statement to the Consistory, embodying an accusation against the ministers Nicolaas Carineus and Petrus Delenus, in which he claimed to be able to prove his standpoint with miracles and stated that he would do so at the next session of the "prophesy". This threatened to lead to a commotion in church. In order to prevent this, Delenus and Utenhove went to the Bishop of London who promised to help them. Before the day on which the service was to be held, Velsius was taken into custody [2]. Ruytinck relates that Velsius in one of his appearances as a "prophet" threatened the Bishop and all his other enemies with the judgment of God. It ended by Velsius being deported. His wanderings after he left England cannot be traced with any degree of accuracy. We only know that he stayed in a number of places in Holland. To an increasing degree he fell into fanatical fantasies, being perpetually in conflict with the religious and civil authorities, "in delirium lapsus". He died after 1581.

Action against such a fanatic, who was probably perfectly sincere, could easily create the impression of dogmatic intolerance. But apart from what we have said above concerning the necessity of maintaining a close confessional bond, in considering this question, account should be taken of the danger arising from mistaken views regarding the Community on the part of a more or less hostile world. Significant in this respect is what the Ambassador to England of the Governess Margaretha, d' Assonleville, wrote to his mistress in April oft hat year: "C'est une grande confusion de la multitude des nostres qui sont icy fuis pour la religion. On les estime en Londres, Sandwich et co-

---

[1] *Kerkeraads-protocollen 1560–1563*, p. 478. Cf. the statement by Strype, *Life of Grindal*, in J. Bonet Maury, *Des origines du Christianisme unitaire chez les Anglais*, Paris 1881, p. 64: "Il soutenait que Jésus Christ est Dieu en homme, ou plutôt homme, Dieu, et que tout chrétien peut, à son example, devenir par la foi homme-Dieu".

[2] *Kerkeraads-protocollen 1560–1563*, pp. 481 et seq.

marque adjacente de XVIII à XX mille testes. Il y en a plu-
sieurs qui désiroient retourner" — and then he quotes Velsius
as his informant (the report was certainly incorrect): "comme
Velsius a dit à moy" [1]. Where such relations existed, it was not
to be wondered at that the leaders of the Dutch Church were
rigorous in their judgment concerning the purity of the doctrine
taught and in the matter of admission to membership. In April a
certain Rolandus Over applied for membership. He was asked to
state his view on the subject of the Anabaptists, who did not accept
the doctrine of God having become fully man in Jesus Christ.
He replied that he would not deny them salvation, but that
he, personally, would not dare to grant them salvation on the
strength of such views. To-day we would say, a humane, wise
and tolerant Christian pronouncement. But not so the leaders
of the Church: he was not admitted "because of his half-heart-
edness in such weighty matters" [2]. These were times, not of the
golden mean, but of violent extremes, not of an "and-and",
but of an "either-or" attitude in such matters.

Behind this small case, however, there lay a much bigger
matter, of which it really was an offshoot: the Van Haemstede
case which shook the Community to its foundations. Adriaan
van Haemstede, on his father's side probably a descendant of
the Counts of Holland, was born about 1525. He studied in Louvain. Possibly his family was one of the first to emigrate to England. In 1556 he was active as a preacher in East Friesland,
and thereafter he laboured in the Southern Netherlands, especially in Antwerp, in circumstances fraught with peril and po-
verty. A price had even been set on his head. He proceeded to
Aachen, but after a short stay, was one of the first to help the
Community in London after the change in conditions there.
In May, 1559, we find him preaching in London. It is evident
from the confession of faith which he sent from there to the
fugitives in Aachen at their request, that he was not an ardent
Calvinist. The document, which hardly touches on the typical
Calvinist dogmatics, is in composition and manner of expression reminiscent of Melanchton, whilst it was rejected by some
as being too Zwinglian. Van Haemstede was certainly no man

---

[1] Gachard, *Correspondance de Philippe II sur les affaires des Pays-Bas*, Vol. II,
p. 247.
[2] *Kerkeraads-protocollen 1560–1563*, p. 398.

of dogmatic extremes and so it was that his sympathies could go out even to those step-children of the Reformation, the Baptists (Mennonites). The London Community, which was itself fundamentally opposed to Anabaptist ideas, also had the example of the English Government before it in this respect. In 1560 an edict was issued by Queen Elizabeth, ordering the Anabaptists to leave the country within 20 days [1]. The authorities were no less afraid of the Anabaptists' principle which aimed at the dissolution of the State than of that which favoured the dissolution of the Church; were they not looked upon as the anarchists of the Reformation? Van Haemstede was unable to agree with this action and he took up the cudgels on behalf of the persecuted. However, in doing so, he made a distinction between two kinds of Baptists, namely the revolutionary, disrupting Baptists, who had ceased to exist after the dramatic happenings in Münster, and the quiet Baptists of the type of Menno Simonsz, sectarians, certainly, but not dangerous to either Church or State. Admittedly they taught a peculiar doctrine regarding the incarnation of Christ, which we have already met with in connection with the question submitted to the above-mentioned Rolandus Over. They held the view that the flesh of Christ was not identical with that of Mary, but built up through the special creative activity of God. But, said Van Haemstede, this was merely an interpretation of the matter and of no importance, as no principle was involved. Very soon the Church Council received a complaint to the effect that Van Haemstede was said to have had meetings with the Anabaptists and had solemnly undertaken to intercede on their behalf with the authorities and the Bishop. When at last he complied with a summons of the Church Council to appear before it — even the ministers did not escape the Church's doctrinal discipline, they were perhaps even more subject to it than anyone else — he admitted having extended his hand to the Anabaptists, though only from a brotherly disposition and not because he agreed with their ideas. However, the Council rejected his plea. Van Haemstede was held to have been at fault by recognizing the others as brothers and as weak members of the body of Christ [2].

---

[1] J. ab Utrecht Dresselhuis, *Adriaan van Haemstede*, in *Archief voor Kerkelijke Geschiedenis*, VI (1835), p. 65.

[2] See the reply to the questions put to him by the Consistory in his letter to Acontius, *Archivum*, II, p. 54.

Moreover, and this point will undoubtedly have weighed heavily, the position taken up by him encouraged "suspicion and hazards for our Community with the English and the others" [1]. The matter now assumed ever growing proportions: the minutes of the Church Council are full of it. The Council suspected Van Haemstede of having connections with heretics of greater or lesser importance, and his irenic refusal to condemn certain heterodox individuals out of hand contributed not a little to this suspicion. In addition, he adhered to his view that differences of opinion concerning certain aspects of doctrine were mere incidentals, "hay and stubble," a "throwing of the dice for the cloak" [2]. On September 2nd, 1560, a disputation took place between Petrus Delenus and Van Haemstede in the presence of the Church Council [3]. On that occasion Van Haemstede was supported by the Italian Jacobus Acontius who was greatly esteemed by the Queen on account of his engineering activities, though his religious views rendered him fully suspect. For Acontius was just another of those typical Renaissance figures, the "omnis homo", versed in all contemporary sciences, an advocate of tolerant humanism, opposed to all confessionalism and inclined towards a relativist standpoint. As Van Haemstede did not recognize the other ministers of the churches (both the French and the Dutch) as judges in his case, the complete case was submitted to the Bishop, who declared himself competent to pronounce judgment. Van Haemstede does not appear to have been disliked, for the Bishop, was pressed to treat the accused (who had meanwhile been suspended from the ministry) with leniency. The Bishop, on his part, promised to exercise moderation in his judgment. There were also friends who pointed to the financial consequences which all this might have for Van Haemstede, and the danger which he would run if he should ultimately become known as a heretic [4]. He persisted in declaring himself prepared to confess his guilt if he could be convinced of his error in a public debate, but this debate was refused him. Finally, on November 17th, 1560, he was excommunicated by the Bishop [5]. Before another

---

[1]) *Kerkeraads-protocollen 1560–1563*, pp. 6–11.
[2]) *Ibid.*, p. 25.
[3]) *Ibid.*, p. 38.
[4]) *Ibid.*, pp. 50, 65.
[5]) The pronouncement in *Archivum*, II, pp. 142 et seq.

month had elapsed, Van Haemstede had left England. Meanwhile news of the sentence had been sent to all related churches
on the Continent: Emden, Antwerp, Frankfort, etc. A sentence
on account of religious liberalism had serious consequences in
those days!

The case would have ended there, but for Van Haemstede's
not inconsiderable following in the Community. A striking feature was the readiness with which complaints were forthcoming
to the effect that Van Haemstede had been badly treated: doctrinal discipline was all very well, but there was also such a
thing as freedom of speech! A woman, Janneke Satler, declared: ,,even if she had been cut off from our Community, she
had not been cut off from God's Community" [1]. Here we come
face to face with the true individual, unclerical point of view
which looks upon church and church community as purely incidental in the light of the holy, invisible Church which at all
times transcends all visible institutions. Meanwhile the Church
remained on its guard against Van Haemstede's teachings. For
instance, a certain Cathryn Luck was severely reprimanded
because she had mixed with "Haemstedians" [2]. Amongst these
"Haemstedians" was to be found, along with others, the well-
known historian Emanuel van Meteren, who was "cut off" on
account of his opposition to the Church Council — an excommunication which lasted until 1571, when he recanted [3]. But
what was worse, in July, 1561, Van Haemstede returned to London and reappeared in the Church, a change of attitude in his
favour having been held out to him. Coming from Emden, he
had journeyed from Groningen in the company of a certain
Godfried Hieronymous, who hailed from that town and carried
a letter from the Emden Community, pressing for Van Haemstede's case to be settled amicably. To this the Church Council replied that it concerned not only Van Haemstede and the
Church, but also the French Church and the Bishop [4]. Van Haemstede, however, had also brought letters from Emden for the
London ministers. He opened them and made their contents
public, even communicating them to the Bishop, before deli-

---

1) *Kerkeraads-protocollen 1560–1563*, pp. 136, 111.
2) *Ibid.*, p. 287. She was denied admission to Communion, p. 302.
3) See W. D. Verduyn, *Emanuel van Meteren*, The Hague 1926, pp. 80–97.
4) *Kerkeraads-protocollen 1560–1563*, p. 333.

vering the letters into the hands of those to whom they were addressed [1]. The rumour of his return immediately caused a great deal of commotion. The Bishop wished the authorities in London to arrest him. The French and Dutch Church Councils conferred together, seeing as much danger in his being made a martyr as in his opportunity "so he be free to strew his venom". The French were in favour of arrest and so it was decided, but the Dutch begged the Bishop to arrange for the letter of apprehension to the authorities to come from him "so that our Community might not be blamed" [2]. The Church was evidently very cautious lest any odium should attach to it. News of the case had spread abroad, both in England and on the Continent, and Acontius took the matter up on behalf of Van Haemtede. The French, on the other hand, were bitterly opposed to him. In the meantime the Bishop had sent the prisoner a form for recantation of his errors, having first obtained advice from influential theologians [3]. Van Haemstede refused to recant what the protocols term "die gruwelen Adriani Hamstedii" (the horrors of Van Haemstede). Sentence was pronounced on August 21st, 1562. He was ordered to leave England within 15 days on pain of death and in the meantime had to abstain from all utterances and disputations.

This ended the Van Haemstede case for good, although, as we have seen, his influence in the Community continued to make itself felt for some time [4]. We may assume that the London Community, though in accordance with the times anything but averse to heresy hunts, in this case was particularly moved by outside pressure from the side of the English authorities — another indication of the Community's dependent position at that time. Van Haemstede returned to East Friesland, where he appears to have died in the same year — a martyr and persecuted for

1) *Ibid.*, p. 336.

2) *Kerkeraads-protocollen 1560–1563*, p. 332.

3) The form can be found in Ruytinck, *Gheschiedenissen*, pp. 31 et seq., followed by the words: ,,Deze bekentenis en stondt Hamstedio niet aan" (Van Haemstede did not like this confession) — which we can readily understand.

4) See also the account given by Van Schelven, *De Vluchtelingenkerken*, pp. 144–152, and the references here and in the published Protocols to *Archivum* and Ruytinck. Little or no evidence can be found there of the sly part which, according to Van Schelven (pp. 149 et seq. of his book), Acontius is supposed to have played in this affair. For that matter, he received his own share of the application of doctrinal discipline in the French churches; see le Baron F. de Schickler, *Les églises du refuge en Angleterre*, Tome I, Paris 1892, pp. 121 et seq.

his convictions, — he, who in his celebrated book, "History and Death of the Pious Martyrs", of 1559, recorded the courage and devotion of the witnesses of the Faith with so much piety for later generations. This book has been reprinted many times.

Another matter was looming up on the horizon, smaller and rather trivial in its origin, but bigger in its repercussions on the Community, namely the case of Van Winghen [1]. A violent plague epidemic, which ravaged Europe in 1563 and spread to England, in London alone caused the deaths of over 21,000 persons, according to Ruytinck. The Dutch Community did not lag behind in taking measures to combat the disease. Doctors were charged with the medical care of the poor, watchmen were made to nurse the sick. They also had to assist in laying out the dead and in burying them, a task which normally fell to the deacons [2]. Among the dead were the two ministers Petrus Delenus and Nicolaus Carineus, the latter having arrived from East Friesland only the year before. The minister of the sister community at Sandwich, Godfried van Winghen, declared himself willing to help the London Community and henceforth acted as its minister. He was born in the district of Liège, and had come to England as a fugitive in the early part of the struggle, acting as tutor to the sons of à Lasco. He had taken part in the wanderings of the exiles and at last found a refuge in London, where he occupied himself in translating the Bible. It is by this translation that he is best known [3]. Held to have qualified thereby for the office of preacher, he served the "Churches under the Cross" in Flanders, amongst others. In 1562 he received a call to Sandwich.

One of the first actions of the minister was to arrange for a regulation to be passed, by which a father, when applying for the baptism of his child, had to submit a declaration by two persons who were willing to act as witnesses at the baptism. It was intended to be a guarantee that the child had been born of parents who, by their confession of faith and their way of life, could claim baptism for their child. There was ample justifi-

---

[1] Here we follow in the main the detailed account of Van Schelven, *De Vluchte-lingenkerken*, pp. 153–178. The representation by Dr. A. Kuyper, *De Hollandsche Gemeente te Londen in 1570* in *Voor Vierhonderd Jaren*, from which some complementary details have been taken, is less correct on certain points.

[2] *Kerkeraads-protocollen 1560–1563*, pp. 42 et seq.

[3] Compare p. 28.

cation for such a measure in those days, considering the continuous stream of new members from the Continent. Moreover,
the measure was no novelty, but had been known already in
the early years of the existence of the Church. However, there
was opposition on the part of the deacons, and it seems likely
that a private feud on the part of one of them, about whom Van
Winghen had previously had reason to complain, was not un-
connected with this. In fact, there was also a matter of principle involved in this opposition. The majority on the Church
Council, when framing the rules of baptism, had done so on the
pattern of the English Church baptism. This dependence on
that Church was a thorn in the flesh to many who based themselves on a strict Reformed standpoint. Two parties presently
came into being, one composed of elders, including Van Winghen, which favoured the measure of witnesses to baptism, and
one composed of the younger deacons, each party having its
adherents in the Community. This resulted in a division within
the Church, which grew to dimensions far exceeding the relative unimportance of the original point at issue. Want of tact,
and a certain obstinacy on the part of the Van Winghen group,
were contributing factors. The deacons even resigned *en bloc*.
The elders thereupon elected new officers in accordance with
their right to co-opt and in the end submitted the whole question to the Bishop, who put them and Van Winghen entirely
in the right. The opposition turned in all directions for support,
but in November, 1564, rather unexpectedly, a settlement was
arrived at, partly through the intervention of the Superintendent. The deacons' party reconciled itself with the settlement,
and Van Winghen and his followers promised to exercise moderation. Presently, however, the struggle broke out anew. Once
more the Bishop intervened, this time with a direct "formual
pacificationis" by which the existing position was maintained
on the whole. In the pending matter of the increase in the number of elders he held out the prospect of an early election. Those
who did not wish to submit to this pacification, had to leave
the Community, but could join an English parish church. From
this it may be concluded that the general expectation was that
the result of the election would be in favour of the anti-Van
Winghen party. However, this decree also failed to bring peace.
The sister community at Emden now intervened and sent de-

legates who were to act as mediators. They were the well-known
preacher Cornelis Cooltuyn and a certain Hendrik Schonenberg.
The Bishop gave them a free hand, but it was not without difficulty that they succeeded, in March 1566, in reaching an agreement, which on the whole favoured the Van Winghen group.
A number of deacons proceeded to attend the services of Anglican preachers whose views corresponded with theirs, but this
did not last long, for it was just those Anglican divines who
disapproved of "the white surplice and sundry similar ceremonials" who about this time were deprived of their office by the
authorities and placed under arrest.

The old antithesis flared up once more, most probably as the
result of a sermon delivered by the Rev. Van Winghen towards
the end of 1566, in which he inveighed violently against the
revolutionary proceedings of the iconoclasts and church pilla-
gers in the Low Countries, in Ruytinck's words "against a business which defies God and the authorities". At the back of
this was a question of principle, one which had previously presented itself for consideration by the Community: the question as to how far it was permissible to oppose the authorities
for the sake of one's belief. In 1563 the Church Council had already had occasion to take action against a certain Cornelis
Riemslager and his friends. They had expressed the opinion
that "it is permitted to oppose the authorities who come to
arrest the brethren, yea, that one need not recognize evil authorities as authorities" [1]. Such a mood of rebellion-for-the-
sake-of-God savoured of revolutionary Anabaptism — though
it need not be identical with it — and was certainly likely
to arouse suspicion on the part of the English authorities. The
question was a burning one in the southern Netherlands and it
became even more so in this "miracle year" of 1566. Across
the water opinion was also strongly divided. The radical standpoint on the question of rebellion was certainly not in keeping
with the views of Calvin, but among the violent Calvinists, who
had emigrated to England and other countries in large numbers
just during these months, Van Winghen's sermon had the effect of oil poured on to fire. It was the period in which certain
changes began to show themselves in the composition of the
London Community as a result of the arrival of these turbu-

---

[1] *Kerkeraads-protocollen 1560–1563*, pp. 391 et seq.

lent elements. This development has been dealt with earlier herein (see page 32). This meant that the deacons' party was encouraged in its opposition. The most recalcitrant elements even decided to leave the Church, and they went to Norwich, there to join the Dutch Community among which they apparently found a number of kindred spirits. From sheer reaction this had the effect of making the Church Council adopt an autocratic and dictatorial course of action. In a document consisting of 27 articles it formulated its attitude in sharp terms. The old controversy was revived once more, but the right to rebel was at the same time emphatically curtailed. The Church Council of Norwich was informed that, unless they lodged an objection, application would be made to Geneva, also in its name, for approbation of these articles. Norwich thereupon sent delegates to Geneva, but these did not gain much information. The delegation from London also arrived, and Geneva expressed agreement with the articles, though condemning their tone. Application for advice was made also to other Reformed centres (Lausanne, Zürich. Bern, Heidelberg). On the whole the replies were not unfavourable to the London Church, but the need for a conciliatory attitude was stressed on all sides. Reconciliation was actually arrived at. It was even decided to replace the entire Church Council by means of free elections. Possibly the party of Van Winghen realized that it had gone too far and that it no longer had the confidence of the Community. In any case, the election went against it. The entire Church Council, now enlarged to 12 elders and 14 deacons, henceforth consisted of persons who were not in sympathy with Van Winghen. The number of ministers was also increased. The new ministers were Domini Barth. Wilhelmi, Octavius Selnavus and Georgius Sylvanus (Joris Wybo). All this happened in 1569.

Van Winghen had lost the battle, certainly a bitter pill to swallow for one of his undoubtedly imperious disposition. He tried to make up for it by continuing to attack the iconoclasts in his sermons. Complaints and interrogations followed until at last he was suspended as a preacher on July 15th, 1570. He would not acknowledge himself beaten, but adopted a sulky attitude, did not attend the Council meetings and during the services sat amongst the congregation. The Council decided to apply to the Coetus of the three foreign communities for a ruling, but at about the same time Van Winghen asked the Bishop to arbitrate. The Bishop's verdict was in Van Winghen's favour, as might have been foreseen. It was on this occasion that the Bishop exercised his right of veto. He gave Van Winghen a letter of inhibition (see page 32). By this action the case was taken out of the hands of the Coetus. In his capacity of Superintendent, the Bishop gave an order that his verdict be read from the pulpit in Dutch and in Latin, and that this must definitely be the end of the controversy. The verdict is characteristic of the maintenance of public authority, which was such a feature of the English Church. No private person would be allowed to change abuses in the Church unless he were specially moved by the Holy Ghost, but this was not to be made a general rule. Even unbelieving and papist magistrates were to be acknowledged and honoured, and believers imprisoned by the authorities were not to be forcibly liberated [1]. This verdict certainly did not breathe the spirit which characterized the revolt even then flaring up in the southern Netherlands. On the contrary, caution and moderation continued to be exercised. As late as 1576, the Colloquium discussed the attitude to be adopted in the case of the "Water Beggars," "who go on the sea, pirating and forageing". The question was: were these people acceptable when they carried letters from the Prince, and could they be admitted to the Communion table? [2]

Thus ended — but for a few final rumblings — the thunder storm of the Van Winghen quarrels, an unattractive chapter in the history of the Church in London. The lengths to which people went in the struggle can be gathered from the story of the behaviour of the elder Jan Engelram, a difficult person who was an ardent follower of Van Winghen, no less violent and tenacious than he. He caused the Community a great deal of trouble. Threatened with expulsion, he tried to get the proceedings against him terminated in his favour, again by a letter of inhibition. But this time it did not work. The Chancellor of the Bishop pronounced verdict against him, and Engelram was forced to make public confession of guilt. A short time afterwards, in April, 1571, he applied for a letter of commendation and mo-

---

1) *Kerkeraads-protocollen 1569–1571*, p. 259.
2) *Colloquia*, p. 30.

ved to Canterbury [1]. If at the end of it all we ask ourselves
the question as to where, or with whom, the fault lay of all these
upheavals, no simple answer can be given. It is certain that
there were faults on both sides, though it is equally certain that
Van Winghen's autocratic and unbending nature exerted an
evil influence. All the same, he does not deserve the violent con-
demnation pronounced on him by Dr Kuyper. Moreover, Dr
Kuyper's presentation of the case is too much coloured by a
contemporary controversy on church politics in Holland. It
is an anachronism to want to see in Van Winghen the typical
adherent of the principle of centralized church government,
as opposed to that of autonomy. Not long afterwards, in 1572,
Van Winghen left England (the Prince had asked for preachers),
but he did not succeed in finding a living. In 1574 he returned
to London where he continued to act as pastor until his death in
1590. That he had not lost the confidence of the London Community is evident from the refusal, in 1579, of a request that
he should be lent to the church at Courtrai for a short time. The
reply stated that he was the only capable regular minister
and could not be spared. In the following year the Council decided to give him a gratuity of £ 6 in recognition of his faithful
services [2]. Finally, as to the question of "taking witnesses in
the matter of baptism of children", which had been one of the
causes of the quarrels in connection with Van Winghen, time
soon smoothed the sharp edges. In the Colloquium of 1576 it
was decided "that everyone was free to do as he wished in so
far as this can be done with propriety in each community and
without coercion of conscience" [3].

By 1570, however, the general situation was not yet so advanced. Careful watch was being kept to ensure that there was
no deviation from the Confession of Faith to which members
had subscribed on joining the Community. It is questionable
whether this maintenance of the Church's teaching was always
realized without "coercion of conscience". Whenever there was
any suspicion of dissentient views, the Church ordered an ex-

---

[1] See Kuyper, *De Hollandsche Gemeente te Londen in 1570*, pp. 165–168; Van
Schelven, *Johannes Engelram*, in *Stemmen des Tijds*, V (1916), 3, pp. 172–305. The
Acta of those days are full of the name of Engelram.

[2] *Acta* V, on Oct. 15th, 1579, and May 20th, 1580.

[3] *Colloquia*, p. 22.

amination into the faith, "examinatio fidei". By the very nature of things, London was bound to be a meeting place of preachers of unorthodox tendencies, exiles unable to find another place of refuge on account of their heterodox views. We already came across one such in Justus Velsius. In 1569, a certain Petrus de Bert [1] was summoned to appear before the Church Council after he had submitted written objections to the Church's teaching. He declared that he found "certain absurdities" in the teaching embodied in the Confession of Faith which he had signed. In a second hearing he maintained his objections against the doctrine of the Holy Trinity "because of the peculiar qualities ascribed to the Father, namely the principle of the creation of all things, which pertains to all the Three Persons". There is no mention of how this matter was resolved [2]. In the same year there were proceedings against a certain Martin Tay, a glazier by profession, who had been received into the Church ten years earlier, although he had openly declared that in the matter of Communion he held to the Lutheran view. Meanwhile he abstained from taking part in the Communion services and when on one occasion there was an opportunity in one of the Embassies to participate in a Communion Service in accordance with Lutheran ritual, he availed himself of it. This was immediately followed by the lodging of a complaint on the part of those who had not yet forgotten the harsh treatment from the Lutheran side which had been meted out to the exiles in their winter wanderings. But Tay, not to be beaten, defended himself on the ground that à Lasco and Utenhove, when in Germany, had also taken part in Communion services with "Martinists", Lutherrans, albeit under protest. On the subject of baptism, too, Tay held views which could not pass muster with the Reformed Church. His excuse was accepted in the end, much to the disgust of his accusers [3]. Naturally, a watch was kept for popery. A certain Abraham der Kinderen was accused of having allowed his children in Antwerp "to take part in popish services" with surplices and pluvials, but this accusation was proved to have no foundation [4]. We already saw that individualistic

---

1) Erroneously no distinction is made in the published *Acta* between him and Pieter de Bert who was an honourable elder and visitor of the sick.

2) *Kerkeraads-protocollen, 1569–1571*, pp. 72, 81.

3) *Ibid*, pp. 73, 96, 114, 119, 121, 129.

4) *Ibid.*, pp. 88, 97.

and Baptist heresies were being guarded against. Booksellers were warned not to stock the writings of Sebastiaan Francq, Hendrik Niclaesz and others [1]. As early as 1561 the Dutch Church had made an approach to the Bishop, pressing him to prohibit the printing in London of the dangerous books of Sebastiaan Francq [2]. The decision of the Colloquium of 1576 that no books should be allowed to be printed without the permission of the Church Council points in the same direction [3].

However, as the years went by, the anxious watch from the point of view of doctrine on the views of members of the congregation gradually became less pronounced and the inquisitorial interest in the safety of the teaching of the Church receded into the background, slowly it is true, but unmistakably. It was a general symptom of the gradual slackening of the ropes of intolerance, though there was no intention of letting them go entirely as yet. We can observe this process developing slowly after the advent of the 17th century. The sentence of expulsion or excommunication, which was regarded as a kind of spiritual death sentence, had, in actual practice, been hedged in by all kinds of protective reservations. It was seldom pronounced and certainly never without careful consideration. Thus, in 1623, in the case of a certain Lowys van Holbroeck, who was excommunicated "because of his shameful apostasy in the abominable superstition of papacy". Two years of negotiation, argument, trial and admonition preceded the pronouncement of the sentence, and both the Colloquium and the Bishop had been brought into it [4]. Doctrine and doctrinal discipline remained, but their character gradually became less formal. The realization that the variations in the teaching were of a relative nature was beginning to make its way, though it did so with great difficulty and under constant opposition. In the case of the Dutch communities in England, a special circumstance contributed to this development. With the passing of the years, the dogmatic significance of London to the home country, and vice versa, was diminishing. Life in general was no longer influenced by religious struggles to the same extent as before,

---

1) *Ibid.*, p. 187.
2) *Kerkeraads-protocollen 1560–1563*, p. 156.
3) *Colloquia*, p. 23.
4) *Acta* VII, on the years 1620–1622.

and there was certainly no longer any need for London to be
regarded as the stronghold of the faith. Not that the relations
with the Low Countries were becoming less close, but the religious, at least the dogmatic element in them, was losing its
significance. Circumstances contributed to the London Community becoming gradually rather isolated in matters of religion, and we may take it that the English surroundings with
their particular religious and ecclesiastical problems, tended to
make the Community in the long run more indifferent to these
questions at home. The Arminian quarrels, for instance, which
during the truce with Spain led to such violent party struggles
at home, caused no commotion in London. The Reverend Ruytinck seems to have been personally interested in these events,
as is shown by his History. In 1611 he preached extensively on
the subject of Acts 15, in order to demonstrate that synods are
particularly well suited to settle differences in the Church [1].
Of course the consistories took some notice of the matter. In
the Colloquium of 1612 the question was asked as to what should
be done with a member who has unsound ideas on the question
of predestination. It was decided that, if such a person persisted
in his error, he should be suspended, and that the Community
should be warned against the danger to which he might expose
it [2]. Six years later the question came up once more, but from
the wording of the minutes it is clear that it was no longer of
vital interest — and this at a time when the drama had reached
its climax in the home land! — "whereas the condition of the
communities across the sea is such that some have been infected
with Arminian sentiments". It was decided that those arriving
with letters of commendation from Arminian ministers should
be put through their paces before being accepted [3]. A year previously, in 1617, the Reverend Regius and an elder, with two
dignitaries of the French Church, on one occasion went to the
Bishop of London, as they were anxious about possible infection
with the views held by the Arminians, by people coming from
overseas: could the Bishop give them some advice as to what
should be done about such people? The Bishop promised to
discuss the matter with the Archbishop and to give a reply "in

---

[1] Ruytinck, *Gheschiedenissen*, p. 267.
[2] *Colloquia*, p. 174.
[3] *Ibid.*, p. 226.

due course". The minutes maintain silence about this step. This will cause no surprise to those who know something about the disposition of the Anglican clergy [1]! We must not, however, underrate the earnestness with which the Arminian question was treated within the Dutch Community. A young woman, a domestic servant, who in 1629 asked to be admitted to Communion, but revealed that she taken part in Communion at Utrecht with the Remonstrant (i.e. Arminian) Community, was examined on her beliefs. In the matter of Free Will she declared her adherence to the doctrine of the Church. The other points were "of so high a matter" that they were quite beyond her. The Church Council was satisfied with this, also because of her promise never again to go to the Arminians. With this, the danger of this particular infection was considered to have been exorcized [2].

Remarkably mild and accommodating — at least in comparison with analogous cases of three-quarters of a century earlier — was the attitude, in 1644, towards a woman who had married a Roman Catholic without first informing the Church and, therefore, without public announcement. She will have to be watched (it is known that she means well), but at the same time there is understanding of the fact that she must also preserve the peace with her husband! However, if it should transpire that he prevents her from attending Communion, she will be taken in hand and, if need be, brought before the Alderman [3]! Even more remarkable is a pronouncement by the Colloquium of 1646: "that the denial of child baptism is really no heresy, but certainly a very harmful error", even if the attitude adopted towards Antinomians and Anabaptists is one of opposition [4]. No less remarkable was the case in the same year of the well-known drainage and land reclamation specialist, Cornelis Vermuyden. He and his wife were reprimanded by the Church Council because they had not had their child baptized sufficiently promptly and because she sometimes worshipped in the English Church. He replied that the christening had only been postponed because his wife was considering having the child baptized in the Eng-

---

1) *Acta* VII, f° 70 v°.
2) *Ibid.*, f° 192 v°.
3) *Acta* VIII, f° 126 r°, 130 r°.
4) *Colloquia*, p. 335.

lish Church. He added that he himself sometimes went to the English Church, not because he did not agree with the Dutch Church, but for "additional edification." Prove to me, he said, that the censorship applies to me because I attend another church, for this reason [1]. This was a new note! Although the Council was prepared to show consideration to prominent people like the Vermuydens, yet Mevrouw Vermuyden had all the same to appear before it. Her defence reflected a state of mind which was not exactly orthodox. It had a strikingly individualistic side to it. She repeats, basing herself on the principle of Christian liberty, that she is free to go where she thinks she will find edification and contests the idea that, by so doing, she would cut herself off from the Dutch Community; for did she not remain within "the True Church?" She even insists on having the refutation of her standpoint in writing, but this is refused her. When the Reverend Calandrinus takes her in hand, she asks for the re-return of her letter of commendation! This is declined on the ground that she is under censorship. However, although a few more complaints are made in the Church Council to the effect that "Lady Vermuyden" detaches herself from the Church, there is no evidence of any further action [2].

In 1645, a certain Ahasverus Fromenteel actually dared to oppose the Church Council in the matter of adult baptism. He even had himself and his wife re-baptized the following year. The Council, whilst mentioning "the awfulness of their sin," for years tried with circumspection and endless patience to keep them in the Church. Although this case was made public as of one who had cut himself off, no mention was made of the name of the person involved. At this time there existed in the Community a certain amount of interest in the question of baptism and in the sectarian movement. This was undoubtedly connected with the Independentistic currents in England prior to and during the Commonwealth. But with the further passage of time all traces of differences in matters of dogma and church

---

[1] *Acta* VIII, f° 152 v°, 154 v°, 164 v°. The departure from the old adherence to principe is also evident from the following incidental circumstance. The Vermuydens originally intended to have their child baptized without witnesses. This had come to the knowledge of the Church Council and the case was carefully considered. The following solution was found: "If they turn up without previous notification, we will not refuse baptism, but if they announce their intention beforehand, we will refuse".

[2] *Archivum*, III[II], pp. 1965, 1967, 2009, 2026, *Acta* VIII, f° 139 r°, 141 r°.

teaching gradually disappear from the chronicles. In the world of Cromwell, man saw around him so much sectarianism, so much religious particularism, that he became accustomed to, and even familiar with, heterodoxy and lost sight of the distinctions between the many forms of religious beliefs. In 1657 the Church Council still devoted some attention to our remarkable religious pioneer and colonist, Peter Plockhoy, who was then in London, and called him — not entirely correctly — a Quaker. The fact that he obstinately refused to remove his hat during prayers in church may have led to this [1].

That, as a matter of fact, already in the 16th century when inquisitorial tendencies were still rampant, the London Community considered that a limit should be set to the mania for persecution, and that it was opposed in particular to the putting to death of heretics, transpires from the history of the Anabaptists who were arrested and executed in 1575. During the years 1571–1575, the Baptist elements in London were numerous and they made many converts. The authorities, however, kept a strict watch, and at Easter, 1575, they surprised a meeting in Whitechapel, outside the City gate, and arrested 27 persons. These were interrogated by Bishop Grindal on the well-known points: the manhood of Christ, child baptism, the oath, obedience to the authorities. As the prisoners understood neither English, nor Latin, and since they appeared to be Dutch, he made use of the services of the Dutch ministers, Van Winghen, Wybo and Regius. Five of the prisoners recanted their errors; eleven women and a young man were put on board a ship and transported across the sea, the young man not before he had first "been somewhat scourged in the street". When the others were threatened with capital punishment, the Church Council delegated one of the ministers and an elder to deliver letters of supplication addressed to the Queen and the Privy Council, embodying an elaborate argument against the prisoners being punished by death. This petition is remarkable for the humane and yet practical, sober spirit which it reflects: something like "what good does it do?" The intervention was in vain. On July 22nd, 1575, the two who had been most vocal and had persisted

---

[1] *Archivum* III[II], p. 2361. On the subject of Plockhoy: J. Lindeboom, *Stiefkinderen van het Christendom*, The Hague 1929, pp. 378–381; C. W. Roldanus, *Zeventiende-eeuwsche Geestesbloei*, Amsterdam 1938, pp. 139–146, 148–151, 176.

most in their convictions, were burned alive. Even when they
had been tied to the stake they refused to recant. What had
moved both the Queen and the Privy Council most to pass this
sentence, was the prisoners' refusal to recognize them as Christian Authorities [1]. This case gained much notoriety, also in Holland. Rumours were spread of Dutch complicity in the sentence,
because, during the trial, the Church Council had seen fit to
express agreement with some articles, five in number, against
the Anabaptists, of which the fifth spoke of the right and the
duty of putting heretics to death [2]. Protests poured in. The Council of the Reformed Church at Antwerp pressed for an explanation
and pronounced the London Community to be in the wrong.
The London Council replied that it had signed the articles
after pressure by the Bishop as a mark of loyalty to the authorities and not from conviction: their own point of view was sufficiently well known to the Antwerp Council [3]. Another enquiry
came in 1577 from the Council of the Reformed Church at Fran-
kenthal, which had been taunted by the Baptists with the reproach
that its London co-religionists had been accomplices in the
deaths of the two victims [4]. Six years after the event, the Council was once more asked for information , this time by the Dordrecht minister, Hendrik van den Corput. A full reply was sent [5].
Even as late as 1618, the London Community received a warning
from Haarlem to the effect that slanderous rumours were being
spread by the Baptists about complicity in the execution of
1575. Apparently the best the London Council could do by way
of answer was to send a copy of the letter sent years earlier to
Van den Corput [6]. Making due allowance for the times and for
the prevailing conditions, no blame attaches to the Dutch
Community, although its attitude in the matter of the fifth
article should have been firmer. The whole case reflects the
subordinate relation of the Church to the English Church and
the temporal authorities.

---

   [1]) An account is given in Ruytinck, *Gheschiedenissen*, pp. 107–113, and also, rather
more circumstantially, in a letter to H. van den Corput, to which further reference
will be made. The letters of supplication in *Archivum*, III[1], pp. 315–319.
   [2]) Letter from the Church Council to Sandwich, June 27th, 1575, asking what they
should do in this matter; *Archivum*, III[1], pp. 313 et seq.
   [3]) *Archivum*, II, pp. 252–258.
   [4]) *Archivum*, III[1], p. 420.
   [5]) *Ibid.*, p. 611; the reply in *Archivum*, II, pp. 700–708.
   [6]) Ruytinck, *Gheschiedenissen*, pp. 314 et seq.

In relating these developments which led up to a gradual slackening of the reins of doctrinal control, we have somewhat anticipated events. Let us, therefore, return for a moment to the first
decades of the Church's existence. The attention given so far to
cases of deviation from the Church's teaching and thus to the negative aspect of the life of the Church, must not blind us to the
fact that, on the positive side, the Church was deeply concerned
with the building up of the Faith. This could not be done without
ministers, but in those days the ever recurrent problem was
where to find capable preachers. It should be realized that, as
yet, no facilities existed for official, academic training, either
in England or in the Low Countries where the Church was still
struggling to reach a more definite form and organization. Those
who acted as ministers were either former Roman Catholic cler-
ics or monks, or "prophetically" inclined, self-taught men who
had prepared themselves as well as they could for the task to
which they felt themselves called. Some had studied abroad
(Geneva, Zürich, Heidelberg, or elsewhere) for a shorter or longer period. There was as yet no University in the Low Countries,
based on Reformed principles. As we have seen, the first pastors
of the London Community came from the Continent. It was
inevitable that the supply should slow down as the need in the
home country increased. The London Church, therefore, took
the matter in hand at an early stage. Presumably it was thought
at first that the "prophesy" could also be made to serve this
end, but as we have seen, it was not satisfactory in the long run.
Later, various schemes were mooted by which preachers would
train themselves and others in the knowledge and interpretation
of the Bible. The ministers Barth. Wilhelmi and Octavius Selnavus, who acted in this capacity in 1569, had been trained within
the Community and so had Johannes Cubus and Jacobus Regius
who replaced Wilhelmi and Van Winghen in 1572. Regius had
already served the Coventry Community, an offshoot of the
London Church, whereas Cubus had previously worked in the
London Church as deacon and school teacher. At the meeting
of the Consistory on December 4th, 1572, the necessity of appointing "a common teacher of theology" for the three churches
was voiced. The money would be found by the ministers when
visiting the members, by exhorting these to greater liberality [1].

1) *Acta* V, f° 6 v°. Cf. De Schickler, *Les églises du refuge*, T. I, p. 201.

The Council even succeeded in finding a teacher in no less a person than Loyseleur de Villiers (who later became Court preacher), the London Community contributing £ 15 per annum for this purpose [1]. In 1581 three persons were available who could be considered for the post of minister [2].

It was thus that the care of the Community extended to the problem of teaching, not only of more advanced teaching which benefited the training of ministers, but also the more elementary teaching which indirectly helped to build up the Community. There were schools for ordinary elementary teaching (it was, in fact, very elementary) and some for more advanced instruction where French and Latin was also taught. Constant appeals were made to parents from the pulpit to send their children to school. For those of slender means the school fees were paid by the deacons [3]. In 1621 the Colloquium pressed the point that each Church Community should have a good school teacher [4].

---

[1] *Acta* V, f° 15 r°.
[2] *Colloquia*, p. 61.
[3] Kuyper, *De Holl. Gem. te Londen*, p. 140.
[4] *Colloquia*, p. 253.

CHAPTER III

MAINTENANCE OF MORAL DISCIPLINE AND PHILANTHROPIC AND SOCIAL ACTIVITIES

The term "corpus corporatum et politicum", by which the Charter of King Edward VI characterized the refugee community is almost untranslatable. However, even untranslated, the word "politicum" is sufficient indication that in this case more is involved than what would be understood by a church community to-day. The term "corpus corporatum et politicum" bound the members together into a kind of civic corporate body. To begin with, this explains why in the correspondence and in Ruytinck's "History" — and, though to a lesser degree, in the Acta — the "nation" occupies a great place, sometimes an even greater place than the "church community". On the other hand, nation and church community were one and the same conception, or rather two aspects of the same conception. For a good understanding of the matter, it should be borne in mind that in those days fugitives outside their own country were without the protection of the law. Neither written nor unwritten laws, nor treaties guaranteed their protection. Whether or not they were admitted and tolerated depended upon the goodwill of the ruling sovereign or of the government of the country where they sought refuge, and this goodwill was, to a great extent, dependent upon existing political relations. It was to be expected that those authorities who granted hospitality required guarantees of the good faith and reliability of the fugitives. Such a guarantee could now be found in the fact that the fugitives were united by a spiritual tie with its special obligations. This spiritual tie offered assurance of unity of (admissible) convictions and acceptance of certain moral norms of order and discipline. For these reasons people like the Dutch and French refugees were considered fit for admission; moreover, there was a certain prospect of gain which might result from their admission. The fugitives, on their part, tried to make the expectations entertained of them come true by paying strict attention to the unity of conviction and the uniformity of behaviour and way of life resulting therefrom — to which they were the more inclined as this unity was entirely in line with the spiritual ties which bound them together. The unity in faith and the religious moral discipline found by them in Holy Scripture and as formulated in their Faith and Order, were the guarantees of a strong ecclesiastical unity within, and of recognition, help and liberty, without.

The preceding chapter dealt with this unity in faith and with the defences put up to guard it against false teachings. We will now consider the procedure followed to combat aberrations in behaviour and way of life as also the positive ethical and social labours of the Community. "Forma ac ratio" and "Christlicke Ordinanciën" had provided the biblical framework for the last-named activities. In the organization of the Community on the model of the old apostolic communities, the aim had been to preserve not only this model, but also the original purity of morals by the imposition of strict discipline. This discipline, though exercised by men, was not regarded as being human in origin, but, as it was based on Scripture, as a divine means of correction. It was for the dignitaries of the Church, i.e. the Ministers of the Word and the elders, to exercise it. Coming, as they did, from within the Community, they acted by virtue of the powers delegated to them by the Community — a system which was, therefore, totally different from the English episcopal system. Their admonition was brotherly admonition, their punishment, brotherly discipline. Its ultimate object was purity of morals and, with it, the well-being of the Church, and therefore, after admonition and non-admission to Communion, there was the penalty of expulsion or ex-communication. We, with our modern views on such matters, must not think lightly of these disciplinary measures. He, who was excluded from Communion, stood outside the circle of the Community; he, who had been excommunicated, stood outside the "corpus corporatum et politicum", with all the perilous possibilities attaching thereto. And let us not forget that excommunication signified more than a symbol in the modern sense of the word. It was a spiritual reality which meant a forfeiting of eternal blessing and bliss for the soul. It is only by keeping these circumstances well in view that we can gain any idea of the earnestness with which the discipline was administered and the docility with which it was accepted.

Was there occasion for such severe maintenance of discipline? Even without going into details, one can easily imagine that the occasion was there in full measure. Picture to yourself the composition of the refugee community. It contained people of deep religious conviction, to whom the purity of their faith and the possibility of confessing that faith in accordance with the indications of Holy Scripture, meant everything. In their Confession of Faith and in their way of life, they felt themselves to be God's own people. But there were also the turbulent and passionate natures with violent impulses, who were driven more by love of adventure and obscure passions than by any religious fervour. For these, existence in the foreign land was full of pitfalls. Torn loose, as they were, from tradition and from any restraint to which they might have been subjected at home, they were an easy prey to their own sinful inclinations and outside temptations, such as a great city offers in large measure. Remember, in this connection, the naturalistic, often little civilized attitude to life, which easily led to excesses [1]. This explains the numerous cases of unfaithfulness, adultery and bigamy, of immorality, drunkenness and dissoluteness, of quarrelling, calumny and fighting, of deceit in business dealings and trade. The Church Council conceived it as a sacred duty, laid upon it by God, to take action against these evils, and a preponderant majority in the Community supported them in this as a matter of course. For the same reasons, applications for membership were closely scrutinized; the promises made by godparents were treated with the utmost seriousness; admission to Communion was limited by a "censura morum", contraction of marriage was hedged in by all manner of guarantees, greed and carousing were warned against. Advice was tendered in all sorts of cases which troubled conscientious members, or in which they felt uncertain as to how they should act. These were the preventive measures; repression was effected by disciplinary

---

[1] What can one say of a drinking party in the house of a victim of the plague, in the company of the visitor of the sick? *Kerkeraads-protocollen 1569–1571*, p. 122.

action. What all this involved is shown by the Council minutes
covering those first decades. Whereas there is a certain scarcity
of detail in the descriptions of actual incidents, the minutes
are filled with accounts of the disciplinary measures taken. These
were recorded in great detail: names, circumstances, everything connected with the sentence was placed on record. The
almost endless length of these accounts does not detract from
their importance, often it actually lends them the colourfulness
of a *chronique scandaleuse*, but it does result in a certain mono-
tony.

Let us look at the facts more closely. Provided we do not
interpret them from a pre-conceived standpoint, these accounts
contribute to the picture which we are able to form of the position which the London Church occupied in the social life of the
Community. For, by the exercise of discipline, the Church had
gradually built up its social structure and imparted to it a shape
peculiarly its own. We will confine ourselves to the consideration of a few examples selected from the extensive material a-
vailable. The Council is continually being notified of intended
marriages. Each case is investigated with careful regard to any
objections which may have been lodged following the public
announcement. Permission for the marriage to take place is
given or withheld, as the case may be. In the latter event there
must be a confession of guilt by one of the parties, or by both,
before the matter can be proceeded with, unless it transpires
that the objections are insurmountable. Take, for instance, the
case of a certain Pieter de Brune, in 1570. Objections to his proposed marriage were lodged on account of an earlier promise
of marriage to a woman in Ghent, with whom he was alleged
to have had illicit intercourse. De Brune denied these allegations
and challenged the objection on the ground that the woman
in question was a lady of easy virtue. The Council treated the
case with the utmost seriousness. The man was told that he
must submit a declaration made before a notary to the effect
that the woman concerned was known to be a prostitute. Furthermore, he had to declare before a notary and witnesses in
London that, before contracting a marriage there, he wished
to be cleared of the supposed promise of marriage, and that
he would submit to the lawful decision of either the Bishop-
Superintendent or the Church Council. Finally, the notary and

the woman in Ghent had to be apprised of these matters with the intimation that, failing any reaction on her part, her claim would lapse after three months [1].

The cases which presented themselves for consideration were not always as complicated as this one. It might just be a simple enquiry as to whether a Christian was allowed to attend a Roman Catholic marriage service (which apparently was not regarded as being Christian). A case of this kind was considered to be sufficiently important to justify a consultation with the French brethren. There is no record of the decision, though there is every reason to believe this to have been in the negative [2]. Often a case would end with a simple confession of guilt. This was, for instance, the end of the case of Elizabeth Warwick whose marriage had been solemnized in the English Church and, to make matters worse, to a man who had long ago severed his ties with the Dutch Church. She confessed her guilt before the Consistory, and this confession was to be proclaimed from the pulpit with full mention of names [3]. This kind of confession, which was a feature of the disciplinary system, was in the nature of an intermediate form between private and public confession, for a distinction was made between these two types of confession [4]. Penance for a transgression of which no knowledge had spread abroad, was done within the body of the Consistory, whereas in the case of a transgression which had become public property, confession was made in the church before the congregation. The most rigorous form, which the latter type of confession took, was that it was read from the pulpit, the penitent standing in a separate place on a raised platform ("opt hoighte" — on the elevation), and affirming it with a publicly pronounced "yea" [5]. The verdict in the case of Elizabeth Warnick was, therefore, less severe. Even less severe, because apparently no name was mentioned, was the treatment of the case of a woman of the name of Wittewrongel. To quote from

---

[1] *Kerkeraads-protocollen* 1569–1571, pp. 85 et seq. Two other cases, *Ibid.*, pp. 27, 69, 70 and 70–72, 104, 117, 121, 153, 158; extensively rendered by Kuyper, *De Holl. Gem. te Lond. in 1572*, pp. 146 et seq.

[2] *Kerkeraads-protocollen* 1560–1563, p. 14.

[3] *Kerkeraads-protocollen* 1569–1571, p. 54.

[4] An elaborate exchange of thought on the subject of which sins are to be considered as private and which as public is to be found in the correspondance with the Community at Antwerp, end of 1575, in *Archivum*, III[1].

[5] *Kerkeraads-protocollen* 1560–1563, p. 409. See also *Acta* V, for 11th Nov., 1572.

the minutes: "The Community will be informed that there is a certain sister of the congregation, who in her house had transgressed the limits of propriety, so that many persons who had been scandalized have become suspicious, and publicity has been given to many more matters than were found to be true after diligent investigation, of which carelessness she, admonished before the Consistory, has confessed her guilt and to many others who might have knowledge of the case. Of which a statement, signed by her, was read out" [1]. It was altogether a queer case. The woman ran an inn, the husband often being away from home. On those occasions she had intimate relations with a young man, his care of her even extending to his acting in the capacity of a midwife.

That the discipline exercised by the Church Council was a means not only of relieving the souls of the transgressors and protecting the Community from "spot and blemish" but also of guarding people against the evil consequences of deeds committed in ignorance, is shown by the case of a certain Amele Bleychers who asked for public announcement to be made of her intended marriage. It transpired that some time before she had had illicit relations in Heidelberg with a man whom she had seduced. The bridegroom-to-be was warned, and he was told that he need not consider himself bound by his promise of marriage. For that matter, he had already had intimate relations with her. The woman had to confess standing "on the elevation" (see page 65). It appears that the two got married all the same some time later [2]. A similar case was that of a woman who declared that, on the strength of a promise of marriage, she had had intercourse with a man. The matter was investigated in great detail by the Church Council, when it turned out that the whole tale was pure invention [3].

Astonishing conditions certainly did obtain from time to time in this circle of believers. The case of Matheux Verhaege is not devoid of humour. Meeting an English woman who was a neighbour, he invited her to go for a walk with him. They went outside the town, had a few drinks and became so intoxicated that, staggering along, they landed in a ditch. They were

---

[1]) *Kerkeraads-protocollen 1569–1571*, p. 114.
[2]) *Kerkeraads-protocollen 1560–1563*, registre, i.v. Amele Blakers.
[3]) *Acta* V, on Aug. 1st, 1583.

rescued by some soldiers and taken into custody. Naturally Matheux had to do penance, in public at that, but he asked for some moderation to be exercised, because he said he knew that the woman's husband would willingly give a crown if he could get to know who had been out with his wife. Matheux's own wife also pleaded on his behalf, and the Council, not wishing to be harsh, was satisfied with the reading of a declaration in which the names were suppressed [1]. On the whole, however the Council was severe in its judgment and rigorous in its measures. The Community was carefully "fenced in". A former monk, hailing from Middelburg, who applied for membership, was certainly not admitted without further investigations [2]. One Alit Boefken, who came from Emden, became the subject of closer investigation, having been accused of harlotry [3]. A hangman's assistant, who came to say good-bye to the Council, asked for letters of recommendation for the churches overseas, but these were refused him [4]. A woman married to a man who had been expelled, was denied admission to Communion. Her husband was the historian Emanuel van Meteren, an adherent of Van Haemstede [5].

Attention was also given to the sins of greed and intemperance. The same Cathryn Luck whom we have met before (see page 44) as a follower of Van Haemstede, was accused of having given too lavish a wedding feast on the occasion of her marriage [6]. One Hans Stel, who caused a great deal of trouble — the minutes for the years 1570–1585 repeatedly mention his name — was reproached for having permitted dancing at the wedding of his daughter. Investigation revealed that no one belonging to the Church had taken part in the dancing. It was found that the bride was pregnant and that "she had not more than three months (to go)". The bridal couple were summoned to appear before the Council, but did not comply [7]. On the other hand the Council decided to bear the cost of a modest wedding breakfast for the Reverend Petrus Delenus [8]. He

---

1) *Kerkeraads-protocollen 1569–1571*, p. 180.
2) *Kerkeraads-protocollen 1560–1563*, p. 396.
3) *Ibid.*, p. 427.
4) *Ibid.*, p. 350.
5) *Ibid.*, p. 393.
6) *Ibid.*, p. 287.
7) *Acta* V, Dec. 5th, 1583.
8) *Kerkeraads-protocollen 1560–1563*, p. 116.

had certainly previously asked for permission to get married, as laid down in the rules. The members of the Council and the deacons were not spared either. One deacon had to do public penance in the church for drunkenness and fighting [1]. In December, 1583, the Council was told by a certain Jan Verbeke that on the Exchange people were saying that some of the elders were engaged in overseas trade by means of a passport issued by the Spanish Ambassador. All the members, on being questioned, protested their innocence. Despite these denials, the Council decided to try and find out whence this rumour originated, so that the matter might be probed to its foundation [2].

This will suffice, though the subject has by no means been exhausted. Moral discipline continued to be exercised even though, as the years went by, it took on less rigorous forms. In 1613 the Church Council considered the incident of the wedding of one of its members, at which there had been dancing. There had been many transgressors. Some excused themselves by saying that they had not realized how great was the sin they had committed. The Council decided that transgressions of this sort would in future come within the purview of the Church's discipline and that this time there would be no more than an admonition on the occasion of the minister's visit which preceded Communion [3]. But the Council continued to keep an eye on its people, as Willem Textor found to his cost. He had committed misconduct with a member of the Community, who, incidentally, had confessed. He left the country and went to France, but returned after some time had elapsed. Soon afterwards he received a summons to appear before the Council. This was in 1632. He, too, reconciled himself with the Community, and an announcement was made from the pulpit without mention of his name (the reference was to "a certain brother") [4]. However, it appears that in the case of women, moral discipline was maintained with greater severity. Thus a maid-servant, who had been violated by a baker's assistant, had to confess in public, whereas he was refused admission to Communion [5]. For the rest, the case fizzled out. Neither party appears to have

---

1) *Ibid.*, p. 138.
2) *Acta* V, Dec. 5th, 1583.
3) *Acta* VII, f° 38 v°.
4) *Acta* VIII, f° 7 v°.
5) *Acta* VIII, f° 25 r°.

been excessively penitent. The man consoled himself with Communion in an English parish; the woman, it seems, was familiar with this particular sin. She became reconciled with the Church six years later, after public confession [1].

Public confessions gradually became the exception rather than the rule. In the years 1645–1647, the Church Council dealt with an involved case of a broken marriage vow, immorality and blackmail, in which, besides a somewhat gay and imprudent widow, a certain Georg Schorstick played a reprehensible part. He was finally, albeit with great difficulty, induced to make full confession, but was told that his confession need not be read out [2].

From what has been said before and even more so from a perusal of the minutes, one might easily conclude that the average moral standard of the Community was pretty low. We should, however, take into account that in such reports attention is focussed in a very one-sided way on the negative aspect, the dark side, whereas no mention is made of the predominant bright side, the positive good. Even then, was the extent of the evil, considered not only relatively but absolutely, really so great? Dr. A. Kuyper, writing his commentary on the Acta (minutes) for the years 1569-1571, which were published by him, took the trouble to compile statistics of all the cases involving discipline, which had come before the Council. They were as follows: 9 cases of sexual immorality, 15 of drunkenness, 5 of dissoluteness, 4 of fighting, 3 of quarrelling, and disturbances, 2 of domestic quarrels, 2 of slander, 2 of persistent neglect to attend Church, 2 of enforced marriage, 3 of clandestine marriages, 1 of separation, 1 of disturbance of the service, 1 of gambling, 1 of a new marriage within a month, 1 of bearing false witness, 1 of forgery, 1 of ill-treatment of children, 1 of a dispute concerning a will, 1 of imprisonment for debt, 1 of attending Mass [3]. Considering all the circumstances, this does not amount to so very much, either relatively or absolutely. We should also bear in mind that, owing to the peculiar position of the Community as a "corpus corporatum et politicum", cases came before

---

1) *Ibid.*, f° 38 r°.
2) *Ibid.*, f° 148–180 pass.
3) Kuyper, *De Holl. Gem. te Lond. in 1570*, p. 156.

it which by to-day's standards would not come within the jurisdiction of the Church Council.

So far we have been considering the exercise of discipline. Not less important was the theoretical aspect of discipline, the framing of general rules. For it was necessary for pronouncements to rest on fixed standards, derived from the Bible. Inversely, cases were always tested in the light of Scripture. It was altogether desirable to have uniformity in these matters in all the communities in England. This necessitated correspondence. The correspondence of the London Community with the sister communities is full of special cases in regard to which there was exchange of counsel and of decisions. The Acts of the Colloquia of the Dutch communities in England are also full of decisions relating to discipline. In this way a complete set of canon law gradually came into being [1], but the more the system was perfected, the less use was made of it. Or it might, perhaps, be more correct to say that, as time went on, broader views were gradually being adopted. For, whilst measures relating to the purely doctrinal aspects of the life of the Church were applied less and less from dogmatic motives, the field of social and pastoral intervention by the Community on its own behalf and on that of its co-religionists, was being extended. Not that this social work had at any time been neglected. When, however, in 1661, the Council occupies itself with the case of a woman who claims having at one time married an Englishman at Ouderkerk [2], which is denied by the man concerned, and it then transpires, as a result of correspondence with the Consistory of Ouderkerk, that the woman's story is true, we here have a clear example of a case of interference in marriage matters which is no longer concerned with discipline based on doctrine, but one which has quite defenitely become a matter of social and pastoral care [3]. The causes of this change and more particularly of the slowly diminishing attention paid to moral discipline based on doctrine, did not lie exclusively within the confines of the Community. To begin with, the existence of a number

---

[1] As an example which also touched upon the maintenance of doctrine, may be cited the decision of the Colloquium of 1609: that a woman has no cause for divorce if her husband is a ,,Bruinist", i.e. an adherent of the Rev. Robert Browne; *Colloquia*, p. 110.

[2] In Holland.

[3] *Archivum*, III[II], pp. 2450 et seq.

of Dutch communities in the Kingdom, each with its own special circumstances, which often differed considerably from those obtaining in the sister communities, tended to complicate matters and to render cases less capable of uniform treatment. Above all, however, the system of rigorous enforcement of doctrinal teaching and moral discipline can really only be maintained within the sect, where there is at least some possibility of preserving the apostolic purity of the Church "without spot or blemish". In the long run, however, it was inevitable that the system should suffer shipwreck on the rock of sober reality; moreover, it came into collision with the demands imposed by Reformed Church law. Furthermore, the system was undermined within the Church Community by the difficulties inherent in consistency in such matters. We met the word "suspicie" (suspicion). Insinuations, backbiting and rancour struck root only too easily in the field of church discipline in which denunciation and tale telling played such a large part. A rigorously applied system of doctrinal and moral discipline digs its own grave. In addition, times were changing, and so was the mental outlook of the Community. The process of secularization, which made its appearance soon after the beginning of the 17th century, was not on easy terms with the more or less clericalistic limitations of the discipline [1]. The time was passing when religious struggles demanded the participation of tightly closed groups, each fighting the Lord's battle with the utmost regard to religious principle. With the disappearance of the bitterness which had characterized the religious struggles, went the need for the warring parties to be closed theocratic entities. Lastly, the difficulty of maintaining the original standpoint in a world which acknowledged entirely different ideas, was becoming increasingly evident. This antithesis led to conflicts in which, gradually, the tendency developed of avoiding violent struggles by compromising, be it with reluctance, in the direction of the totally different sphere of the Anglican Church. Especially in the days of Archbishop Laud, when the doors of the English Church were so to speak, thrown wide open — not without a "force them to enter" — the Dutch Community was obliged, against its in-

---

[1] Remarkable is one of the explanations given by Norwich in 1627 to account for the reduction in numbers there: besides the high cost of maintaining the Community, there is the (Church) censorship; *Colloquia*, p. 296.

clination, to moderate the strictness of its discipline, for fear of losing members to the English Church. Whether one liked it or not, one had to study the customers who were about to patronize the shop next-door.

We now come to that part of this chapter, which we have designated "Philanthropic and Social Activities." This branch of the Church's activity was the particular concern of the deacons and elders; it grew in importance with the years. As previously stated, it goes back to the very beginning of the Church. The Church Council at Antwerp in 1563 gives a recommendation in favour of a certain Peter die Rauweel, who was formerly with the Baptists, but has now joined the Reformed Church and intends to seek work as a brewer's drayman [1]. A couple who wish to get married in the Church are told to wait "until they are in better health" [2]. Of the same nature is the action taken a little later, in 1612, in connection with a rumour that certain members are suffering from venereal diseases. The Council decided to investigate the matter (the names were to be withheld), and invited the individuals concerned to appear before it [3]. In 1625, in consequence of complaints made, it was ruled that persons "with sores and open wounds" had better abstain from attending the services as long as they suffered in this way or, at least, they should sit apart. They might "cause great fright to other people" [4]. Care for the physical health of the congregation is also apparent from the pronouncement of 1599 that "honest exercises of the body", such as ball games, shooting, etc., are permissible, provided "due regard is taken of what is edifying" [5]. It was always the aim of the deacons and the Church Council to give assistance to those in need. In 1570 a man and a woman of the working class wanted to get married, but they lacked the means. Their employer had an idea: he addressed a request to the Council, asking for permission to hold a collection at the Church door on the day of the wedding. The request was granted, and an announcement of the proposed collection was

---

[1] *Kerkeraads-protocollen 1560–1563*, p. 378.
[2]. *Ibid*, p. 434.
[3] *Acta* VII, f° 22 v°.
[4] *Ibid.*, f° 127 v°.
[5] *Colloquia*, p. 94.

made from the pulpit [1]. Six years later there was a former Augustine monk, who had fled from Ypres and found employment as a woolcomber. It is messy work which he will come to dislike in the long run. The Sandwich Community writes that he is better suited for work connected with some kind of study and asks London to have him taught bookbinding [2]. A girl, who was left an orphan with no one to look after her, was sent to Emden, where her grandmother was said to live. Emden wrote, saying that no grandmother could be traced and that they had quite enough poor people to look after. So the girl was sent back — one case out of many [3]. In the same year, 1577, the elders of the Community at Maidstone sent to the elders of the London Community a former nun, hailing from a convent in Ghent, "still very young in the religion of Christ, but belief will come with hearing". Her worldly possessions consisted only of 3 or 4 shillings which the deacons at Maidstone had given her [4]. The following year the Community at Zierikzee requested the London Council to pass on to the Bishop of London a letter asking for financial help. No suit was given to this request, as the Bishop was wont to refer poor Dutch persons to their own Church communities. The Council replied that those nearest should help first. (Is it possible that Zierikzee was in distress as a result of the "Spanish Fury", the revolt of the Spanish troops in 1576?) Yet there was a desire to do something, and a collection was held which yielded £ 10 [5]. A similar answer was returned to a request from the Church communities in West Flanders. All the same, a sum of £ 25 was collected and sent. At the request of the "Classis" of Brabant, £ 100 was remitted in 1579 [6]. A totally different case was the following. A certain Captain Ten Hove of the Dutch States army writes from Ypres in 1580 that a soldier in his company has violated a girl and robbed her parents. As he has fled to England, the assistance of the Church Council is invoked to get him delivered into the hands of justice [7].

---

1) *Kerkeraads-protocollen 1569–1571*, p. 124.
2) *Archivum*, III1, pp. 455 et seq.
3) *Ibid.*, p. 465.
4) *Ibid.*, p. 473.
5) *Archivum*, II, p. 610.
6) *Acta* V, April, 1579.
7) *Archivum* III1, p. 596.

From time to time the Council and the deacons were confronted with most unusual cases. In 1631, Jane Wattkines, a Dutch
woman, addresses a petition to the Lord Mayor of London for
help, so that she may be released from the debtors' prison where
she had been held for the last year and a quarter. Her husband
was killed in battle near the Isle de Ré; the little money she
had has gone towards her keep in prison. She needs £ 50 on surety, and she now asks for intercession on her behalf with the
"Dutch Company" which might, perhaps, give the money. The
Lord Mayor passed on the request and at the same time made
an appeal to the Church Council, because if she were not soon
released she would "be turned over to the Common Gaole where
she shall be likely to perishe" [1]. The wording of her letter does
not give the impression that she was a very active member of
the Church, but what a measure of misery lies behind this tale,
and how clearly it shows that the Dutch Church was often the
only or the last refuge of people who had suffered shipwreck
in the world. The Church has to this day continued in this good
work. — How very sad is the letter which Neeltje Cornelis wrote
to the Church council in 1645. Her son, now fifteen years old,
went to sea with his father three years before. Both were taken
prisoner by the Turks and taken to Algiers "in miserable sla-
very". With the aid of a few wealthy people, she has managed
to collect £ 200 and with this sum she has succeeded in ransom-
ing her husband. But now the Turks ask for another 600 reales
for her son. She adds a devout argument: the boy is being tempt-
ed to renounce his Christian faith, "the soul of her child is at
stake". A heartbreaking case, even without this — somewhat
doubtful — argument [2]. There were more of these pitiful tales
behind which we can picture a world of personal and social misery. What are we to think of those two prisoners in "Nieugat"
(Newgate) who ask for the minister to visit them, otherwise
they must die [3]! Then there is the widow from Bremen, who
was taken prisoner by a Dutch warship and robbed of her money,
an arm and a leg broken. She has pawned her late husband's
testament for £ 6 with a Scot living in Holland, and asks for
assistance to travel to Dunkirk or Utrecht, where the Scot now

---

1) *Archivum*, III[II], p. 1505.
2) *Ibid.*, pp. 1967 et seq.
3) *Ibid.*, p. 1914.

lives [1]. A somewhat unlikely tale? Perhaps, but the Council
had no alternative but to investigate the matter, a task which
it discharged with devotion and in a painstaking manner, as
was their wont in all such matters. In the same year 1645, the
Community in Sandwich had taken in a number of very poor
fugitives from Flanders and now were at a loss to know what
to do with them. Sandwich wrote to London as a matter of course.
Almost by return of post the answer came, indicating likely
possibilities of employment for different kinds of manual workers, and containing the following observation which does honour to the sentiments of the Council members of that time:
"In these fugitives from Flanders we may behold the condition
of our ancestors and the foundation of our Churches in this
Countrie" [2].

We shall see in greater detail how London, again and again,
had to assist the other communities by word and deed. The
following is a pleasing example of social assistance of a construct-
ive, educational character. The small Reformed Community
in Mortlake was very poor. They approached London with the
somewhat original proposal that London should place an order
with them for the weaving of a carpet — it was apparently a
case of another weaving community. The carpet was to repre-
sent a scene taken from the Acts and would cost £ 375. This
idea was favourably received and an order was placed for a carpet which was to cost £ 540. The transaction turned out to be
a bad bargain for the deacons, who evidently played a leading
part in this matter. Six years later, in 1651, they had a deficit
of £ 500, and this was partly due to the loss made on the carpet,
notwithstanding the fact that the scene depicted had been
changed to a hunting scene, this being more likely to appeal to
English taste than would a scene from the Bible [3].

The wars between England and the Dutch Republic of 1652-
1654 and 1665–1667 caused the London Community many difficulties of a philanthropic nature. There is no evidence of direct hostile interference on the part of the Government or the
population; for this the Church was in too small a degree a "piece

---

1) *Ibid.*, p. 2251.
2) *Ibid.*, p. 1991.
3) *Ibid.*, III[II], pp. 1992, 1995, 2197. The Mortlake tapestry was famous. In the Rut-
land Chapel of St. George's Chapel at Windsor there hangs a carpet (restored later)
made in the reign of Charles II.

of Holland in England," being rather an English group of
Dutch origin. Prisoners of war, however, were brought to England, and these had to be cared for, which meant expenditure
of time and money. After the first war with England, the Ambassador, Van Beverningk, made every effort to get the London
Church reimbursed by the States General for the moneys ex-
pended in this way. He was successful, and £ 600 was refunded [1].
The London Community similarly rose to the occasion during
the second war with England. A lovely story is that of the Church
Council at Groningen, which had heard that there were men from
the province of Groningen amongst the prisoners. A sum of 600
florins was collected for them in the town of Groningen and
remitted for distribution, but, so read the instruction, to no
other than the men from Groningen [2]. Real provincial chauvinism!
After the conclusion of this war, the Ambassador, Michiel van
Gogh, also tried to obtain a refund for the Church of the amounts
spent on the care of prisoners of war [3]. Similarly, after the Peace
of Nymegen in 1678, on the occasion of the ceremony to welcome the Ambassador, Coenraad van Beuningen, the Council
pressed him to promote the refund of the moneys spent on the
care of prisoners of war. From this it is obvious that also during the second war the Church had been extending its care to
the prisoners of war [4]. Taking it all in all, this material bears
witness to the high sense of the duty to dispense Christian charity, which existed in the Community. It is true that the possibility of rendering aid was apparently present in great measure,
because of the wealth of many of the Church members. Though
the deacons might sometimes see the bottom of their money
chest, the willingness to help on the part of the members was
great. The money spent on assistance and on poor relief came
from current income and was not realized capital. However,
charity was dispensed even when there was little money available,
as for instance in 1571, when the Church was glad to receive a
gift of £ 10 for its poor from the House of Commons [5]. Four
years later, when there seems to have been an influx of people
without means, the Privy Council pressed the Church to refuse

---

1) *Archivum*, III[II], p. 2276.
2) *Ibid.*, p. 2534.
3) *Ibid.*, p. 2547.
4) *Acta* IX, f° 11 v°.
5) Ruytinck, *Gheschiedenissen*, p. 86.

aid to non-members. The Church considered that this would
be harmful to the Christian cause and appealed to the Bishop
of London for intervention and support. The Privy Council
proved to be accommodating and declared itself satisfied as
long as aid was refused to those who were not "of the religion,"
and the others referred to other Dutch church communities.
The Church Council was content with this decision and resolved
to see to it that only bona fide believers were admitted into
the Church [1]. Religious tolerance was anything but all-embracing!

As has been noted, the financial position of the Church was
none too favourable in the early years. The Church owned no
property, the number of indigent persons and persons in need
of relief was great, and the time of the large fortunes and in-
comes had not yet arrived. In December, 1570, the ministers and
elders proposed that the sums received for poor-relief from gifts
and legacies should be applied as to one half to general church
activities and as to the other to poor-relief, but the deacons
refused to entertain this [2]. By degrees the Community increased
in well-being, that is to say, a section of the members achieved
a state of prosperity which enabled them to give generously,
both for the Church's own purposes and for charity on a large
scale. This is not the place for detailed enquiries into the sources
of this prosperity. The numerous, well-preserved records contain
abundant material for a historical study of the economics of
the period. We may, however, point to two factors which throw
a light on these developments. We have in the first place the
factor of the energy and spirit of enterprise which one may expect to find in the case of colonists, who, from spiritual motives,
faced the uncertainties of emigration. The other is the "inner-
weltliche Askese", so typical of Reformed Protestantism during
the time of its growth and when it had reached its peak: the
sense of vocation which urged men to take hold of the earthly
possibilities and utilize them in work and sober living, not in the
first place in the service of personal advantage and well-being,
but "ad maiorem Dei gloriam": to the greater glory of God.
However this may be, the prosperity came and, with it, the
readiness, yes, more than that, the sense of duty, to give and

---

[1] *Ibid.*, pp. 103–105; cf. *Archivum*, II, pp. 499–503.
[2] *Kerkeraads-protocollen 1569–1571*, pp. 249–253.

to help. When in later years, in the still unsettled first half of
the 17th century, we read of substantial help being given to
causes outside the Church, this refers to the proceeds of collections for which an appeal to the generosity of the members was
never made in vain. To those of ample means it was a question
of "service." As far back as 1582, we find a reference to a striking method adopted by the Council when an appeal for help
for the Service of the Word was received from Brussels. It was
decided to ask only the more prominent members of the Community to contribute and to spare the common man [1]. Those
members who were considered to be in a position to give were
simply told that they must give.

The 17th century still made great demands on the generosity
of the wealthier members. The scene of the religious wars had
shifted. It was no longer in the Low Countries that persecution
was rampant and distress had to be alleviated, but more particularly in Germany, where there was great suffering as a result
of the Thirty Years War. The archives of the Dutch Church in
London are full of letters written in those years, asking for help,
and of proofs that such help had actually been distributed. Here
we can mention only a few examples, though it would not do
to be too niggardly with them. As early as 1583 a collection was
held, jointly with the French, for Geneva. This collection "on a
plate", at the Church door at Easter, yielded £ 72, to which
Sandwich added £ 4 and Norwich £ 14 [2]. In 1602 a sum of £ 310
was made available for Geneva which was then being threatened
by Roman Savoy [3]. In 1620 £ 52 was collected for Heynsberg
and Gulik [4]. When in 1624 the Palatinate was laid low by Tilly's
army, the Leyden faculty of theology made an appeal to the
London Community on behalf of its students from the Palatinate [5]. The Palatinate suffered terribly, and so did Bohemia,
and the sympathies of the English King went out to those afflicted. Possibly his concern was not unmixed with dynastic
considerations, for a sister of Charles I was married to the un-
fortunate Elector of the Palatinate, the Winter King of Bohemia.
The King ordered that collections be made throughout the length

---

1) *Acta* V, December 17th, 1582.
2) *Acta* V, July 25th, 1583.
3) Ruytinck, *Gheschiedenissen*, pp. 166 et seq.
4) *Ibid.*, p. 395.
5) *Archivum*, III[1], p. 1310.

and breadth of England on behalf of the persecuted, particularly the pastors and their families, and the Dutch Church in London became the centre from which the moneys were distributed [1]. A Royal proclamation of February 8th, 1628, called for collections to be made in all the churches of the Kingdom, the money to be sent through the intermediary of the Bishops of the various dioceses via the Bishop of London to the Dutch Church [2]. In the same year £ 210 was remitted, intended for the pastors who had been expelled from the Palatinate, later another £ 300, then again £ 200, followed by yet another £ 300 [3]. These amounts were intended for the Lower Palatinate and were sent to Hanau. Other sums went to Nuremberg and were destined for those expelled from the Upper Palatinate, who had formed a refugee colony in that town. In 1629, 2000 florins were remitted through the Amsterdam Church Council which also acted as intermediary in special cases [4]. And so on, with larger and smaller amounts. Another instance was the £ 600 from moneys collected, which was sent to the people in the Lower Palatinate during the months December, 1631, January, 1632. This was all money from English sources (though the task of handling these sums fell to the Dutch Church), but the Dutch did not stand aloof either. At one morning service £ 163 was collected [5]. For these collections, the Church Council frequently adopted the method, referred to on page 78, of calling together the more prominent members for the purpose, as, for instance, on the occasion of a collection for the Upper Palatinate in 1626 [6]. In 1631, the Council decided to invite capable teachers from Hanau and Nuremberg to give impetus to the appeal [7]. The need was very great. The letters from Hanau and Nuremberg fully confirm the reports which have come down to us of the calamities of the Thirty Years War, though they also throw a

---

1) *Archivum*, III[II], pp. 1547, 1633.
2) *Archivum*, III[I], pp. 1365 et seq.
3) *Ibid.*, pp. 1382, 1400, 1411, 1430.
4) *Ibid.*, III[I], p. 1458. The previous year the Amsterdam Church Council had asked if it might extend the distribution to school and other teachers and to Bohemian nobles, but London replied that, for the time being, it should comply with the Royal charge; *Archivum* III[I], p. 1395; *Acta* VII, f° 179 r°. Shortly afterwards it was decided not to apply for an extension of the scope of the Royal charge, the need to be filled being already excessively great; *Ibid.*, f° 181 r°.
5) *Archivum*, III[II], p. 1543.
6) *Acta* VII, f° 138 v°.
7) *Acta* VII, f° 240 r°.

peculiar light on the conditions which obtained in that greatly harassed country. The archives of the Church contain a remarkable letter from Hanau, dated May 11th, 1632. At that time (Lutheran) Swedes had thrown themselves into the struggle with the object of helping the threatened Protestant cause. Just then, the Swedish king was on his triumphal march through Bavaria, but the Swedish troops which had remained behind were not a whit better than the Spanish troops as far as ferocity of conduct and love of plunder were concerned [1]. In 1633 the fugitive ministers began to return to their posts, but they complained about the unmannerly conduct of the Swedish general towards those of the Reformed Church — the old antagonism between Lutheran and Calvinist, with which we are familiar from the wanderings of the exiles in 1553. It is most remarkable that in none of the letters from the Palatinate do we read of any reaction to the death of Gustav Adolph, which must have been a heavy blow to the Protestants in Germany. There was an other appeal, this time in 1636, by the widow of Frederick IV, the Elector Palatine, Louise of Orange, daughter of William the Silent, on behalf of the pastors and school teachers of Zweibrücken, their widows and orphans, and it was not made in vain [2].

Not only the distribution of the money, but also the acknowledgments, caused all sorts of difficulties. For instance, the exiled pastors from the Upper Palatinate received a reminder that, though they had sent letters of thanks to the King, the Archbishops and the Bishops, they had not yet written to the Lord Privy Seal (then Henry, Earl of Manchester). But, continues the letter, first give us an idea of what you propose to write. Speak only of the charity received, but make no reference to the Emperor, nor to the Antichrist, nor to the papists, nor even to the Jesuits [3]. These were the days of Laud, when the Government steered an episcopal, catholicizing course from which, incidentally, the Dutch Community was to experience much misery.

As mentioned, the Bohemian Protestants also benefited by this generously conceived scheme for giving succour. A number

---

1) *Archivum*, III[II], p. 1554.
2) *Ibid.*,   1730.
3) *Ibid.*, p. 1633.

of the exiled Bohemian ministers were living at Lesna, in Poland. Among them was the great Johan Amos Comenius, then, and also later, a national Czech figure, theologian, pedagogue, champion of oecumenical Church unity, a man with an international reputation. He himself wrote a letter of thanks from Lesna [1]. In 1632 a couple of Bohemian students came over to render thanks in person and to impart more detailed information to their co-religionists [2]. The giving of help to the Bohemians continued for many years. As late as 1641 the Bohemian brethren, writing from Lesna, asked for help for 80 preachers. They mentioned that eight years previously they had vainly applied for help to the English Church. Could Laud's policy have been behind this? The letter, of which Comenius was one of the signatories, took eight months to reach its destination. In reply, the Dutch Community sent £ 140, the proceeds of a collection [3]. A few years later Comenius came to London in person with a special aim in view: to help in the reform of school teaching. However, owing to the troubled times through which England was then passing, the work of the committee set up to study this question never came to anything. Before his departure Comenius wrote a letter of thanks to the London Community [4]. In 1656 he gave a letter of introduction to London to a couple of poor students from Moravia. They were each given $\frac{1}{2}$ £ "out of the purse" [5] Some time later, at the invitation of Geneva, the Dutch Community interested itself in the Waldenses in Piedmont. This was in the days of Cromwell who, as is well known, greatly favoured the Protestant cause in Italy. A sum of £ 200 was collected [6]. In 1659, the "Protestants in the valleys" (Waldenses) repeated their cry for help [7]. As a matter of fact, in 1624 the Community had organized a collection for the persecuted co-religionists in Valtellina and the Grisons, which brought in £ 154 [8].

Gradually the distress of the Protestants on the Continent grew less. The religious wars were coming to an end, a state of

---

[1] *Ibid.*, p. 1633.
[2] *Acta* VIII, f° 8 v°.
[3] *Archivum*, III[11], pp. 1852 et seq.
[4] *Ibid.*, pp. 1887 et seq.
[5] *Acta* VIII, f° 237 v°.
[6] *Archivum*, III[11], pp. 2256 et seq.; cf. *Acta* VIII, f° 221 v°.
[7] *Archivum*, III[11], p. 2429.
[8] Ruytinck, *Gheschiedenissen*, pp. 451–462.

equilibrium between the various creeds was coming into being, and cases of expulsion of dissenters were becoming more rare, though they did still occur, as in the case of the French Huguenots. When in 1677 the Dutch Community at Glückstadt in Denmark asked for a gift of money and were given £ 15, this was not on account of any distress caused by persecution [1]. Whatever the motives, help continued to be given whenever it was asked for, even though the needs were no longer of the kind by which mankind is moved. The times of tranquility and repose, prosperity and equability, were drawing near. All the same there continued to be suppliants who had gone through the pitiful experience of some form or other of persecution for the sake of their religious convictions: a Spaniard who submitted a document in which he related his sufferings through the Inquisition, a converted Roman Catholic priest, a Greek-Catholic divine, a Hungarian pastor who was freed from the galleys by Admiral De Ruyter — none ever appealed in vain. In 1761 we find a donation of £ 5 being made, on the recommendation of the Leyden professor Schultens, towards the building of a Reformed church at Permasenz (Hessen) [2]. In 1807, when the world, certainly the Dutch-speaking part of it, is appalled at the news of the disaster in Leyden, caused by the explosion of a ship carrying a cargo of gunpowder, succour is sent amounting to no less than £ 3000, which sum King Louis, brother of Napoleon, places at the disposal of the Leyden authorities [3]. Throughout the 19th and 20th centuries the prosperous London Community has continued to extend a helping hand to institutions in Holland, founded for the purpose of rendering spiritual and moral aid. We will single out one instance, because it illustrates the religious orientation towards which the Community had been moving, namely that of theological modernism and to which, beginning with the Reverend Adama van Scheltema (1874-1901), the ministers of the London Church have inclined ever since. In the 'eighties, a few modernist theologians in Holland conceived the plan of having a new translation made of the Old Testament, in which the latest findings of the researches into Biblical history would be embodied. This undertaking would cost money,

---

1) *Archivum*, III[II], p. 2614.
2) *Acta* IX, f° 212 v°.
3) *Archivum*, III[II], pp. 2859 et seq.

and Professor Abraham Kuenen, the eminent Old Testament scholar, made a successful appeal to the London Community. The Community's help is acknowledged in the "Leyden Translation" of the old Testament [1]. Thus the Church's philantropy was adjusted to the changing needs.

All this goes to show that the Community's field of activity and working methods were being continually extended towards a broad acceptance of social responsibility and that the religious and moral charge which the Church knew to have been laid upon it, in no way remained confined to the narrow limits of its own circle in order to make this a model of Christian life. Indeed, from the very beginning there has been an important social side to the activities of the Church. It lay in the nature of the Church as a "corpus corporatum et politicum" that its governors should perform all manner of functions which nowadays fall to the task of ambassadors, consulates, chambers of commerce, employment and enquiry bureaux. The Church acted as notary public, arbitrator, intermediary, justice of the peace, in all sorts of cases in which the parties concerned could not, or would not, appeal to the English authorities. In the earliest years we already find the Church looking after wills, making copies of them and undertaking their safe custody [2]. In 1589, the Church is asked to assist someone who is coming over to recover a sum of money which the Reverend Fontanus of Arnhem had lent to an English sea captain [3]. In 1605, the magistrates of Deventer invoke the aid of the Church Council in the collection, on behalf of two orphans, of an inheritance left to them by an uncle who had died in London [4]. In 1625 the Church helps to secure the release of a surgeon from Maidstone who had been impressed into the Navy [5]. In 1639 Sir Cornelius Vermuyden, the well-known land-reclamation specialist, asks the Council to help bring about his release from the debtors' prison to which he had been committed, partly through the action of Lamotte, an elder of the Church, who was associated with him in his somewhat over-ambitious undertakings [6]. Thus the curiously representative position of the Dutch Church again and again led to its having

---

1) *Index to vols. 28 and 29, Arch.* (Letters 1823–1900), no. 4950.
2) *Kerkeraads-protocollen 1560–1563,* p. 490.
3) *Archivum,* II, pp. 888 et seq.
4) *Archivum,* III[1], p. 1162.
5) *Acta* VII, f° 125 v°.
6) *Archivum,* III[11], pp. 1794 et seq.

to take action in purely mundane affairs. It is self-evident that this brought with it a danger of worldliness, of "becoming like the world", as the old Dutch has it. How real this danger was, is perceived when reading Ruytinck's History of the Church and even more so the works of his successors. Their contents are of a rather secularized character to the neglect of ecclesiastical matters, and there is an almost exaggerated interest in mundane affairs. However, we must bear in mind that Ruytinck intended to write "Gheschiedenissen ende Handelingen van de Nederduytsche Natie ende gemeynten" (Histories and Acts of the Netherlands nation and church communities). Is there, perhaps, an echo of the "corpus corporatum et politicum" in this emphasis on the nation? For the rest, we need not look far for the cause of this leaning towards the profane aspect of his subject. Ruytinck used a manuscript of the historian Van Meteren, which contained many references to commerce and similar items of information [1]. It may be said that, as a rule, the leaders of the Community were on their guard against a process of oversecularization within the Church. They did their best to "keep the world outside the Church". The Church remained the church. This may be illustrated by quoting two decisions. A request for permission to hold a sale in the Church was refused [2]. At the end of 1626, the sexton's announcements, made after the sermon on Sundays, of the days on which sales were to be held, were discontinued, "rightly judging this to be a frivolous mixing of the church and the market" [3].

That the Church, in its anxiety to give help outside, did not forget its own poor, is so universally known that we need only mention it in passing. The accounts of the deacons, which have been preserved, bear eloquent witness to this fact. In the annals of the first years of the Community's existence we already find mention of a "poor-house", apparently a rented dwelling house. This caused trouble, when in November, 1562, notice was given of termination of the lease. We may assume that this did not terminate this part of the Church's care for its poor. It cannot be said that the needy were always anxious to be admitted. In 1633,

---

1) Verduyn, *Em. v. Meteren*, p. 17. For a time there was in London a kind of chamber of commerce, a corporation of Dutch merchants, of which Van Meteren was one of the two heads or consuls; *Ibid.*, p. 74.
2) *Kerkeraads-protocollen 1569–1571* p. 61.
3) Ruytinck, *Gheschiedenissen*, p. 499.

the deacons asked the Council to help them by trying persuasion [1]. In 1685 the Church obtained the use of the "almshouses" in Sun Street, Moorgate (Parish of St. Leonard's); three years later it was decided to purchase the site [2]. The deacons acted as trustees. The houses remained in use for nearly two centuries. As late as the beginning of last century, the oldest minister lived there rent free [3]. From a letter written in 1667, applying for the post of "house master", it might be concluded that at that time there was a kind of hospital attached to the place [4]. In 1865 the houses were expropriated for £ 7000 on behalf of the London & North Western Railway Company [5]. Their place was taken by the almshouses at Old Charlton near Greenwich, built specially for the purpose, on an ample scale. They were opened in 1867 and considerably enlarged in 1885 to accommodate aged people and invalids. During the summer months the houses were also made available for children of needy Dutch people. Actually, the new Charlton was also intended to serve as a convalescent home. At the beginning of this century, from 1905 to 1918, the Community established a kind of household school there. It is these "hofjes" which, known as the Dutch Homes, have contributed so much to the good name which the Dutch Church enjoys. The second world war put an end to the existence of the Homes.

To end this chapter, we once more go back in time, in order to consider another kind of care of the Community, namely the question of the study for the ministry and the steps to be taken to promote these studies. Admittedly this activity was not of an exclusively disinterested character, for, as we have seen, in the initial stages it aimed at remedying the shortage of ministers in the Dutch churches in England as well as overseas. Later, however, from the beginning of the 17th century, when the Dutch churches in England looked to the Continent for their ministers, the aim came to be mainly the assistance of the sister churches overseas, and it became increasingly so with the passage of time. As early as 1577, a schoolmaster at Norwich, Joh. Ruytinck, was being considered for training for the ministry,

---

1) *Acta* VIII, f° 20 v°.
2) *Acta* IX, f° 27 r°; *Index to vols 28 and 29*, no. 4668.
3) *Archivum*, III[11], p. 2861.
4) *Ibid.*, p. 2548.
5) *Index, etc.*, nos. 4603, 4607.

but, though deeply grateful, he preferred to decline this offer because he was too conscious of his own lack of ability [1]. Another man, Assuerus Regemorter, who later became minister of the London Church, was studying in "Nieuwstadt" in 1579 and asked for permission to stay another year. It is not expressly stated whether he was studying at the expense of the Church, though this is probable. The request was granted, provided that the Church "of the fatherland" could spare him for so long [2]. In 1583, a young man was sent by the Consistory to Leyden for preliminary studies. The Leyden Consistory, however, wrote that he was making no progress and was dull, and they advised that he should be recalled and taught a trade [3]. In the same year the Council decided, on the ground of unfavourable reports, to discontinue the support of Pieter Lambregts who was studying at Ghent [4]. A certain Livinus Cabelliau was then studying at Ghent, also at the expense of the Church, but with much better results [5]. However, in 1583 the students at Ghent were asked whether it would not benefit their studies if they were to be transferred to Leyden [6]. The fact that the accounts for 1582–1583 show an excess of income over expenditure of £ 80, whilst the following year receipts exceeded expenditure by £ 116, would seem to indicate that considerable amounts were involved in the help given to students [7]. In 1603, a certain Jacobus de Roo — most probably the son of a minister of the London Church — was studying in Leyden where he lived in the house of Professor Gomarus [8]. Two years later another protégé of the London Community, Tobias Regius, probably also the son of a minister of the London Church, was likewise cared for in the house of this famous man [9]. In 1625, one Bartholomeus Hulsius, a nephew of Ruytinck's, studied in Leyden [10]. However, as already indicated, the London Community was not always lucky with its foster-children. Take, for instance, the case of Ruytinck's son,

---

[1] *Archivum*, II, pp. 593 et seq.
[2] *Acta* V, Aug. 16th, 1579.
[3] *Archivum*, III[1], p. 696.
[4] *Acta* V, March 14th, 1583.
[5] *Archivum*, III[1], p. 719.
[6] *Acta* V, Dec. 5th, 1583.
[7] *Acta* V, July 16th, 1583.
[8] *Archivum*, II, pp. 416 et seq.
[9] *Archivum*, III[1], pp. 1164 et seq.
[10] *Ibid.*, p. 1312.

Simeon jr., who was at Leyden in 1629 and was given permission to go also to France. He was still there two years later. Such a course of study would cost the Community 700 florins per year [1]. From the letters one gets the impression that Simeon jr. was a good hand at talking, but also that the Community gradually came to see through him [2]. Joh. Ruytinck, probably a younger brother, who also studied in Leyden, did better [3]. Prior to this, he had studied in Cambridge, but in 1637 he wrote from there: "The examination for which I must sit, is simply a question of money; for £ 10 you get your degree". He preferred, therefore, to return to London and finish his studies there [4]. In 1645 another minister's son, Arnold van Laren (his father was the Reverend van Laren who had died a few years previously) sent his thesis from Utrecht and the Council rewarded him with a gift of £ 10 in Flemish money [5]. The London Church Council never failed to show interest. Poor students of diverse nationalities seldom appealed to it in vain for help [6].

---

[1] *Archivum*, III[1], p. 1488.
[2] *Archivum*, III[11], pp. 1583 et seq. For further information concerning this S. Ruytinck, see *Nieuw Nederl. Biogr. Woordenboek*, Part IV.
[3] *Archivum*, III[11], p. 1651.
[4] *Ibid.*, p. 2912. Johannes became minister in Zuidland in Holland, 1638, and later in Yarmouth, 1641.
[5] *Ibid.*, p. 1976.
[6] *Acta* VII, f° 272 v° et seq.

CHAPTER IV

THE RELATIONS WITH OTHER REFORMED
CHURCHES IN THE LOW COUNTRIES AND IN
ENGLAND

The Dutch Reformed Church in London has, from the very
beginning, been a completely independent body, a "phenomenon
sui generis". It has never, in the true sense of the word, formed
part of a wider church community. It was an independent church,
yet it could not be reckoned to fit into the general form of Nonconformity, for the church has always denied emphatically having
any affinity with the pronounced sectarian type of Baptists,
Brownists and similar social expressions of Christendom. In
the same positive manner it sought contact, and to a certain
extent community, with pronouncedly ecclesiastical bodies:
the Reformed churches of the Low Countries and France, as
also, be it with a certain reserve, with the Church of England.
If one were to examine the academic question as to whether
the Church conformed to the church-type or the sect-type of
religious organization, the answer would undoubtedly be in
favour of the former, though as far as the Church's utterances
and outward forms of manifestation are concerned, one can
point to many features typical of the latter type. In any case,
the Church has entertained direct and friendly relations with
the churches mentioned. It has for long periods even maintained
a real fellowship with these churches.

As this chapter treats of the relations with other churches,
the Reformed Church in the Netherlands, the Walloon or French
Reformed Church and the other Dutch churches in England
will be reviewed. This will be done in the order stated. It might be
objected that the oldest and closest formal connections have
been those with the Walloon Reformed group, but the relations
which existed between the London Church and the Reformed

Church at home were even closer, and these relations have best withstood the passage of time. We have seen that there was a period during which the London Church meant more to the Church at home than vice versa. These were particularly the years prior to 1571, before the Church at home was fully organized, being at that time still in "statu nascendi", whereas the London Community was by then organized and had its doctrinal teaching and liturgy, its books of instruction and service books, its own translation of the Bible, and its own rhymed version of the Psalms. All these achievements came only slowly to the Reformed Church at home during the gradual process of consolidation, and there was a time when the London Church, the first to make use of the Dutch language in its outward manifestations [1], earned the pronouncement made later by the Reverend Festus Hommius "mater et propagatrix omnium reformatorum ecclesiarum belgicarum", mother and nursery of all Netherlands Reformed churches. In subsequent years the roles were divided differently: the Church in the Netherlands sought its own outward forms of manifestation, and these have in London replaced the forms which had been in use there. We also discussed the abandoning of Van Utenhove's rhymed version of the Psalms and of his translation of the New Testament. à Lasco's "Compendium doctrinae" was soon replaced in the Low Countries by the Dutch Confession of Faith of Guy de Brès, the "Confessio Belgica". If we enquire into the cause of this, the answer must point to the greater significance of the latter as a concrete, sharp definition of the deep values underlying the Reformed Confession of Faith. The clearly defined and unequivocal standpoint of opposition to the Anabaptists also favoured its adoption. Finally there was the factor of the French origin of the Belgica, from the "Confessio Gallicana", which made its adoption in a church which had had its origin in French-speaking parts almost a self-evident matter, and so it did not last long before the Dutch ministers in England, in common with their colleagues at home, subscribed to the 37 articles of the "Confessio Belgica". The "Korte ondersoekinge des gheloofs" maintained itself for a considerable time (till 1611) in the Low Countries, but the "Kort Begrijp", which took its place, still clearly shows its influence,

---

[1] Woudstra, *De Holl. Vreemdelingengemeente*, p. 98.

sometimes by the actual incorporation of matter from it [1]. The Emden Small Catechism has not had any direct influence in the Low Countries, but it is universally known and it has been demonstrated by experts, that it, and the "Korte ondersoekinge" already mentioned, have contributed to our so valuable and popular Heidelberg Catechism [2]. Also the London liturgical writings had soon to make room in the Low Countries for those by Datheen and others who followed in the wake of his rhymed version of the Psalms. For that matter, the London liturgical writings had not been published in a form to make them suitable for use in church [3]. Of the forms drawn up by Datheen for baptism, Communion and marriage, the forms for baptism and marriage, in contrast with the forms for Communion, bear the imprint of the strong influence of Micron's forms which were used in the London Church, to the extent of the incorporation of actual passages [4]. Of the other four forms, those for the ordination of ministers, installation of elders and deacons, expulsion and reinstatement, the first two show clear traces of influence by London, and these are not lacking in the other two. One should bear in mind in this connection that Micron's "Christelicke Ordinanciën" were still being reprinted in Delft in 1582. Finally, the action conducted in the home country against the use of the organ apparently emanates from the London Community [5].

The influence of the London Community on the home church, therefore, has left certain traces, even though in later years the direct effect was only limited in scope. Conversely, the (direct) influence which the Church at home had on the London Church, is also evidence of the close relations which have existed between them. In 1575 the signing of the "Confessio Belgica" in the Dutch and French texts, by ministers on their first ordination, was made obligatory [6]. This was a case of the Dutch example operating. When in 1599, on the occasion of the Colloquium of the Dutch churches held in London, the question is asked: "Does there exist a church order on which the Dutch churches in this Kingdom

---

[1]) Van Schelven, *De Vluchtelingenkerken*, p. 206.
[2]) M. A. Gooszen, *De Heidelberger Catechismus, textus receptus met toelichtende teksten*, Leiden 1890, pp. 56–61.
[3]) Van Schelven, *De vluchtelingenkerken*, p. 208.
[4]) For particulars see Woudstra, *De Hollandsche Vreemdelingengemeente*, p. 117–122.
[5]) *Ibid.*, p. 123–127.
[6]) *Colloquia*, p. 19.

regulate themselves?" the answer is: "Yes, namely the Netherlands church order which will be followed as closely as possible" [1].
The matter was once more raised in the Colloquium of 1609,
and on that occasion the answer was clarified by the observation
that the churches in England had joined the synod of Dordrecht
of 1578, and of Middelburg of 1581. The statement was added
that from the decisions taken by these synods and by the Colloquia, which decisions amounted in fact to a set of Canon law,
a "Corpus Disciplinae" would be extracted for submission to
the congregation. This "Corpus Disciplinae" appears in full in
the appendices of the Acta of this Colloquium [2]. It was accepted
with the proviso that a Colloquium could later introduce revi-
sions. In 1627 it was actually decided to revise it somewhat and
to add the pronouncements under Canon law. A remarkable
feature is the stipulation that account will have to be taken of
what is to be found in the old oecumenical synods and in the
English Church Constitutions (book of Canons), if it can help
in stiffening discipline, and provided it is in line with the ordinances of the Church itself, and of the churches overseas [3]. In
those years the prevailing wind blew from the direction of the
English Church. It became more and more threatening; was it
a case of setting one's sail to the prevailing wind?

It must be acknowledged that the work of à Lasco and Micron
had by then receded into the background. Four years later the
London Community asked in the Colloquium whether it would
not be recommendable for the new Corpus Disciplinae to be
added to the church order drawn up by these two leaders. It
was decided to take from the work of à Lasco and Micron whatever fitted into the Corpus, and to add this to the latter [4]. Thus
the original London material was in future to sail in the wake
of the home Church. That there existed a readiness to reckon
with the churches across the sea, also transpires from the decision
by the same Colloquium to ask the (provincial) synods for copies
of their resolutions "in so far as they touch on the welfare of
the churches". In 1624 the London Church Council had emphatically determined that at the Communion Service the customs

[1] *Ibid.*, p. 99.
[2] *Ibid.*, p. 104.
[3] *Ibid.*, p. 297 et seq.
[4] *Ibid.*, p. 301.
[5] *Acta* VII, f° 117 v°.

of the churches overseas should be followed [5]. In 1638, on the
example of the home Church, the translation of the Bible made
by order of the States General of the United Provinces was adopted [1] and a century and a half later, in 1776, the action of the
Church at home in taking into use the new rhymed version of
the Psalms, was followed [2].

All these relations, which were more or less firm, could only
come to full fruition through the common activity of an all em-
bracing church communion. What was the position in this respect? It was only natural that the important synod of Emden
held in 1571, which was of such great significance for the process of organization of the Dutch Reformed churches, attracted
much attention on both sides of the sea. As far as London is
concerned, we know this from a report in the minutes that the
minister Ysbrand Balck (Trabius) appeared in a meeting of the
Consistory for the purpose of communicating to the Consistory
the contents of a letter which spoke of a coming general synod
for all "who are attached to the religion", which synod would
be held at the instigation of the Prince of Orange and of the
Elector Palatine [3]. It is known, and this report makes it even
more understandable, that there was no time for arranging
for the London Community to be represented at this synod which
was timed to begin about October 4th, There was no lack of
encouragement for London to join the community which was
brought into being at Emden. On the strength of decisions taken
there, the Dutch and French communities in Sandwich proposed
in 1572 to proceed to the formation of a "Classis;" they declared their willingness to sign both confessions, the "Belgica"
and the "Gallicana" [4]. Moded made a similar proposal in the
name of the Dutch Community of Norwich [5]. From Holland,
Dathenus pressed in the same year for complete agreement and
co-operation with the organization created in Emden [6]. We may
take it that there was no lack of interest in London, but they
were not free. The English authorities had little mind for these
close relations which might encroach upon their own centralized
system. In 1574, the provincial synod of Dordrecht once more

[1) *Acta* VIII, f°. 67 r°.
2) *Acta* IX, f° 244 r°.
3) *Acta* III, on 2nd. Sept., 1571.
4) *Archivum*, III[1], p. 155.
5) *Ibid.*, p. 166.
6) *Archivum*, II, pp. 394, et seq.

pressed for the formation of a "Classis." At long last the brethren
in England gave ear to the hint, and decided to hold "gatherings" or Colloquia, and to send delegates to the next general
synod, though with strict injunctions to do nothing which might
prejudice the freedom of the churches in the Kingdom [1]. Thus
it was that in the Colloquium held in 1578 the decision was taken
to delegate Ysbrand Trabius, minister at Sandwich, and the
London elder, Van Roo, to the general synod at Dordrecht of
that year. Points from the previous synod were subjected to
scrutiny; amongst other matters it was considered desirable
that Datheen should once more review his rhymed version of
the Psalms — in truth, no idle decision. The Council was prepared, however, to conform to the decisions to be taken by the
coming synod, but "subject to the approval of the superintendents" [2]. A striking feature of the invitation received from the
home country is the request for time and place of the coming
synod to be kept as secret as possible [3], an injunction which
reflects the perilous conditions of existence in Holland at that
time. The synod realised the difficulties which obtained in England, and recognized the reservation, which was to the effect
that London could not undertake to be bound by the ceremonies and rules of the home Church, beyond what they could
accept "with the goodwill of our superintendents and for the
peace of our community in this realm" [4]. The Colloquium also
sent delegates to the synod of Middelburg of 1581: a minister
from London and an elder from Sandwich. They also were given
instructions. One of these instructions is remarkable because
of the light which it throws on the "English" mentality which
had come over the churches. The proposal was for overseers to
be appointed, who would exercise supervision of the churches
and of their ministers. They would retire on the occasion of each
three-yearly synod, but would be eligible for re-election [5]. Ad-

---

1) *Colloquia* p 6. Compare also the letter from the "Classis" Walcheren in answer
to London's letter: it is well understood in the home country that London must
reckon with the "strict laws of the Realm of England"; ,,and also what you write
about the impossibility of observing the (Reformed) Church Order, both in respect
of grouping into "classes" as well as in the matter of ceremonies .... we quite
understand"; *Archivum*, II, pp. 510 et seq.
2) *Colloquia*, pp. 40, 42, 49.
3) *Archivum*, II, p. 614.
4) *Archivum*, III[1], p. 525.
5) *Colloquia*, p. 59.

mittedly this is not fully in accord with the English (and German) system with its overseers appointed from above. The representative character was thus preserved. All the same it was a remarkable compromise between Calvinistic and Anglican conceptions.

And so we gradually approach the time of the Arminian disputes and of the synod of Dordrecht of 1618–1619. The relations of the London Church with the prominent leaders of orthodoxy in the Dutch Republic were good. In 1611 the influential Leyden minister, Festus Hommius, dedicated to the London Community his "De Jesu Christo servatore libri IV contra Faustum Socinum", the writing of which had been occasioned by the sensational appointment in Leyden of Professor Vorstius, who favoured the Remonstrants. There was every reason for expecting that the churches in England would be invited to send delegates to that large church gathering, seeing that both sides attached value to the maintenance of the relations which had been established, but it was necessary to reckon with the ambiguous figure of the English King, who was an important theologian in his own estimation (also he had written against Vorstius). The King was desirous of exerting his influence in the coming synod, although he was anything but inclined to encourage the synodical-presbyterial system of church government in his own realm [1]. Saying that the King looked upon the Dutch churches in England in their independence of the English State Church as a necessary evil, is hardly putting it too strongly. The States General of the United Provinces, who were the promotors of the synod, attached value to the presence of delegates from the English State Church — in no small measure from political considerations — but, for this very reason, considered it undesirable to invite in addition the Dutch communities, the more so as the King had made it known that he would not give permission for their representation. It is evident from a letter which Festus Hommius wrote to the Reverend Ruytinck, probably in the second half of 1618, that this political line of action was, for several reasons, not to the liking of the Dutch theologians in the home country. Ruytinck is asked in this letter to use his influence with the Archbishop of Canterbury, so that the delegates, who will be sent by

---

[1] See for the double-faced church policy of the King as regards the foreigners amongst other works De Schickler, *Les égl. du refuge*, T. II, pp. 361 et seq., 367.

the Government, shall be men "not loving truth less than peace",
as it is known that amongst the Anglican theologians there are
such as do not entirely oppose the views which today cause disturbances in the Dutch churches, men like Overall and Richardson. Hommius adds that he has on several occasions pressed
the States General for the Dutch churches in England also to
be invited to attend the synod. The reply is that originally one
had not thought of it, and that it is now too late. If they were
invited, the Dutch churches in Germany would also have to be
invited, and these, anyway, lacked the means in these critical
times, to send delegates. Was Hommius entirely sincere in putting it thus? But, he continues, if you still consider it useful or
necessary and possible to send a delegation, let me know, and
I will then approach the States General on your behalf. We do
not possess Ruytinck's reply, but we do have a second letter
from Hommius stating that a repetition of the request by the
States General to the King would be undesirable on political
grounds: if you, churches, still want to get something, ask the
King yourselves, when the States will also give their support
through the Ambassador Noël de Caron [1]. It is a pity that Ruytinck omits to mention the date of this correspondence. We
would otherwise have been able to judge of the real significance
of Hommius's "too late". Also Ruytinck uses these words, but
their true import is not clear: "and the letter of convocation
having on the one hand arrived too late and being on the other
hand somewhat incomplete". The Dutch communities sent no
delegates, but only the London elder, Carolus Liebaert, as ob-
server. He was furnished with a letter containing certain points,
which it was desirable should be brought unofficially to the
notice of the synod.

London had imagined that things would have been very
different. Already on the 5th June the Colloquium, which was
then in session, had decided to send a delegation [2]. Two ministers, the Reverend Ruytinck and the Reverend Proost from
Colchester, as well as an elder, the Liebaert just mentioned, were
chosen and instructions were drafted, everything in the expect-

---

[1] Ruytinck, *Gheschiedenissen*, pp. 321 et seq.
[2] *Colloquia*, pp. 223–226. The invitation from the States General was only sent off
after the 25th June, see W. J. M. van Eysinga, *De internationale Synode van Dordrecht*,
in *Exuli*, Haarlem 1948, p. 22.

ation of the letter of convocation which never arrived [1]. Liebaert
was present at the synod, but seated by himself and having no
right to vote. He had brought with him a kind of letter of cre-
dence, in which the London Consistory, whom the Colloquium
had charged with the management of this affair, points out rather
bitterly that London, as "mater belgicis ecclesiis" had deserved
something better than being given a back seat, and expresses
the expectation that this case will not constitute a precedent;
such a disregard of the tie between the churches will make it
difficult to preserve the unity with the Church in the home country [2]. The synod apparently realised this. After the synod was
over it sent a letter which expressed regret for what had happened, and gave the solemn assurance that on the occasion of
another synod the States General would be pressed with all possible emphasis to recognize the churches in England as being
of equal standing with the other participants [3]. We know that
the opportunity has never presented itself. The Dordrecht synod
was to be the last one held for centuries to come and.....
the ties with the home Church did in fact become less and less
strong, at least in matters of organization. When Festus Hommius, who had been scriba of the synod, came over some time
afterwards to offer the King and the Archbishop copies of the
Acta Dordracena, he honoured the London Community with
a copy of one of his works "Specimen controversiarum belgicarum" to which an essay by Ruytinck had been added. A sop
thrown to Cerberus?

It goes without saying that with the loosening of the ties in
matters of organization, the personal and spiritual ties were not
severed. We have already discussed education. In the early stages
we have the exchange-ministers, who were lent by London to
the home Church for shorter or longer periods. These cases of
loan were so numerous that a few examples must suffice. As
early as 1578, Jac.Regius was loaned to Ghent for three months.
After expiration of this period, a request for an extension was
made. London showed little inclination, but a year later Regius was still in Ghent [4]. All requests were not granted. Thus

---

1) *Colloquia*, p. 237–243.
2) *Archivum*, III[1], pp. 1274 et seq.
3) *Ibid.*, p. 1277.
4) *Ibid.*, pp. 509, 535, 554.

London did not see its way to allow Regius in the previous year
to accept a call to Haarlem and this, despite pressure on the
part of the Prince of Orange. London felt rather awkward about
it. Even so it could defend its attitude by pointing out that four
ministers could scarcely cope with the work in London, that
there was already a vacancy, and that Van Winghen was old.
Fearing that the Prince might be offended, the Council asked
the Court preacher, Taffin, to explain the position to him [1].
Also, when in 1586 no one less than Count William Louis, the
Stadtholder of Friesland, asked for the Reverend Luc. van Peenen to be lent, the Church Council refused. A request in 1588
by the ministers of Dordrecht, Delft, Rotterdam and the Hague
for advice in the following matter, is remarkable. They feared,
on account of their religion, that the Queen would conclude
peace with Spain. They, therefore, wanted to mobilize the "Classes" of the home church for the purpose of addressing themselves
to her with a petition. But the London Community was consulted first. And London replied, very cautiously: that these are
matters which remain within the Privy Council, and no one,
let alone the foreigners, must meddle in this; for the rest the
Council has sufficient confidence in the concern which the Queen
has for the religion [2]. In 1606 the Church Council of Amsterdam asked the London Council to indicate a suitable minister
to fill the vacancy in the English church there, but on no account a Brownist, i.e., an adherent of the "independent sect"
of the Reverend Browne. It transpires from a second letter from
Amsterdam that the London Council had meanwhile exonerated
the Amsterdam brethren from the accusation of supporting
the Brownist movement, an accusation which could have been
inferred from the circumstance that the Brownists (or Bruinisten
in Dutch) had found shelter in Amsterdam [3]. When in later years
the London Community obtained its ministers from the Continent, prominent figures in the home country were always consulted; Gomarus, Voetius, the Theological Faculty of Leyden.
Noteworthy is the advice given by Voetius concerning a certain
preacher not indicated by name, who still secretly serves a com-

---

[1] *Archivum*, III¹, pp. 470, 472.
[2] *Ibid.*, p. 861, 865.
[3] *Ibid.*, p. 1179, 1193. In Amsterdam the alley (close to the Nieuwmarkt) where
they had their small church, continued to be called "Bruinisten gang".

Lindeboom   7

documentary evidence, declared themselves willing, but a decision was not arrived at [1].

In 1605 the French once more renewed their demands for the joint use of the church. We are acquainted with their arguments on this occasion from the comprehensive reply which has come down to us in Ruytinck's "History" [2]. We know from the correspondence that it was most probably not drafted without reference to the advice which the Reverend Regius obtained for this purpose from a certain Joh. Radermaker, then living in Middelburg, formerly in London, where he had shared the vicissitudes of the Dutch Community from its very beginning. In three comprehensive expositions he has expounded to the London brethren their perfect right to the exclusive use of the church [3]. In passing, the French had also pressed for an investigation into the rights which they thought they had on the churchyard. On the Dutch side this proposal was considered to be totally inopportune, but as regards the matter itself they pointed out that the churchyard, under existing conditions, must be regarded either as having been already handed over to another owner, or as still being at the disposal of the King. In any case, it was not considered advisable to open up this question. And now for the main point in the French document, which was, that it followed from the use in the Charter of the word "Germani" that the Dutch had no right to the church. The reply refutes this argument by pointing out that this word embraces "as well the Low German as the High German language": as one speaks in England of the Netherlanders as Dutchmen. In 1560 the church was returned to the Dutch, and to them alone, and it is they who have borne all the costs connected with the church. A proposal to submit the question to arbitrators, "good men and true", must be declined as being inadvisable; for this the question goes back too far in time, moreover it would be impossible to find "good men and true" with sufficient expert knowledge; in any case, it would be a procedure which would drag on endlessly, as was the case with the attempt to arbitrate in 1580, which never led to any result. The French brethren cannot deduce any right from the fact that they have celebrated Communion in the church. This was the

---

1) *Ibid.*, May 31st, June 14th, and Nov. 22nd, 1582.
2) Ruytinck, *Gheschiedenissen*, pp. 201–210.
3) *Archivum*, III¹, pp. 1168–1176.

result of special permission, and it had been made clear at the time that this permission was given without prejudice as to rights. The French had also submitted that the Coetus was always being held in Austin Friars. The reply to this was that the original decision had been to meet alternatively in both churches, the Dutch and the French. Why should we have arrived at this decision if there had existed a joint right to one church? Finally: there does not exist any factual foundation for the argument that the Dutch have always paid one half of the rent of the French church.

It would be wrong to conclude from the fact that each side kept strictly to its own opinion, that the relations between the two churches bore a hostile character. Once a month, on the first Sunday, there was an exchange of churches, a custom which in 1799 was limited to once a year [1]. It was the duty of the sexton of Austin Friars on those occasions to take to the French church on the preceding Saturday the books "and whatever belongs to the religion" [2]. This exchange of church building, which was arranged in order to accommodate the French in their celebration of Communion, for which there was not sufficient room in their own Church [3], probably terminated in 1843, when they occupied their new church in St. Martins-le-Grand, because after that year there is no further mention of an exchange (compare below page 187). Joint meetings took place in the Coetus. When a new Archbishop or Bishop or Lord Mayor took office, a joint deputation paid its respects. On these occasions the French minister used at first to speak for the two churches. Later, the French and the Dutch ministers addressed the Lord Mayor in turn [4], and the same on the occasion of the accession of James I. The Colloquium of that year was also held jointly, but on that occasion two Dutch churches were represented. A proposal to hold a synod of all the foreign churches found little support [5]. In 1606 a joint address on the protection of foreign labour was submitted to the House of Commons [6]. When in 1615 the church was being repaired, the Dutch Consistory

---

1) *Acta* IX, f° 266 r°.
2) *Ibid.*, f° 198 r°.
3) Moens, *The Dutch Church Registers*, p. XLII (after Stow's *London*).
4) *Acta* VIII, f° 282 r°.
5) *Colloquia*, pp. 100 et seq.
6) *Archivum*, III[11]. p. 2898.

submitted a request to the French Community asking for permission to worship in its church on Wednesdays and Fridays, which request was readily granted [1]. In the same year the French repeated the proposal, made previously, that the two churches should meet jointly in Colloquium, but the Dutch raised objections, their argument being, that also in the home country Walloons and Dutch had separate meetings, the language would be an obstacle, and the various church councils would have to be consulted, for which purpose more detailed supporting arguments from the French would be required. The French replied that their Colloquium was so very small, and that it found only very little appreciation amongst the religious communities. Three years later, on the occasion of the next Colloquium, the Dutch rejected the proposal [2]. The troubles and cares in the days of Laud, however, brought the two churches together again. This will be further considered in a later chapter. Noteworthy are the figures of the membership of the two communities, which were quoted at that time. The French then had 1400 members against the Dutch 840. During the major reparation of the church in 1641, the Dutch again met for worship in the French church [3]. We may further mention that in 1647–1648 a joint Colloquium or synod was held after all. It lasted two and a half months and dealt, amongst other matters, with the case of the Reverend Poujade of the French Community in Canterbury, who had been guilty of all kinds of misdemeanour and immorality [4]. Already in 1640 this misguided shepherd had been the cause of party strife in his church. The London Coetus had then been brought into it, and had been successful in finding a way out of the difficulty [5].

How fruitful the co-operation was in those years is shown by the help which the Dutch Church offered to the French in 1652 in connection with the call to London of a candidate to the Ministry, who had not yet been ordained. The case is especially worth mentioning, because of the personality of the candidate,

---

[1] *Acta* VII, f° 56 r°.
[2] *Colloquia*, pp. 197 et seq, 212, 218.
[3] *Acta* VIII, f° 100 v°.
[4] *Archivum*, III[II], pp. 2083 et seq.
[5] On the subject of the case Poujade, which does not concern us, see De Schickler, *Les égl. du refuge*, T. II, pp. 130–138, and the correspondence in *Archivum*, III[II] of those years.

the remarkable Jean Baptiste Stouppe, who died a Lieutenant
Colonel of the French Army from wounds received in the battle
near Neerwinden (1692); in 1672 he served in the French Army
of occupation in the Netherlands [1]. In 1652 the French communities in England could not send delegates to examine the candidate. The French Community in London turned to the Dutch
sister Community for assistance with a view to Stouppe being
examined in the Coetus, and so it happenend [2]. When in 1666 the
French lost their church in the Great Fire, they were, at their
request, given the use of the church in Austin Friars, which
involved some re-arrangement of the times of the services. The
French also asked for a contribution towards the cost of rebuilding their church. This was declined by the Consistory. The
Consistory did give permission, though, for the members personally to be asked for contributions [3]. In 1687, when the French
Community had grown considerably in numbers as a result of a
flood of refugees, it made a similar request "for a long period",
coupled, in case the request were granted, with a request for
permission to build a gallery in the Dutch church. Within a few
days the Dutch were ready with their reply which was in the
negative, "for weighty reasons" [4]. Was there a fear that they
would cease to be masters in their own house? A negative answer
was also returned to the French lady, who lived a long distance
away which caused her to be late for Communion, and who asked
for a reserved seat in the pew for women, with a coat hook. It was
on this occasion that it was decided always to refuse requests of
this nature [5]. In 1725, 1745 and 1780, the French brethren were
again given the hospitality of the Dutch Church when their own
church was under repair [6]. In this way the relations remained
good and undisturbed, without there being any longer any
question of closer co-operation. Co-operation became even less
pronounced with the passage of time, in the absence of common
dangers which called for joint defensive action. But the friend-

---

[1] Concerning him, see C. W. Roldanus, *Een verloopen predikant in de 17e eeuw*, in
De Gids, vol. 96 (1932), I, pp. 215–231; De Schickler, *Les égl. du refuge*, T. II, p. 169–
173, 231–234.
[2] *Acta* VIII, f° 211 r°.
[3] *Ibid.*, f° 274 v°.
[4] *Acta* IX, f° 59 r° et seq.
[5] *Ibid.*, f° 100 v°.
[6] *Ibid.*, f° 142 v°, 182 v°, 239 v°.

ship remained. In 1850 there were joint celebrations in commemoration of the 300 years' existence of the two communities, and when in 1862 the Dutch were deprived of the use of their church through fire, it was the French Community which not only expressed its condolence, but offered the use of its church for services on Sunday afternoons [1].

On many occasions we have mentioned the names of other Dutch church communities in England: Norwich, Sandwich, Colchester, and have spoken about the joint gatherings, the Colloquia, and the time has now come for considering these communities more closely. The reader must not expect to find in what follows, a more or less exhaustive treatment of the material. It only touches our main subject indirectly. Moreover, exhaustive treatment would involve research and description on a scale which is beyond the scope of the present work. The history of the Dutch church communities in England outside London could well be a monograph on its own, and the writing of it would have to be preceded by exhaustive research and study. It would hardly be a stimulating and, from the nature of the subject, a satisfying labour, because on the whole the history of all these communities has been a long tale of woe. A tale of premature formation, of painful efforts at keeping the community alive, of disappointing struggles against all sorts of adverse circumstances, within and without, such as lack of funds, internal dissensions, decline in numbers and interest, all leading to a general decline, and ending in extinction. It is significant that it is really not possible to state with certainty when some of these communities were dissolved. After a period of gradual exhaustion they vanish from the history of the Dutch communities. The fact that the life of these communities was so often prolonged, and that injections of vitality at various times resulted in a temporary revival, is due, most of the time, to help from the London Community, in the beginning the "prima inter pares", later the guiding force and a source of financial and spiritual help. For this reason we are bound to consider these matters, be it only in passing.

The coming into existence of these church communities was closely connected with the civil settlements of which they form-

---

[1] *Index to volumes 28 and 29*, no. 4473.

Plate IV

The interior of the old church about the middle of the 19th century

ed the uniting spiritual element. A grouping of people originating from the same country and speaking the same language, could not be conceived of in those days without the uniting element which the church supplied, and which, at the same time, fulfilled, in many respects, the functions which one associates nowadays with an organized society. The care of temporal well-being and that of eternal bliss were closely connected, and the latter often set the pattern for the former. Not only those, who, for the sake of religion and conscience in the strict sense of the word, sought refuge in foreign lands, but also those who left their country because they saw their liberties threatened in a more general sense, considered it self-evident that their religious interests were taken care of by a church community. The authorities in the new country, being, from the religious aspect, more or less of the same mind, not only raised no obstacles against this, but they even encouraged it very positively, for the religious tie furnished a solid guarantee for the behaviour of the immigrants in civil life. The English Government exhibited the same goodwill towards the exiles and fugitives who went to other places as it showed to those who came to London, because of the community of spirit between them and, in addition, from considerations of the usefulness of the immigrants. We may even take it that the latter consideration came to weigh more and more heavily. The distribution of the industrious foreigners over an increasing number of country districts and towns, promised enhanced material gain from the granting of hospitality, but from the nature of the case it gave rise to increasing interference in the life of the churches.

Dr. Van Schelven has gathered together in his book important material bearing on the history of the other church communities in the initial periods of their existence. Grateful use has been made of this material in what follows. — Sandwich was the oldest outside community. It came into existence as early as 1561 as a result of the settlement there, at the request of the magistrate and with the consent of the Queen, of a number of families who belonged to the London Church. There were many weavers among them. In the first decades of its existence, the Community rose to great prosperity, being served by no fewer than three ministers. In subsequent years it had its share of internal quarrels and party divisions. It started already in 1576 with a violent quarrel between the ministers Balck and Obry. London acted the part of arbitrator and both parties submitted to the verdict [1]. In the years following 1560 a schismatic minister of the French church in Canterbury, Ayton, caused a great disturbance in Sandwich. Once more, as in so many similar cases, it was the London Community which had to intervene with counsel and mediation. Somewhat later there was another dispute in which a certain Reverend Damselius figured. After 1706 Sandwich, which about 1635 still counted 500 members [2], disappeared from the correspondence with the London Community; already by the end of the previous century the membership had greatly diminished.

Colchester was the second fugitive community. It came into existence probably about 1565, as a result of an excess of membership in the Sandwich Community. In 1644 it is still referred to as a flourishing community [3], which need not surprise us, seeing that it was reported in 1635 to have a membership of about 700 [4]; but after the beginning of the eighteenth century this church also is no longer mentioned in the correspondence of the London Church. Also for Colchester, London had been a support and a refuge.

Halstead was a shoot of Colchester. It was founded in 1576, but came to grief already in 1590 through opposition on the part of the local population, and this in spite of the prosperity which the foreigners brought to the district. The weavers of baize returned to Colchester, and none took their place, notwithstanding some urging on the part of the London Church Council that the weavers should be encouraged to return to Halstead [5].

An important community was that of Norwich, opened by patent of the Queen in 1565 for the foreigners, again mostly weavers. Initially its members came from Sandwich. Later on many came direct from Flanders. It has had an important history, according to Van Vleteren's ,,Historie''. It counted in 1635 almost 400 members. Moreover, as was the case with Sandwich, Norwich found a certain measure of support in a French sister

---

1) *Archivum*, III[1], pp. 447 et seq.
2) *De historie vant Synode A° 1635 beschreven door D. Timotheus van Vleteren's eigen hant, p. 84.*
3) *Colloquia*, p. 343.
4) Van Vleteren, *Historie*, p. 84.
5) *Archivum*, III[1], p. 907.

community. Norwich has suffered much distress from the troubles during the time of Laud. Many emigrated to Virginia, others returned to the Low Countries [1]. In the end it has been Norwich which, after London, has maintained itself longest as a foreign church community. In the eighteenth century, when there could no longer be any question of a Colloquium, the mutual relations weakened. However, they were not broken off. Rather did London, when Norwich no longer had a minister of its own, obtain a kind of tutelage over the Community, which gradually assumed a more and more English character. A minister from London preached occasionally, and once in two years Communion was celebrated, for the last time in 1818 [2]. In the course of the nineteenth and until the beginning of the twentieth century, the only tie between the two communities was an annual preaching engagement by the minister from Austin Friars, in order to ensure the continuity of the right of the Community to the available funds which would otherwise revert to the Royal Charity Commission. Actually, this annual service became a mere formality, as it was held in the English language (Dutch was no longer understood in the tiny ,,community''), with a few introductory words in Dutch. The services continued to be held in the large and beautiful old church, Black Friars Hall, even when, about the year 1890, it passed into the ownership of the Norwich Municipality. Eventually these services were discontinued. On July 13th, 1919, the last ,,Dutch'' religious service in Norwich was held. Today the funds are being administered by the entire London Church Council, as trustees.

Maidstone, where a colony of fugitives settled in 1576, remained small. It was seldom served by a resident minister, and then only for a short time. In 1637 there were complaints about increasing loss of members to the English church (the pressure experienced in these days from the Laud troubles was considerable) [3]. In 1660 the Community is referred to as no longer existing [4]. London has also given itself much trouble over this Community.

Yarmouth dated as a Dutch church community from 1569,

---

1) De Schickler, *Les églises du refuge*, T. II, pp. 39 et seq.
2) *Archivum*, III[II], p. 2863.
3) *Acta* VIII, f° 56 v°.
4) *Archivum*, III[II]. p. 2446.

but six years later it was already on the way to extinction. Yet
it was kept alive. It was once more London which put it on its
feet again in 1620 [1]. In 1635 membership was estimated at 28. In
1660 Yarmouth still participated in an address of homage to
Charles II, who had just become King [2]. A short while before, the
Community had proposed that a letter of condolence and of
welcome should be sent to Cromwell's son, Richard [3]. They had
a minister again at that time and, of course, they appealed to
London for support, but for once London advised that they
should cut their coat according to their cloth. As late as 1680
the London Community has furnished financial aid [4]. Shortly
afterwards Yarmouth disappears from the correspondence.

Of Stamford, Ipswich, Thetford, Lynn, Dover and Coventry,
little more can be said than that they have had a short and
uneventful existence during the sixteenth century.

But communities did not only arise during the century of
religious persecution and struggles. Certain communities, having
a very special character, came into being later. They were also
the outcome of religious motives, but less as a result of the
stresses of the time, than of the conviction, equally weighty from
the civil as from the religious point of view, that a certain, say a
Dutch, communal entity should have its appropriate religious
communal structure. The way in which such communities could
be founded about that time on a purely business basis, transpires
from the proposition by an English nobleman, who was a landown-
er in Ireland, contained in a letter addressed to the Consistory
in 1603, offering to have a town founded by the Dutch in the
Province of Munster. No suit was given to this proposition [5].

In a somewhat similar way the Community in Mortlake (Sur-
rey) came into existence in 1621, in close relation to London, i.e.,
as a branch community. They were the Flemish tapestry weavers,
who had been introduced into England with economic intent,
and who had been proclaimed by the Archbishop to be a church

---

[1] *Colloquia*, p. 271.
[2] *Archivum*, III, p. 2436.
[3] *Ibid.*, p. 2405. The Minister of Yarmouth gave a sample in his draft for this
letter of his flowery language: "We have heard that pale death has stamped its foot
on the earthly tabernacle of this great man".
[4] *Ibid.*, III[11], p. 2633.
[5] *Archivum*, II, pp. 924 et seq., III[1], p. 1138.

community, with permission to hold their services in the parish church, or otherwise in the house of Sir Francis Crane, the promoter, under the aegis of the London Community which lent its own ministers for the services at Mortlake. The London Church Council has far from neglected its duties. The minutes from 1630–1640 bear continuous witness to its care on behalf of the branch Community. It was the weavers of Mortlake, on whose behalf the unprofitable deal for the supply of a carpet, which has been related above (page 75) was made. The words of 1655: "members of London living in Mortlake" show that the Community was looked upon as being part of the London Community. At that time there were about sixty members [1]. In 1664 the services were taken by a candidate, but the London Consistory thought it necessary to admonish him because he preached in English. He was emphatically forbidden to do this, as also to concern himself with matters which concern the State or the Church of England, "which might cause great distress to all the foreign churches in the country" [2]. Thereafter traces of this Community disappear from the correspondence, which means: from history.

Efforts to found a community in Hatfield Chase had an interesting cause. This was the district in the north of Lincolnshire to the south east of Yorkshire, where Sir Cornelius Vermuyden, the well-known land drainage specialist, was engaged on his land reclamation and dam construction works. We cannot devote space to him and his important undertakings, and must limit ourselves to a reference to the important work on him by Korthals Altes [3]. In 1637 efforts were made to establish a church community amongst the Dutch emigrants. In the beginning there was great interest in this project in the home country, where men like Jacob Cats, Constantijn Huygens and Johannes van Baerle were among those who were financially interested in this work of land reclamation. We know that the results of Vermuyden's drainage operations did not come up to expectation. The saying "he has bitten off more than he can chew" can be applied to

---

[1] *Archivum*, III[II]. p. 2265.
[2] *Ibid.*, p. 2501.
[3] J. Korthals Altes, *Sir Cornelius Vermuyden, the Lifework of a great Anglo-Dutchman in land reclamation and drainage*, Lond.–The Hague 1925.

Vermuyden [1]. Exaggerated expectations had been raised in the minds of prospective church members. The occupants of the new land and the "participants of the embankment of Hatfield Chase" had promised to build a church, but there was no progress and, of course, it was once more London to which a request for counsel and help was addressed. However, nothing came of it all [2]. Actually there was a French pastor, and it seems that this French element had succeeded in supplying the spiritual needs of both "François et Flamands" for some years. But it was an extraordinary community where in two small churches the services were held in English and the Anglican liturgy was followed. This explains, but does not condone, the fact that in the fifties the Community suffered greatly at the hands of the troops of Cromwell [3]. Many colonists departed after this.

Finally, the Community of Canvey Island in the mouth of the Thames, close to the northern bank. Land reclamation was carried on here. It was a lurid spot. Whoever has seen the drawing in Southerden Burn's book of the small wooden Dutch church, feels a kind of oppression at the thought that ministers and candidates living in that deserted spot amongst an English population, which on the whole was not well disposed towards the foreign workers, had to preach the Gospel to a Community of low intellectual and cultural standing, and such on an annual stipend of £ 30 (partly paid by London at that), which incidentally had to cover the cost of keeping a horse because of the bad roads [4]. It is hardly to be wondered at that often the better ministers could not be induced to go to this island. As already indicated, this Community found its origin in a land reclamation scheme. The scheme had been entrusted to a Dutch contractor in 1622 [5]. In 1627 the need of establishing a church community and of appoint-

---

[1]) Already in 1633 complaints were received by the London Community to the effect that Sir Cornelius Vermuyden failed to meet his obligations. It was decided that a couple of elders would take him to task; *Acta* VIII, f° 21 r°, 38 r°.

[2]) *Archivum*, III[II], p. 1760.

[3]) The explanation of this conformity with English usage is probably to be found in the pressure which in the 'thirties of the 17the century the Archbishop of York had been exerting on the Community, entirely in the spirit and on the instruction of Laud. Because in writing to London, the Community asked very definitely for a preacher ,,conforming to the churches of Geneva"; De Schickler, *Les égl. du refuge*, T. II, pp. 48–55, 178.

[4]) *Archivum*, III[II], p. 2443.

[5]) Burn, *History of the refugees*, pp. 220 et seq. See also Moens, *the Dutch Church Registers*, p. XXXV.

ing a minister, was felt. But there was no progress and in 1631 the Dutch population is said to be "very wild and unruly", owing to there being no minister of religion. However, in 1641 there was a minister, but he appears to have been rather inexperienced. The post was often vacant [1]. In 1706 the Colloquium thought that the Community had ceased to exist, but they were mistaken: a sign of life was received [2]. But we may conclude from the circumstance that in 1710 the deacons of the London Church took on the management of the land attached to the Church of Canvey Island, that the Community as such had by then disappeared [3].

It is a fluctuating number of these communities which were united for over a century in a Colloquium. The name already signified a midway course and a concession. In the home country and given perfect freedom of action, it would have been called a "Classis". But we have seen how the ecclesiastical "Commissaries" of the Queen had pronounced their veto on the holding of organized gatherings (such as the gatherings of the "Classes" would have been within the larger overall church complex), as also the participation in any synod abroad and the underwriting of its decisions. Offence was even taken at the fact that the official reports of the synod held at Emden had formed the subject of discussion at a gathering of the English fugitive churches [4]. The word "Colloquium" hid rather conveniently that in practice the organization was that of a "Classis", for "Colloque" was the old name for the meetings from which in France the "classes" had emerged. Be it merely as a Colloquium, and not as a gathering or "Classis" within a larger all-embracing ecclesiastical body, the first gathering of delegates of the Dutch refugee churches was held on March 15th, 1575. Apart from London, the churches of Norwich, Sandwich, Colchester, Maidstone, Yarmouth and Thetford were represented by ministers and elders. It is a fairly well established fact that the churches looked upon this gathering as a disguised meeting or "Classes", such as the synod of Emden had recommended. It is moreover confirmed by a statement

---

[1] *Colloquia*, pp. 298, 300, 313, 315, 327, 368.
[2] *Ibid.*, pp. 387, et seq.
[3] *Archivum*, III[II], p. 2783.
[4] *Archivum*, II, pp. 194 et seq., 410 et seq.; compare III[I], pp. 150 et seq.

which Ruytinck makes in his "History" [1]. It was resolved, in
conformity with Reformed church law that each community
should have one vote, and that in matters touching doctrine all
ministers, prophets and candidates for the ministry would be
allowed to vote. The authority of the Colloquia was accepted,
by all churches agreeing to be guided by majority resolutions.
This was by no means an empty phrase, certainly not in the
early stage. In previous pages we have repeatedly met with
cases in which the Colloquium took action with authority against
a member. Mention may be made in this connection of a pronouncement of the Colloquium of 1577, which instructed London to call the Community of Dover to task for the exorbitant
interest, sometimes amounting to 50%, charged by some of its
members, and to call the Church Council there to account. Those
involved had on a previous occasion declared that a moderate rate
of commercial interest could not be looked upon as usury —
a sound Reformed standpoint! [2] The report is remarkable
because of the evidence it offers of a certain preponderance
of the London Community, and because it is such a striking
instance of interference in a social matter. As a matter of fact,
this preponderance of London is continuously in evidence. London was, as it were, the address to which churches at home di-
rected their communications meant for the communities in
England. When, for instance, in 1580 the communities overseas
were invited to attend the synod of Middelburg, this was done
via the London Church [3]. This preponderance actually grew
with the years to an appreciable extent, not least through the
continuously worsening financial position of the other churches,
which made them dependent on London. It is interesting to
see the ever-growing share occupied by the outside churches in
the minute books of the London Community, like so many
children in need of care.

During the first few years the Colloquium met regularly once
a year. The Colloquium of 1578 decided to send a delegation
to the National Synod which was to be held at Dordrecht.
However, there followed a period of three years during which
no Colloquium was held. Then, in 1581, the question of sending

---

[1]) Ruytinck, *Gheschiedenissen*, p. 106.
[2]) *Archivum*, IIII[1], pp. 442 et seq., 425.
[3]) *Ibid.*, p. 603.

delegates to the National Synod of Middelburg of that year came up for consideration. It was decided to send delegates. But it is a striking fact that Norwich, which did not attend the Colloquium, saw no good purpose served by representation at Middelburg. Changes in church order, so they wrote, do more harm than good as a rule, and if ever we return to the home country it will be time enough to comply with the regulations in force there. To this the Colloquium replied: there is no harm in it, only good [1]. When in the same year another Colloquium was to be held for the express purpose of discussing the resolutions passed in Middelburg, Norwich sent a letter in which they declared that they would not take any notice of Middelburg [2]). These are the first signs of a spirit of opposition, which can be observed to an increasing degree as time goes on in the case of the Norwich Community. As it happened, the subject of Middelburg was hardly mentioned at this Colloquium. Had the first mine been laid underneath the institution of Colloquia? Whatever the position, it was considered necessary to pose the question as to whether further gatherings should be held at regular intervals, or only as the need arose. It was decided to meet at intervals of one year and a half, but in 1583 it was again Norwich which did not consider it necessary to send a delegate [3]. It was the same in 1584 [4]. It would seem that there was a desire to avoid embarrassment for the Superintendent [5]. In 1586 the Norwich Community was represented, though not because of the Colloquium, but on account of a particular measure which was about to be taken. If we view these incidents from a certain standpoint, we can see from them the extent to which support, supervision, and in certain cases compulsion on the part of the authorities, could have significance for an organized church. Meanwhile, the Colloquium of 1586 had been summoned at the request of Sir Thomas Walsingham (who had communicated with the London Community) for the purpose of discussing, among other matters, the necessity of importing as much grain as possible, and of establishing a register of all English workers in the employ of

---

1) *Ibid.*, pp. 636, 640 et seq.
2) *Colloquia*, pp. 65 et seq.
3) *Colloquia*, pp. 69, 71.
4) *Ibid.*, p. 78.
5) *Archivum*, III¹, pp. 751 et seq.

foreigners resident in England [1]. The threat of the Armada was becoming more clearly defined. Thirteen years now passed before the Colloquium met again. Norwich was present in 1599, but on that occasion it was decided to meet in future only "for weighty reasons" [2]. The next gathering was in 1609 and from then onwards the Colloquium met regularly, as a rule every three years, until 1634. The reason for the long interval between the gatherings of 1599 and 1609 was most likely the dislike on the part of the King of this typical expression of presbyterian church government. As Ruytinck puts it: that the King "having come to the Crown of England, revealed himself as thinking better of the hierarchy of England than of the Presbyterate of Scotland" [3], the reason why he forbade the holding of regular synods in the latter country. We have already seen how the synod of Dordrecht of 1618–1619 occupied the attention of the Colloquium. A curious resolution by the Colloquium of 1621 shows that the Dutch churches outside Holland did not attach much weight to the questions of dogma which this synod had been specially called to consider. It was the custom at that time for the ministers who took part in a Colloquium to preach a sermon to the delegates (a similar custom existed in the home country in connection with the meetings of the "Classes"). The text on which the sermon was to be preached had to be submitted in advance. The question arose as to whether in future also the entire sermon should be considered in the light of the synodal five articles against the Remonstrants, which constituted the kernel of the resolutions passed in Dordrecht. The decision was in the negative. It was considered sufficient for the text to be passed, as being ample guarantee against the possible expression of unorthodox views. It was also decided that, whereas the ministers should once again sign the confession of faith in token of agreement, the elders and deacons need not do so, it being feared that the novelty would cause dislike of the Colloquia on the part of the English [4]. Apparently it was advisable to tread warily in the matter of the Colloquia! — The gatherings continued to be held, but at irregular intervals, and with varying attendances.

---

[1] *Archivum*, II, pp. 794 et seq.
[2] *Colloquia*, p. 99.
[3] Ruytinck, *Gheschiedenissen*, p. 233.
[4] *Colloquia*, pp. 247 et seq. — In 1641 it was decided that all ministers would once more by their signature express their adherence to Dordrecht, p. 315.

Every time some of the communities were absent; now this one, now that one failed to attend. The reasons were shortage of money, difficult conditions of travel, or vacancies in the ministry. The latter occurred often in the case of the smaller and poorer communities. The last Colloquium was held in 1706, the only churches represented being London and Norwich — a case of "combat fini faute de combattants"!

In 1644 the Colloquium had resolved to encourage the introduction of the Bible translation made by order of the States General [1]. We saw on page 92 that the London Community had already introduced this translation in 1638.

We should not conclude from this bloodless end that the Colloquia had been without significance. They certainly helped during difficult times to advance the cause of corporate unity and to strengthen its maintenance in the face of the outer world. This was the case to a special degree with the Colloquium of 1634–1635, at which time the existence of the fugitive churches was being endangered by the campaign of Laud. The Colloquia further played an important part in the drawing up of fixed rules for the maintenance of church discipline. After what has been said on this subject in the preceding chapter, especially as far as it concerns the London Community, further reference to it is superfluous, the more so as these uniform arrangements applied to all the communities, and not only to London in particular. The story of the Colloquia is important because it shows how the hegemony of the London Community where the other churches were concerned, was apparent from the start, and how thereafter it grew from strength to strength. London was the great authority because of its numbers and of its financial and cultural ascendancy, but in the degree in which this ascendancy grew, the original character of the gatherings became weaker. This could only lead to a position where the basic principle of Reformed church law, namely that no one church community should rule over another, became affected. Actually the decline of the other Dutch churches in England set in early. A plaint which Norwich, to a certain extent the *enfant terrible* of the family, submitted as early as 1627 to the Colloquium of that year, is instructive in this connection: ,,What must be done to keep the communities in being, as many amongst the members, stiffened by the evil

---

[1] *Ibid.*, p. 327.

example of one, threaten, in the face of all kinds of unpleasant-
nesses to which they are exposed, or because of their being under
church censorship, to leave and to refuse to bear the financial
burdens imposed upon them, to the weakening of the communities
and their eventual extinction?" [1] Even in a hospitable and not
unfriendly country like England, the position of the foreign
residents was not easy. The next chapter will illustrate this
further.

---

1) *Ibid.*, p. 296.

Chapter V

THE RELATION TO CHURCH AND STATE
THE STRUGGLE WITH ARCHBISHOP LAUD

In this chapter we shall deal with the relation in which the Dutch Church in London stood to the political powers, and to the Church Authorities. We are aware that it is possible to raise objections against this method, because, considering the closeness of the bonds between Church and State, these relations can hardly be separated from one another. When the Archbishop and the Bishop of London occupied themselves with the Dutch Community, either to help it or to interfere with it, they also did so in their capacity as indirect organs of the power of the State. Admittedly, the reigning sovereign was not the supreme head in matters of faith, but he was nevertheless supreme governor of the State Church. In consequence, actions taken by the Church Authorities in the name of the State Church, very quickly took on the character of an action by the State, from which it followed that active or passive opposition on the part of the foreign Church Community could easily be held to be a crime against the State. Yet, there were relations which were entirely, or predominantly, political and secular in character. These, however, touched less the Dutch Church than the Dutch Nation. However, as the latter had in its Church Community its only representative organ, and in the Church Council its sole representative, it was, at least during the first century and a half, inevitably the church "corpus corporatum et politicum", which received the favours or experienced the obstruction, and had to resist the latter.

As early as 1567, the Church was given legal status by the authorities, who issued an order for "all strangers abiding in the City of London who professed Christ and the Gospel to join themselves to that church" [1]. Obviously, the object was not to serve the spiritual needs of the Community but to facilitate the supervision of foreigners and to have some warrant that no elements which could be regarded as being revolutionary, such as the Anabaptists and the like, would find their way into the Community. It was not long, however, before the population and the authorities looked askance at the growth of the Community, especially on account of the growing competition in trade. A resolution taken in 1574 by the Common Council prohibiting the taking into service of apprentices whose fathers had not been born within the Kingdom [2], put on the brakes. Two years later it was the Shoemakers' Guild which resolved that an investigation should be made into the question of the foreigners (who as foreigners were due to pay double tax) to determine whether they were denizens and how much tax they paid [3]. In the following year a curious question of international politics, in which the Church Council became involved, presented itself. The Privy Council accused the Prince of Orange of having caused English vessels to be seized in the mouth of the Thames, and the London Community was ordered to abstain from giving support to the Prince as long as the dispute on this question remained unsettled. The Privy Council notified the Church Council to be very exacting in the observance of this order, as the House of Commons was not well-disposed towards the foreigners on account of this incident. The matter was settled through the intermediary of Loyseleur de Villiers, the Court-preacher of the Prince and his diplomatic representative on occasions, but the Community in England had to bear the cost of his mission. Only Norwich, in opposition in this as in so many other matters, refused to contribute, on the plea that Norwich was a "country town", and as such had no interest in a commercial question [4].

Before the end of this year, 1576, further tribulations befell the Community. In the latter part of December, it received a notification, written in Latin, from the Lord Mayor saying that the Privy Council had given orders for watch to be kept on the observance of the rules of fasting. Even among the English population there

---

[1]) Pijper, *Utenhove*, p. 99 (after Strype, *Annals of the Reformation*).
[2]) *Archivum*, III[1], pp. 270 et seq.
[3]) Burn, *History of the refugees*, p. 9. Denizens did not have the status of native born subjects.
[4]) *Archivum*, II, pp. 361–364, III[1], pp. 421, 434.

seems to have been something lacking in this respect. This, said the Lord Mayor, is no question of religion but concerns the "political utility" of the Kingdom, which foreigners also must observe [1]. The degree to which such observation could be enforced was shown in 1587 by an order from the Lord Mayor and the Court of Aldermen, in which the foreigners "within the Cittie or the fredome and Liberties of the same" were enjoined so to arrange their business premises, that passers-by could not see them at work, nor that wares and merchandise lying in the shop would be exposed to view, but subject to their having sufficient light to work by [2]). In 1590 a decree by the Common Council of London prohibited foreign schoolmasters to practise as scriveners, keep an open shop or display a sign [3].

Yet the Court was not ill-disposed towards the foreigners. In 1591 the Queen approached the King of Poland in an endeavour to obtain liberty of religious confession for the Dutch in Dantzig, because, so the request said, these foreigners should be clearly distinguished from those amongst their compatriots, who preach rebellion and anarchy. The incident shows how deadly afraid the rulers of Europe were of the Anabaptists. Elizabeth had been moved to take this step by an appeal from the Dutch Community in London [4]. Another year she ordered that measures taken against "the poor candlemakers and others of the Dutch congregation" should be discontinued. Something similar occurred in March 1599 [5]. It was actually more the middle-class tradesmen rather than the Court or the Government who, in those days, sought to obstruct the Dutch and other foreigners; but then it was, admittedly, these tradesmen who had to bear the brunt of the competition, whereas the result of the promotion of prosperity, which was the Government's aim in protecting the foreigners, could only be realized in the long run and in indirect ways. A bill aimed at the foreigners, and promoted on the initiative of the tradesmen, was passed by the House of Commons, but a dissolution of Parliament prevented further progress being made in this matter. In 1586 and again in 1593, the unruly "ap-

---

[1]) *Archivum*, II, pp. 570 et seq.
[2]) *Archivum*, III[1], pp. 852 et seq. In 1605 the order prohibiting the display of merchandise was still in force; Ruytinck, *Gheschiedenissen*, p. 229.
[3]) *Archivum*, III[1], p. 906.
[4]) *Archivum*, II, pp. 860 et seq.
[5]) *Archivum*, III[1], pp. 939 et seq., 1035.

prentices of London" were the cause of a riot aimed against the foreigners, but the authorities took strong measures to quell it. It was on this occasion that the following poem was nailed to the church door:

"You stranger that inhabit in this land,
    Know this same writing, do it understand,
    Conceive it well for save guard of your lives,
    Your goods, your children and your dearest wives" [1].

These occurrences make it understandable that in 1593 the Amsterdam preacher Plancius, a good business man as well as a good Calvinist, felt moved to suggest a way out to his London colleague, the intention being that it should also be brought to the notice of the other communities in the Kingdom. Seeing how the unfriendly mood against the Dutch in England is on the increase, he counsels a move to ..... Harderwijk (a small town in Holland situated on the Zuiderzee). He knows from experience that there are good opportunities there, cloth weavers are welcome, and a resolution by the Burgomaster, Sheriffs and Aldermen of the town, which is enclosed, guarantees full rights to those who come over [2]. Imagination reels at the very thought of this plan having been carried out! In 1599 the Dutch and French communities had to petition the Queen against trouble experienced from the secret agents. An order followed that these persecutions should cease [3]. It was in particular the tailors, candlemakers and yarn spinners who were the victims of the informers [4]. Despite these continuous difficulties, the Community was fully conscious of the great obligation which it had towards the Government. In 1603, when the Dutch Community in Altona asked London to pray the King to approach the Hamburg Magistrate on behalf of the Reformed church members who were experiencing trouble from the side of the Lutherans (the old trouble!), London replies that it would rather not interfere, they were already beholden to the King for so much [5]. Ruytinck writes about a resolution of the Common Council of 1605 based on centuries-old regulations, which resolution prohibits aliens

---

1) Burn, *History of the refugees*, pp. 10, 191.
2) *Archivum*, III[1], pp. 956 et seq.
3) *Ibid.*, p. 1037; *Archivum* II, p. 901.
4) *Archivum*, III, pp. 1056 et seq.
5) *Ibid.*, pp. 1102, 1109.

who have not been naturalized, from carrying on a trade or industry, but a remonstrance addressed to the Government restored the "freedom to the poor strangers" [1].

In 1616 the Church Council had once more to take up the cudgels on behalf of the craftsmen who were being "sorely tried by the informer and by the tale-tellers". The Council addressed themselves to the King through the Ambassador. The detailed account which Ruytinck gives of these negotiations [2] contains important items of information bearing on the state of the colony. The Council refutes the alleged considerable increase in the number of Dutch people. It replies that there are fewer than there were thirty years ago, not more than 450 families, of which many are denizens or have been born in England. It is simply not true that the foreigners are so excessively prosperous, this is only true of a small minority. Neither is it true that they remit the greater part of their profits to the Continent, as had been alleged; the contrary is the fact. They bring money to England. Further, the denizens must, in many cases, pay double dues, so that it is pure invention to say that other foreigners also profit from these privileges. It is only natural that the free denizens mix with their former compatriots and that they are members of the latter's Church Community. Also, they do not neglect attendance at the State Church. The argument had been advanced that the foreigners had shown lack of gratitude by persisting in intermarrying. The Council replies, not without humour: "Iff a part of thankfulness do consist in mariage with th' English, it is knowen that both of the richer and poorer sorte are so joyned". The accusation had also been made that the foreigners had fled in the year 1588, in the hour of danger, when the Armada threatened the safety of the country. This allegation is refuted as being without foundation. The Community helped the good cause with money and men, in proof whereof they refer to the expression of thanks by the Privy Council. As regards the Dutch "itt is nott their custom to fly when occasion is offered to defend the countrye and to maintain the truth". Finally, documents are submitted to prove that the English over there in the Netherlands enjoy not fewer, but more privileges than the Dutch do here. These protests bore fruit. The foreigners were pronounced

---

[1] Ruytinck, *Gheschiedenissen*, pp. 229 et seq.
[2] *Ibid.*, pp. 290, 302; compare *Archivum*, III[1], p. 1263.

to be in the right. "Whatever may come of this, may time show",
so Ruytinck concludes his tale.

The taxes, certainly, were heavy. In the following year, 1617,
the King wanted to travel to Scotland in great state, and the
subjects had to bear the cost of this enterprise, which amounted
to a complete removal. A demand was also made on the Dutch
Community, and on being urged by the Netherlands Ambassador,
furnished a loan of £ 20,000. "May the Lord protect us from similar vexatious matters", says Ruytinck [1]. For the troubles were
not yet over. In 1619 there was another complaint to the authorities about the large number of foreigners and their prosperous
circumstances. The Church Council, on being summoned to
appear before the authorities, managed to give satisfactory information. It was on this occasion that the Council submitted
statistics. These arrived at a total number of 1613 foreigners,
77 denizens and 882 persons who had been born in England of
Dutch parents. The majority consisted of craftsmen. The larger
number of these (no information in this respect was given for
merchants), lived outside the City [2]. The English objectors did
not let the matter rest. Very soon there were complaints from
that side that the business activities of the Dutch merchants
caused serious harm to the Kingdom. The merchants were said
to encourage the transfer of money abroad, and to help in getting
money concentrated in a few hands. The Attorney General
brought the case before the Star Chamber. Once more an appeal
was made to the King, through the Ambassador, Noël de Caron.
The King sent the appeal to the Attorney General. This had the
effect of oil poured on fire. The Attorney General managed to
obtain a decree "ne exeas" from the Chancery Court on bail
for each merchant to the sum of £ 2,000. This measure was subsequently rescinded, but the evil returned in an aggravated
form.

The £ 20,000 mentioned above had been advanced by the
Ambassador De Caron to the Community under surety, and the
Privy Council had undertaken to be his surety for the repayment
of the sum by the King (it will be remembered that it was said
to have been a loan) with payment of interest at the rate of ten
per cent. per annum for the part not repaid. Apparently the

---

[1] Ruytinck, *Gheschiedenissen*, p. 314.
[2] *Ibid.*, pp. 333–340.

members of the Privy Council expected no great things from this repayment and they were trying to hit on a method of settling with the Ambassador by way of a counterclaim, as the Dutch have it "with closed purses", and thereby ridding themselves of the surety liability. There ensued a complicated financial manipulation of a questionable character, which has been described by Ruytinck, who was a close witness of it all, and by the author of the continuation of his History, the Reverend Calandrinus, in great detail but with insufficient clarity. We cannot here summarize at all extensively the fifty pages, in which both clergymen have recorded the matter [1]. A short summary must suffice, the more so as the question really concerned the colony or the nation more than the Church Community, even though the latter has always taken up the cudgels for the colony and was the centre to which all addressed themselves. The old accusation that the Dutch merchants collected big sums of money and then sent them abroad, causing the country to be deprived of them, was resuscitated. The merchants were in the first instance summoned to prove their innocence of these practices. When this proved ineffective, the Attorney General produced a number of shady individuals, ,,rascally, infamous, irregular people", who declared under oath that merchants, whom they indicated by name, had collected sums amounting to thousands and tens of thousands of pounds and had transferred them abroad. One of them even pretended to reveal that there existed an ordinance in the Community, that members who made publicly known any matter reflecting unfavourably on their compatriots, would be excommunicated. The judges of the Star Chamber, being of the opinion that they had not sufficient material at their disposal for formulating an accusation (not more than involved 18 or 19 delinquents, whereas all the merchants were supposed to be guilty), asked the King for further instructions. The King ordered them to carry on with the collection of the maximum amount of evidence against the maximum number of persons, and additional evidence was found! The merchants protested and declared their innocence. The Ambassador approached several members of the Privy Council on their behalf. The States General submitted a protest through diplomatic channels — it was all in vain. In the end 19 merchants were

---

[1] *Ibid.*, pp. 346–401.

condemned to the payment of a fine of £ 130,000. Once more
the Ambassador intervened, once more the States General
sent a note, the minister of the Church appealed to the Attorney
General — it all availed nothing. The secretary of the King
even gave the Dutch and French Consistories to understand
that the entire colony was considered to be guilty in this matter
and that, therefore, failing speedy payment, all foreigners
would be called upon to pay. At long last, after a lot of arguing,
the Ambassador managed to obtain that the King would be
satisfied with £ 60,000, and that this amount would include —
it was here that the cat was let out of the bag — the sum, which
the King still owed to the Ambassador under surety of thePrivy
Council, and which, with the ten per cent. interest on £ 20,000
over three years, amounted to £ 26,000. This part of the fine
had, therefore, to be paid to the Ambassador who, it will be
remembered, had advanced the £ 20,000 to the Community. In
this manner the King was relieved from the necessity of repaying
the „borrowed" money, the loan furnished by the Community
was converted into a levy, and the Royal Treasury benefited
to the tune of £ 34,000!

The sequence of this story does not give a very favourable
impression of the attitude adopted by the Dutch in this matter.
It can be readily understood that they resented having to pay
to the Ambassador, Noël de Caron, the large sum of £ 26,000,
but they should have remembered that it became part of the
fine which they owed to the Treasury, and that this part only
differed from the rest in the address where payment had to
be made. The Ambassador had to press repeatedly for payment
and was even forced to appeal to the King and to the Privy
Council for assistance, which led to further sharp letters from the
latter. The words used by the Reverend Calandrinus who evidently
was not blind to the more or less shifty attitude on the part of
the debtors, are worthy of note. He wrote: "this the churches have
brought on themselves by their meddling in political matters"[1].
One has to interpret the word "political" as used here, in a somewhat wider sense than that current today. Was it possible that
the merchants were not entirely blameless in the matter? A
single, but significant utterance by Ruytinck: "some who possibly had been somewhat negligent, relying on their simplici-

1) *Ibid.*, p. 397.

ty" [1] makes us suspect this. The question of the claim by De Caron dragged on until 1624. Two years previously the craftsmen had been in trouble, when an endeavour was made to force them to accept repressive and unfavourable guild conditions. A petition to the King had a partial result: a repeated attack failed [2].

Did the churches draw any lessons — needed or not needed — from these incidents? One could come to this conclusion from the words in which the Reverend Van Cuilemborgh, who continued the work of Calandrinus, describes the position after King Charles I had come to the throne. At that time, the Community, he says, was "in a fairly undisturbed state", "not the least of the cause being that it has avoided as much as possible making requests to the Court, becoming involved with the Government, bragging overmuch about the age and the privileges of our Church, putting on airs, but has behaved in a more humble and peaceful fashion, judging its strength to lie in quietude and faith" [3]. Moreover, in 1621 the question was raised in a Colloquium "in how far Ministers of the Word may meddle in matters of politics?". The answer of the meeting was: if they are forced to it from above, for instance through action of the Privy Council, then they must not stand aside, unless it would create unrest in the Community, but the first condition must always be that it serves the interests of the Church [4].

We will pass by the political difficulties in the turbulent later· years of the reign of Charles I. These difficulties are so closely connected with the religious and ecclesiastical relations to Church and State that they are better discussed later. Naturally, the Community became involved in the growing political controversy, whereas up to now relations with the authorities, both civil and ecclesiastical, had been restricted to matters relating to doctrine and church government. On August 18th, 1641, by which time the conflict between King and Commons had become more sharply defined, the latter asked the Church to pray that it might please God to move the King's heart not to depart to the North with the army on the next day [5]. Two years later "the Militia of London" asked for support in the form of men,

---

1) *Ibid.*, p. 349.
2) *Ibid.*, pp. 430, 449.
3) *Ibid.*, p. 488.
4) *Colloquia*, pp. 251 et seq.
5) *Archivum*, III[11], p. 1860.

horses, ammunition and money [1], and in 1644 the Westminster Synod, "Assembly of Divines", addressed a call to the ministers to co-operate in the collection of money for the enlistment and upkeep of the forces under Sir Thomas Middleton [2]. With all that, the wind was by now beginning to blow from a quarter favourable to the Church. Both Church Assembly and Parliament were inspired by the same puritan spirit as was the Dutch Church, and the presbyterial-synodal system of church government came to be generally acknowledged. A proclamation by the Lord Mayor in 1649, calling on the citizens for strict observance of the Sunday and of the days of fasting and prayer, which proclamation it was requested should be read from the pulpit, will not have met with much opposition in the Community. If, in the same year, Dutch craftsmen were sorely tried, this will probably have been due to professional jealousy. It caused the Community to petition the House of Commons [3].

Also during the time of the Commonwealth conditions were unfavourable to the Community. Broadly speaking, those in power sympathized with the Reformed spirit which inspired the Community. It is certainly remarkable that there is so little evidence of difficulties experienced by the Church from the side of the authorities and the populace during the first war with the Dutch Republic. This may have been partly due to the greater mutual understanding in matters of the spirit. Moreover, belligerents had by then not as yet advanced so far in civilization that they considered it to be their duty to torment peaceful citizens of the opposing side in all circumstances and in all possible ways! In 1652 there was talk, following a hint from Cromwell, of a petition from the Community to Parliament, pressing for peace and recommending itself to the goodwill of Parliament. Cromwell had given the assurance of his personal goodwill towards the Reformed church communities [4]. The correspondence does not reveal whether the petition was actually submitted. For that matter, great care was exercised in those days. In 1653 or 1654, the other Dutch communities were opposed to the holding of a Colloquium: it might be misinterpreted, they said. But the

---

[1] *Ibid.*, p. 1913.
[2] *Ibid.*, p. 1926.
[3] *Ibid.*, p. 2173.
[4] *Ibid.*, pp. 2210–2213.

relations remained good. We know, moreover, that on religious grounds, Cromwell was on principle no enemy of the Dutch Republic, and that he was most anxious for peace between the two countries, as it would help him in furthering the cause of Protestantism which lay so close to his heart. When the peace of Westminster had been concluded, relations improved even further. In 1655 Cromwell presented a sum of £ 100 to the Community, from a legacy, the money being intended for the Dutch poor [1]. In the same year the Lord Protector and the Privy Council once more commended the foreigners to the special care of the Lord Mayor and Aldermen, after another complaint had been received about obstructions having been put in their way [2]. At the time of Cromwell's death, the Community sent an address of tribute to his son and successor, Richard, to which a reply was received promising permanent protection [3]. But also after the Restoration the good relations were on the whole maintained, even though at that time the episcopalian church had again been re-instated. In 1670 we read of a petition to the King by the Dutch and French churches, on behalf of poor Protestant weavers from Flanders and other foreign parts: they experience difficulties from the side of the Weavers Company and their protection is asked for. As a matter of fact a somewhat favourable arrangement for the admission of the foreigners into the Guild was arrived at, through the intervention of the Privy Council [4].

Taking the wide view, when we pass from the relation of the Community to the political authorities to its relation to the ecclesiastical authorities, there is no big jump. What in her time Queen Elizabeth intended to attain with the State Church, and what that Church itself desired, was an ordered society. What the Tudors have brought into being is not so much an English faith as an English Church. As the sovereign acted, not as supreme head, but as supreme governor, opposition to, even dissent from the Church's teaching, could be interpreted as a crime against the State, and procedure by the State need not take the slippery path of an inquiry into the faith of the accused. Whatever

---

1) *Acta*, VIII, f° 227 r°.
2) *Archivum*, III, p. 2213.
3) *Ibid.*, p. 2408.
4) *Ibid.*, pp. 2565–2570.

gave offence or was unacceptable in the church services of the
foreigners, could be sanctioned by the royal favour, but such
sanction was greatly influenced by the direction in which the
English Church leaders of a particular period guided the Church.
We must clearly realize that in English eyes the religion of the
foreigners did give some offence and that it was more or less
unacceptable. It was a form of Calvinism which in the days
of King Edward VI might have had some chance of becoming
the religion of the State Church, but which, actually, failed to
answer the needs of the greater part of the people and the spirit of the Anglican Church. As a seventeenth century pamphlet
has it later: "Calvin's religion was too lean, and the catholic
religion too fat" [1]. The Puritanism of the foreigners, their aversion
to anything which, however remotely, reminded them of the
papacy, was, however, less an outcome of dogma than an attitude of mind, and it was this that made the foreigners tolerable
in English eyes. Their presbyterian church order was admittedly
in no way that of Elizabeth's State Church, yet it could be regarded as a form of state church. Thus it was that for the continued
existence of the church of the foreigners, submission to the authority of the State was a *sine qua non*. This submission gave
them a feeling of safety, and on the other hand, the authorities
felt protected from Anabaptist rebellious tendencies and revolutionary disturbances. That there was no lack of submission
we have seen on several occasions. It was the basis of the relation
of the Dutch Church to the authorities which came definitely
into being in 1560 and which differed in some important respects
from that of the first years after 1550. The Church had most
definitely to reckon with the figure of the Bishop of London
in his capacity as Superintendent, and it did so.

Within the framework of this relation of submission there
was ample room for differences, large and small. The former
were to occur more particularly during the reign of Charles I
when episcopalian aspirations began to display totalitarian
tendencies. The smaller differences were almost daily occurrences. One of the issues was the "desertion" by members of
the foreign Church Community to the State Church, whenever
they quarrelled with their own church, it being most of the time
a matter of the censorship. On the whole the authorities adopted

---

[1] Byrne, *Elizabethan Life*, etc., p. 159.

a loyal attitude in such cases, and they watched against the State Church becoming a refuge for those whose position in their own church had become impossible as a result of their misbehaviour. In 1561 the Bishop of London made a declaration which was occasioned by a request of this sort, to the effect that persons who had left the Dutch Church Community otherwise than by mutual consent, may not be accepted into his Church [1]. In 1574 a conference was held with the Archbishop on the subject of marriage of Dutch people outside their own church. On this occasion the Dutch Community was recognized in its own marriage discipline and the Archbishop undertook to notify his clergy that they must not solemnize marriages of foreigners, if these could not submit a proper letter of commendation from their own church [2]. In the following year, the Bishop of London, on receipt of a complaint from the Community, repeated this instruction: evidence of written consent from the Community and from the Archbishop must be submitted. The complaint seems to have referred in particular to the fact that in the English Church no preliminary announcement was made, which fact encouraged clandestine marriages [3]. In 1586 a certain Aeg. Raet, who was debarred from Communion, complained to the Archbishop. The Archbishop urged the Council to be satisfied with this man's confession of guilt [4]. In 1509 the question was raised in the Colloquium as to how to deal with a schoolmaster who kept a school without the consent of the Dutch Church, but under licence from the English ecclesiastical authorities. It was a delicate question. The result of the discussion was: "the matter will be submitted in all quietness to the commissary" [5]. That "deserters" were an ever present problem is evident from a petition which all the Dutch communities addressed to Archbishop Abott in May 1611: people under censorship go over to English parishes to take part in Communion there. The Archbishop is asked to refer such people back to their own church, so long as there is nothing in their church order which is at variance with the King's laws or with the ordinances of the English

---

1) *Kerkeraads-protocollen 1561–1563*, p. 137.
2) *Acta VI, f° 41 v°.*
3) Ruytinck, *Gheschiedenissen*, p. 105.
4) *Archivum*, III[1], p. 818.
5) *Colloquia*, p. 111.

Church [1]. In 1615 the Colloquium once more debated whether or not to approach the Archbishop on this point, but it was considered preferable to consult in the first place the chancellor of the Bishop of London. He considered it to be a reasonable request and promised his support [2]. With the passage of the years these and similar questions receded into the background. More important points of dispute were coming to the fore and the significance of the censorship as a point of dispute became less, possibly in part owing to the difficulties to which the censorship could give rise.

We know already that the Bishop of London acted as Superintendent after 1560. We have also seen on more than one occasion, that this office embodied a very real exercise of authority, even though, ostensibly, its holder was elected by the Community, in accordance with the terms of the Charter. Without actually being subservient to the Bishop, though cases of subservience did occur, care was taken to remain on good terms with him and every consideration was given to his views. When in 1570 a dispute arose between one of the ministers and a member of the Community, steps were taken to ascertain the wishes of the Superintendent [3]. There was admittedly a certain element of subordination in the relation, though in most cases the Council will not have had any difficulty in accepting the position. A case in point is the letter from the Bishop in 1579, when a fire had destroyed a part of Portsmouth, calling on the Church to contribute towards the cost of rebuilding, in common with all London parishes [4]. We may take it that in this and similar cases, whether of lesser or greater importance, the wish expressed carried the weight of an order. In 1579 a member of the Community, a certain Conr. Reynolds, had a quarrel with his wife. The couple made it up, but it seems that some elders fanned the dispute afresh. This time the Bishop was brought into it. An official on his staff warned against any further steps being taken without previous consultation with the Bishop [5]. In 1581 it occurred to a creditor of the Community to appeal to the Bishop for support of his claim. The Bishop called on the Church

1) *Archivum*, III[1], pp. 1225–1229.
2) *Ibid.*, pp. 1260–1263; *Colloquia*, pp. 204–266.
3) *Kerkeraads-protocollen 1569–1571*, p. 75.
4) *Archivum*, II, pp. 639 et seq.
5) *Archivum*, III[1], p. 560.

Council, a discussion of the matter ensued [1]. In 1612 the Community experienced much trouble from a hysterical woman and this time the Council called on Bishop King with the the request for him to take measures against her [2]. Then there was the question of the ownership of the Church spire (of which more in a subsequent chapter). The Bishop was called in by the Reverend Ruytinck who made use of the opportunity to send him a long exposition on the Arminian disturbances in the Republic [3]. Great care was taken to avoid giving offence to the English authorities. In the Colloquium of 1612 the question was discussed whether an Englishman, who was a member of his own Church, could be admitted to Communion. The cautious conclusion was: if it can be done without opposition from the English clergy, well and good, in the opposite case it is inadvisable [4]. The Colloquium of 1621 had to answer the question as to whether it was permitted to engage a preacher who, by his signature, had signified his acceptance of the ceremonies and ordinances of the English Church. The answer, couched in cautious terms, was in the affirmative: they have nowhere been pronounced to be contrary to God's Word and — second argument of a less profound but more positive character — refusal might be construed as an unfriendly act towards the State Church [5]. All the same, when a principle was in danger, the reaction was quite definite. In 1619 the Norwich Community complained that it had received a notification from the Chancellor of the Bishop that it must in future celebrate Communion in a kneeling attitude. London suggested a form of protest which had the desired result [6]. Another case involving a question of principle was that of the English clergyman, who asked his Dutch colleague to assist him in administering Communion. The best thing to do, so it was judged, was to "decline politely" [7].

We will see presently how significant and fraught with danger were the relations to the English Church and to the superintendents in the days of Archbishop Laud. It is self-evident that the office of Superintendent lost much of its significance during

---

1) *Ibid.*, p. 646.
2) *Ibid.*, p. 1239.
3) *Ibid.*, pp. 1246 et seq.
4) *Colloquia*, p. 161.
5) *Ibid.*, p. 250.
6) Ruytinck, *Gheschiedenissen*, pp. 328 et seq.
7) *Colloquia*, p. 250.

the Commonwealth. After the Restoration, when the antithesis between Episcopalianism and Puritanism became less sharp, the office does not appear to have been formally re-instated. The "obedient subordinate" relationship gradually disappeared. Nevertheless, it is anything but clear what the actual relationship was during these years. In 1660 the point arose as to whether it would not be a wise move, so that "patent and privileges" might be strengthened, to appoint a superintendent, either by electing such a functionary from within the Community, or by accepting the Bishop of London, "as is customary", in that office. A week later, however, it was decided "not to give first consideration" to the appointment of a superintendent, as inspection of the "statute book" had shown that the "patent" (the Charter) was unassailable [1]. In 1668 the question of the office of superintendent comes up for discussion, merely as a matter of form [2]. The report of the interference, in 1692, by the Bishop in the following matter, makes curious reading. In that year December 25th fell on a Monday. The Bishop asked whether it would not be recommendable to dispense with the service on December 26th. This was agreed to [3]. In 1703 in the case of the Reverend Van Cuilemborgh (about whom more in the next chapter), when there was a danger of the Community being split in two, his adherents appealed to the Bishop of London and asked the latter, in his capacity as Superintendent, to act as judge in the dispute [4]. Van Cuilemborgh also appealed to the Bishop [5]. It ended with Van Cuilemborgh being suspended by the Bishop, who, when giving his decision, made no reference to his office of Superintendent. [6] Also in the detailed account of this case, which is included in Hessel's Archivum, although there is mention of the action by the Bishop and of his efforts to bring about peace, as also of the support he gave to the Community against Van Cuilemborgh's party, there is nowhere any evidence of the Bishop's having acted specifically as Superintendent. Rather does one get the impression of a feeling of embarrassment on his part, because of his inability to do more for the Community

---

1) *Acta* VIII, f° 257 r°.
2) *Archivum*, III[II], p. 2548.
3) *Acta* IX, f° 84 r°.
4) *Archivum*, III[II], p. 2742.
5) *Ibid.*, p. 2758.
6) *Ibid.*, p. 2759.

than what he actually did and this, although Van Cuilemborgh's
lawyer had tried hard before Doctor's Commons, though without
success, to have the case brought within the jurisdiction of the Bishop [1]. But when on October 9th, 1703, the Bishop delivered his
final verdict, by which Van Cuilemborgh was dismissed, he did
so in the function of "my Superintendency" [2]. In 1721, in a
lawsuit concerning the property rights of the Church, it became
evident that it was desirable for the Church again to have its
superintendent, in conformity with the stipulations of the Charter, and that it should be the Bishop of London [3]. This explains
why in the following year the appointment of Bishop John Robinson as Superintendent of the Community was approved by
the King [4].

In its relation to the English Church, the Dutch Church Community gradually became more autonomous, but the figure of
the superintendent continued to retain its value as a resort to
which appeal could be made in cases of internal differences.
In 1820 William Hawley, Bishop of London, acted as intermediary in a difference between the two ministers of the Community.
It does not transpire whether he did so specifically in his capacity as Superintendent, but in any case, on the occasion of his
appointment in 1813 as Bishop of London, he had been acclaim-
ed by the Church Council as "inspector superintendentis ti-
tulo" [5]. Apparently the tie with the superintendent had by then
become so greatly loosened that the appointment of a minister
was no longer notified to him, but only to the King, through
the Home Department. This procedure was also followed by
the French Community in London, at least so the Dutch told the
Bishop on the occasion of his efforts at mediation in the above-
mentioned dispute between the two Dutch ministers.

In our review, through the centuries, of the history of the office
of superintendent, we have somewhat anticipated our account
of the relation of the Dutch Church Community to the English
Church. The puritanical orientation of the Dutch Community
inevitably led to the authorities' looking upon it, more or less,
as the least acceptable amongst the co-religionists or as the most

---

1) *Ibid.*, pp. 2729–2736.
2) *Ibid.*, pp. 2933 et seq.
3) *Ibid.*, p. 2795.
4) *Ibid.*, p. 2796; *Acta*, IX, f° 137 v°.
5) *Archivum*, III¹¹, pp. 2867 et seq.

acceptable among the opponents. This was especially the case
in those times in which the High Church outlook and episcopalianism predominated. If it was not the Community itself which
the authorities eyed with suspicion, it was rather that they were
not entirely satisfied that it would not be used as a jumping-off
board by kindred elements much more dangerous to the Anglican
Church. Already in the days of Queen Elizabeth, Puritanism
had begun to develop within the State Church on the theological
and specifically ecclesiastical plane, initially not progressing
beyond propagating the presbyterial-synodal church order as
against the episcopal order of church government. However,
in their wake there followed the much more direct enemy, the
followers of Robert Browne, with their idea of a church freed
from all State ties, who were, therefore, regarded as being completely revolutionary and dangerous to the State. A church
like the Anglican, intent as it was on the maintenance of the
Catholic church tradition and of the hierarchy, could not do
otherwise than look upon Brownists and their like as prime enemies. It is well known with how little consideration, actually
with what harshness, Church and State have treated the Brownists. It is, therefore, understandable that the Privy Council
addressed a warning to the Church Council in 1573, against
allowing any foothold to the rebels who wanted to introduce
new ideas dangerous to the State. We can, so the Privy Council
wrote, justify certain deviations in the ceremonies, because in
the end we serve the same God to whom the whole world belongs
We approve your ceremonies, but want to ask you not to
be misled by a certain measure of similarity in belief, in af-
fording an opportunity to those who are intent on sowing
dissension in this realm and enabling them to gain adherents.
The Church Council accepted the warning and gave assurances
of its loyalty, promising that it would not admit such elements
into the Community. In actual fact it had up till then not had
any such among its members [1]. As we might expect, given this
attitude by the Council, we find no evidence during the reign
of Queen Elizabeth of serious clashes with the State Church
in this domain of the life of the Church. It was very different
under her successor, less through any fault on the part of the
Community, than through the ambiguous attitude which this

---

[1] *Archivum*, II, pp. 456–463, 482–485; Ruytinck, *Gheschiedenissen*, pp. 92–97.

capricious figure, with his pronounced episcopalian sympathies, adopted from the start. Perhaps the change was partly due to the fact that the puritanically inclined in the Kingdom had expected different things from a Scottish King. He, however, did not leave them long in uncertainty. Already in 1604 there was a disputation in the presence of the King. On that occasion James gave clear evidence of his dislike of puritanical ideas. He had had enough in Scotland of puritan-calvinist preachers. A supplication from twentytwo preachers in the Kingdom, who inclined towards Puritanism, for liberty of preaching, drew from the King the remark: "no Bishop, no King" [1]. It would hardly be possible to express more clearly the alliance between the episcopal form of Church Government and State Authority. Storms were gathering, also for the foreign church communities. Immediately after the King's accession, they had turned to a few members of Parliament, who were sympathetically inclined towards the foreign communities, and had appealed to them for support in maintaining their well-being, whereas those in London were to seek contact with their Bishop, with a view to receiving timely indication of any threat of a measure which might endanger their liberty.

It is only natural that the foreign church communities tried from the earliest time onwards, and especially during these and following years, to obtain official confirmation of their privileges. Remember: the Charter was a "grant", not a „gift." These efforts invariably led to the desired aim, but the practical application of that aim was not always in conformity with it [2]. Among such confirmations must be reckoned the above mentioned letter from the Privy Council of 1573, and a resolution by this Council of the following year, whereby foreigners who had moved to other parts of the Kingdom, were guaranteed the same liberties and rights as the foreign church Communities already in existence possessed. In 1603 King James, in answer to an address of homage on the occasion of his accession to the throne, had promised the same protection as the churches had enjoyed under the government of his "sister" (?). In 1616 the

---

1) *Ibid.*, p. 178–189.
2) Summary of these efforts in a note of February 23rd, 1635 in *Archivum*, III[11], p. 1688. It is also to be found in Van Vleteren, *Historie*, pp. 66–70. Another, shorter, summary of May 3rd, 1645, in *Archivum*, III[11], p. 1967.

King once more confirmed this in a letter addressed to all the courts of justice. In no wise different was the action by King Charles I when he came to the throne in 1625, which action even allayed the disquiet which his marriage with a French Roman Catholic princess had aroused. In the following year he repeated his assurances in a letter to the judicial authorities. Meanwhile, in fact as early as 1615, there had been signs of intentions on the part of the authorities, of detaching the English born descendants of the emigrants from the foreign church communities [1]. Significant, as illustrating the feeling of disquiet in the Dutch Community, is the decision of the Colloquia to ask the coming Dordrecht synod (at that time the impression still prevailed in the London Community that it was entitled to participation on a footing of equality), for "some forceful arguments", which might help it in defending the presbyterial church system, seeing that the office of elder is being opposed in England and held to count for little [2]. The foreign communities had little faith in the King and his advisers, and they saw the spectre of papistry looming on the horizon — not more than a spectre, for the ambitions of the episcopalians did not stretch so far. When in 1619 the King re-imposed the old prohibition of the consumption of meat on days of fasting and on fixed fish-days, Ruytinck said of it: "it smells of the old dough", and he added that many "had bought licences with some money from the house of the Bishop" [3]. But worse was to follow.

Never has the relation of the foreigners to the State Church been more difficult and more in the nature of a rope that hurts through being drawn too tightly, than in the days of Archbishop Laud, during the reign of Charles I. The image of the too tightly drawn rope is actually too mild. The attitude of the State Church developed into an effort to strangle the life of the Community entirely, and thus to cause its eventual extinction. It was based on a well-conceived plan, the outcome of the nationalist-episcopalian tendencies of Laud, for which he, strong character that he was, had managed to win the weaker King, who, moreover, was himself not averse to absolutism. For Laud has undoubtedly

---

[1] Ruytinck, *Gheschiedenissen*, pp. 286 et seq.; *Colloquia*, pp. 210 et seq.
[2] *Ibid.*, p. 241.
[3] Ruytinck, *Gheschiedenissen*, p. 329.

been a strong figure as a statesman and a prince of the Church, however unattractive he was as a human being. After the death of Buckingham in 1628, having, for all practical purposes, become prime minister, his aim became more and more the advancement of the unity of the realm through the unity of the Church. The Church within which, and by means of which, this unity had to be realized, was, naturally, the State Church, to which all other churches would have to conform. This was not only the self-evident point of departure of Laud's totalitarian endeavours, but no other church than just the Church of England with its hierarchy of Bishops and its centralized form of government from above, was suitable to the same extent for the realization of his plans. "Without Bishops, no Church", this old Ignatian conception reflected also the deepest conviction of Laud. It was not without reason that his theological interest, and that of his contemporaries, was in the Apostolic Fathers! This striving after a High Church naturally involved a strong attachment to the old rites and ceremonies, such as liturgical vestments, candles, crucifixes; in short, the complete Catholic ritual had to serve to anchor the State Church firmly in the past and to make it in the present and for the future a symbol and carrier of the conception of the unity of the State. In this system there was no room for churches having another system of organization or a different type of religious service, for presbyterian, let alone independent church communities. This meant that all non-conformists would have to conform and thus be brought within the Anglican totality. It was, of course, inevitable that Laud should, in this, meet with powerful opposition from the non-conformists, but unfortunately his aim agreed in every way with the views of those who, for many a year, had cast envious glances at the independent position and material prosperity of the churches maintained by the foreigners.

Already in 1623, when Laud was still Bishop of London, he had submitted an elaborate note to the Privy Council: "Report and Remedy concerning the French and Dutch Churches as they now stand in many parts of this Kingdom, first the danger, then the public remedy" [1]. Even if it had been right at the time, so it

---

1) To be found in De Schickler, *Les égl. du refuge*, T. II, pp. 21 et seq.; also in W. J. C. Moens, *the Walloon Church of Norwich, its registers and history*, Lymington 1887–1888, Append. XXIV.

was argued, to have made room for the foreign churches, now
that the members can no longer be regarded as impoverished and
persecuted foreigners, there is no reason why these churches
should be allowed to continue to exist, completely separated
from the "established church", by reason of which they inevitably constitute foreign communities vis à vis the State, and a
church within the Church. The example of these people has a
bad effect, and it undermines the obedience of the people to the
State Church. We will, therefore, so Laud continues, first have to
ascertain their numbers and then treat them in future as foreigners without special privileges; that means imposing on them
double taxes, which will hit the merchant and the well-to-do
among them. It will be seen that Laud made no secret of his
ulterior economic motives. Further, the foreigners must be incorporated in the parishes of the State Church and, on pain of
excommunication, be compelled to follow the English liturgy.
In conclusion he expresses himself as confident, that possible
opposition on the part of the few can easily be overcome and that
the great mass can be won for all this without difficulty. So
spoke the man, who no longer looked upon the persecuted from
the Palatinate as brothers in the Faith, and who showed clearly
that in the last resort his allegiance to Rome was greater than
his allegiance to puritanical Calvinism. The times of Archbishops Grindal, Parker, Sandys, Abbott, who had all been well-
disposed towards the foreigners, were past. Laud became Archbishop of Canterbury in 1633. With his ability and stubborn-
ness it was to be expected that he would do his utmost to realize
his totalitarian plans. The resistance from the side of the foreigners would certainly not have much effect upon him, who ignored
the opposition on the part of English authorities, because among
the latter were many who were in no way enamoured of the
idea that the well-to-do foreigners should become detached from
their own church and thus in the long run from their community,
which might result in the colonies of foreigners becoming a
charge on the parishes [1].

Laud began his attack in the early part of 1634, and thus
began a struggle which continued for some years, a struggle
which caused the Dutch and French communities many an
anxious hour and which ended eventually with Laud's tragic

---

[1] H. D. Trevor Roper, *Archbishop Laud, 1573–1645*, Lond. 1940, p. 198.

defeat. We possess a good deal of information on the subject of this controversy from what the Acta of the Colloquia and, of course, the correspondence of the Dutch communities tell us about it, evidence of the attention then devoted to it, as to a very important event. There has come down to us a printed document from the hand of a contemporary French minister in Canterbury, Jean Bulteel, who, being himself closely involved in these events, was greatly interested in them, especially from the standpoint of the French churches [1]. Of significance also is an unpublished manuscript by a minister of the Dutch Community in London, Timotheus van Vleteren [2], who has also been a close witness of the struggle of Laud against the churches of the foreigners. De Schickler has devoted much attention to this matter in his book on the French churches in England [3]. In a letter to the Archbishop dated April 10th, 1634, King Charles I had ordered the Archbishop and his staff to take all necessary measures for an investigation into all churches, schools and similar institutions with the object of ascertaining in how far the unity of worship and discipline was being maintained. The King stated that he did this in his capacity of "defensor fidei", defender of the true Catholic Christian Faith [4]. Laud did not allow the grass to grow under his feet. Only a few days later the French churches of Canterbury, Maidstone and Sandwich, as well as the Dutch church in the latter place, which were all inside his diocese, received three questions for answer. In the first place, which liturgy did they follow and why was the service not held in the English language, further how many of the members had been born in England, and finally, were the members born in England prepared to conform with the State Church. This is how the Church Council of the Sandwich Community reported the case to the London Council, the oracle and source of help for all foreign church communities. At the same time they proposed, also in the name of the French churches mentioned, that a joint meeting be held with a view to agreeing as much as possible on a uniform line of action. The reply which the four communities sent jointly

---

[1] Jean Bulteel, *Relation of the troubles of the Three Foreign Churches in Kent caused by the injunctions of W. Laud*, Lond. 1645.

[2] "*De historie vant Synode A° 1635*" beschreven door D. Timotheus van Vleteren's *eigen hant*. Manuscript in the archives of the Church.

[3] De Schickler, *Les égl. du refuge*, T. II., pp. 21–47.

[4] *Archivum*, III[II], p. 1644.

to the Archbishop on the advice of the Coetus, and in which reference was made to the Charter, did not satisfy him, understandably enough[1]. In the place of a kindly request, there now came a command to appear at short notice before a commission of enquiry. In the event of non-compliance "we would soon be made aware as to whether we come under his jurisdiction or not" [2]. On December 19th, 1634 the delegates appeared before the commission of enquiry which was headed by the Vicar General of the Archdiocese, Sir Nathaniel Brent. There they were told that the members of the communities, who had been born in England, should in future join their respective Anglican parishes and attend the services held there, and that those who had not been born in England would be allowed to continue to meet in their own churches, but that they would have to follow the English liturgy, at least in the Dutch (or French) translation [3]. It was decided to call a Colloquium of all foreign churches as quickly as possible. This has actually been the first and the only real synod of the united French and Dutch churches which has been held in England in the course of the centuries. The synod met in London on February 15th, 1635, deeply conscious of the impending threat. Two elders, who had been to see the Archbishop in connection with the collection on behalf of the Palatinate, had had an additional opportunity of noting his firm resolve to carry out his plans, whatever the cost. On February 10th, which was a Saturday, the delegates of the four communities in Kent had spoken with the Archbishop on the question, but he had not shown any great friendliness. He had cut short the address by the Reverend Bulteel of Canterbury, saying he had no time now, the gentlemen had better come back the day after tomorrow (Monday the 12th). But on the intervening Sunday he had expressed the view, so it transpired, that it was really too absurd to continue to regard as aliens, foreigners established in the country up to the fifth generation: was it not a fact that in some communities scarcely ten persons could be pointed out who were real foreigners? [4] There was something in what he said — Laud was not stupid. This transpired on the Monday, at the renewed hearing. In reply to the

---

1) *Ibid.*, pp. 1647 et seq.
2) *Ibid.*, p. 1667.
3) *Ibid.*, pp. 1669.
4) Van Vleteren, *Historie*, pp. 11, 15 et seq.

statement that the children did not know enough English to be able to follow the services, he observed that this was merely an idle excuse for standing aside, because of their view that the English liturgy played into the hands of the papists. The delegates retorted, taking good care not to upset the mighty personage whom they confronted, and who certainly did not want to be thought a papist, that this argument only applied to papists abroad, at which the Archbishop became somewhat more amenable and admitted that the papists had in fact stained with superstition the only redeeming teaching there was. Laud showed further displeasure at the fact that the foreign churches had no hierarchy of ministers, but that all the ministers were equal, that at their Communion the communicants sat together "as in a drinking house", that in the existing circumstances they were as a state within the State, and that the foreign communities were an occasion for repeated obstructionism. No exception could be taken to Laud's attitude at this interview; he even offered his apologies for having dismissed the gentlemen two days earlier, but as regards the matter at issue he maintained his point [1]. We thought it well to reproduce rather fully what was said at the interview, because it conveys Laud's standpoint in such a striking manner.

The synod, therefore, met. Only the French Community of Southampton and the Dutch Community of Yarmouth failed to send delegates, but Yarmouth thought it could offer a good piece of advice, namely "to offer the Archbishop's Commissary some courtesy or gift"! [2] The French pastor in London, Pasteur Primerose, was elected chairman. The Reverend James Proost of Colchester (he later served the London Community) became scriba and the Reverend Regemorter of London, assessor. It was decided to send a petition to the King [3]. A few days previously, contact had been established with the Ambassador of the Republic, Joachimi, with the Duke of Soubise and with Monsieur Turquet de Mayerne, with the request that they support the cause at Court, but Joachimi, who was of the opinion that a petition would do more harm than good, preferred to abstain from such action. It was, therefore, decided for the time being

---

1) *Ibid.*, pp. 20 et seq.
2) *Archivum*, III[II], p. 1679.
3) The petition and the draft *Ibid.*, pp. 1684–1688.

not to call on the good services of the Duke of Soubise, who was incapacitated by foot-trouble, but who was perfectly willing to be taken to Court. Further, delegates called in pairs on members of the Privy Council, in the hope of creating a favourable atmosphere within that body. Everything points to the synod being more or less in a mood of desperation. It was proposed to issue an order for a general fast, but it was apparently found impossible to arrive at a decision. One member of the synod proposed that it should here and there make financial provision for the ministers, in case the communities "should come to nought, which God forbid", as this would strengthen their ability, by the removal of material cares, to maintain their standpoint in the matter of the liturgy [1]. February 21st had been fixed as the day on which the petition would be presented. It was decided, on the advice of well-wishers at Court, that no elders should form part of the deputation [2]. This decision shows how vividly it was realized that such a manifestation of presbyterial-synodal church law might act on the High Church Anglicans as "a red rag to a bull". But that day, with the Lord Chamberlain absent (he was still asleep "because of the revels on the previous night") and the deputation itself hesitating as to the right moment for presentation, they did not succeed in passing the document surreptitiously into the hands of the King "passing from the chapel to the table". The action that day was a failure. The next day they were more fortunate. The King accepted the petition, which he immediately handed on, but he did not wish to listen to the address by the French pastor, Marmet. The text of this address was sent after him through an intermediary at Court. Soubise managed to find a suitable moment for pointing out discreetly to the King what the political consequences might be: "the King of France will certainly not tolerate two religions in his realm, if you, Sire, refuse to tolerate two kinds of ceremonials". Soubise got the impression that the King was unaware of the demand in the matter of liturgy, and that he only insisted on: "one church for those born in England". For the rest, the King seemed rather helpless in the face of the impelling action by his powerful Archbishop, and he seemed to comfort himself and others with the thought that "l'exécution ne sera pas si rude

---

[1] Van Vleteren, *Historie*, pp. 58–61.
[2] *Ibid.*, p. 79.

qu'ils craignent" and that the strangers "went in fear of greater punishment than they actually received" [1]. The fear amongst the foreign residents was, in fact, very great, not only in the communities in Kent, which had been immediately seized, but also in London and in the other communities, because it was realized that if the measures could be carried out with any degree of success, they would not be restricted to the archdiocese of Laud, even though the Bishop of Norwich, to give one instance, was sympathetically inclined towards the foreign residents [2].

The prospect which faced the foreign churches was gloomy in the extreme: uncertainty of membership, a complete break with the churches' own tradition, a denial of Reformed principles, and a reduction of the sacraments, leaving only Communion and even this in the garb of a foreign ceremonial, i.e., not gathered round the Communion table, but standing before the altar. However, the intervention with the King at least seemed to have had some result. Archbishop Laud asked Sir Nathaniel Brent to tell the Kent churches that he was willing to receive the delegates once more. It also became known that there was a certain tendency within the Privy Council to be more accommodating towards the foreign residents. The foreign churches drew the conclusion from this that they would be well-advised to allow matters to take their course, and also that it might be a good thing if they were to show solidarity with the Anglican parishes by occasional attendances at Anglican services. Political considerations very probably had had something to do with this more accommodating attitude. The authorities had evidence of rising unrest and opposition amongst the Reformed Scots "who agitated greatly against the ceremonies" [3]. The action by the well-known peacemaker in church affairs, Johannes Duraeus (John Dury), may have been a contributory factor in this change of attitude. This remarkable idealist, whom we shall meet again in a subsequent chapter, when his relations to the London Community will be considered, had just then returned to England from Germany, where he had been acting as mediator between the Reformed and the Lutheran churches. Duraeus, whose spiritual labours invariably attracted the attention of the political figures

---

1) *Ibid.*, pp. 82 et seq.
2) *Ibid.*, p. 88; compare Roper, *Laud*, p. 200.
3) Van Vleteren, *Historie*, p. 100.

of his day (which is not surprising, seeing how closely religious differences nearly always touched political and national differences in those days), had influence in high circles. He appears to have made use of these connections to let it be known that the attitude of the Archbishop might do great harm to the cause of Protestantism [1].

On March 17th the gentlemen from Kent had their interview with the Archbishop. He was not unfriendly, but complained about the rumour touching himself, to the effect that he had been hard in his attitude towards the delegates, and that he had declined to recognize them as "ministers". On the contrary, he declared in effect, I regard you as "teachers", but our church order is closer to the Evangelical order than yours, and the fact that you have no hierarchy is due to Calvin's action in eradicating it from the Reformed churches. The Archbishop repeated the old objection, that as things were, the foreigners constituted a church within the Church and a state within the State. What will become of our baptism, asked the delegates, if presently the second generation is already considered to be English and subject to English church order? Laud tried to satisfy them by pointing out that in any case they would retain the "potestas baptizandi", a poor consolation if this potentiality could never be translated into fact. "We would have the power to baptize but not the exercise thereof". Their request to the Archbishop for intercession on behalf of the foreign churches met with a definite refusal: he had initiated the action himself and it had his full backing. However, he declared himself willing to make an exception for the first generation, "of the first descent" [2]. Before the synod dispersed, a discussion took place with the Vicar General, Sir Nathaniel Brent, at which he tried to secure from the delegates to the synod a binding undertaking, in black and white, concerning the celebration of Communion according to English ritual, obedience on the part of the Community, etc. [3] Their answers were non-committal, which drew the remark from Brent: "I fear that you are taking the wrong road" [4]. Shortly afterwards the final decision of the Archbishop was made known.

---

1) *Ibid.*, p. 108.
2) *Ibid.*, pp. 103 et seq.
3) *Colloquia*, pp. 309 et seq.
4) Van Vleteren, *Historie*, p. 109.

It was to the effect that all the members of the foreign communities had to become incorporated in an Anglican parish before April 1st. The synod on its side decided, before dispersing, to maintain the stand taken, and that the delegates would "in no wise be either the messengers or the instruments of the aforesaid injunction, because it aims at the ruin of the aforesaid communities the which they are bound to foster" [1].

However, Laud did not think of yielding. On April 23rd, 1635, the foreign churches in his archdiocese were served with a writ by which all the members were declared to have been incorporated *en bloc* in their respective Anglican parishes and those born in England, including the ministers, for whom it had previously been intimated an exception might be made, were made subject to the ordinances of the Anglican Church. Those who had not been born in England were allowed their own church order. July 1st was fixed as the final date [2]. Of course, it was once again the London Church to which the threatened communities addressed themselves in their plight. Oddly enough, the magistrate in Canterbury intervened on behalf of the foreign residents, basing his plea largely on economic arguments. But the cute Laud had no difficulty in refuting these arguments [3]. There ensued a silent but stubborn struggle which, however, showed a tendency to drag. The communities practised passive resistance, and tried to find excuses, and Laud, though not budging an inch in his principles, saw himself compelled by all manner of opposition to temper the application of his measure. Thus he declared in a letter written in August 1635 to the Norwich Community (the action was now no longer restricted to his own archdiocese) that "natives of the first descent" would be allowed to continue to belong to their own church community, for the sake of the education of their children, and also in order that the new measures may not be applied immediately in full force. Further, "the natives of the first descent" would no longer be allowed to shirk their financial responsibilities to their own original community — which, incidentally, was in no way detrimental to the State Church, because the foreign residents already contributed to it [4]. In September the Dutch and the French communities in London

---

1) *Colloquia*, p. 312.
2) *Archivum*, III[II], p. 1699.
3) *Ibid.*, pp. 1703 et seq.
4) *Ibid.*, pp. 1712 et seq.

received a similar notification for communication to all the sister communities, with the rather meagre concession that the foreign residents might occasionally also meet for worship in their own churches. The promise that the new members of the State Church would not be troubled with guild rules to which they had not been subjected before, and that for this reason they would be safeguarded from the activities of the informers, had more positive value [1].

Actually the application of the measures was not as severe as might have been expected, even though the Dutch Community in London had reason to complain about members going over to Anglican parishes [2]. As already indicated, there was passive resistance on the one side, and on the other side, a might which found itself challenged by this opposition. Laud was fully conscious of the sabotage of his methods. In December 1635 he wrote to the King: "albeit they made some show of conformity, yet I do not find they have yielded such obedience as is required. . . . so that I fear I shall be driven to a quicker proceeding with them".

A year later, he was more satisfied with the way events were shaping. "The Walloons and other strangers in my diocese do come orderly to their parish churches, and there receive the sacraments and marry, etc., according to my injunctions, with that limitation which Your Majesty allowed" [3]. It was not until May 1637, however, that an order was formally served on the London Community. However, by then there was no longer a question of the use of the Anglican liturgy, at least not in the case of those who were allowed to remain exclusively full members of their own community, namely, the foreign residents who had been born outside England and those born in England "of the first descent" [4]. All the time efforts were being made, often with great cunning, to avoid compliance with the order. This transpires for instance from a letter from the minister of the Norwich Community, Caspar van Nieren, to his London colleague, Van Vleteren, which, incidentally, shows how much depended on the particular place in which the injunctions were being applied. We have been ordered, writes the Pastor Norwicensis, to announce

---

1) *Ibid.*, p. 1745.
2) *Acta* VIII, f° 57 v°.
3) Roper, *Laud*, p. 163.
4) *Archivum*, III[II], p. 1749.

the regulations in the church. If you have not been expressly ordered to do so, do not do it. Meanwhile, we continue as of old, but we try to keep friends with the English clergy. However, the rector of our parish was so unmannerly, that at Easter he made house to house calls with his clerk and ordered the people "of the first descent" to attend Communion "on pain of trouble". We have protested against this. Some have obeyed from fear, others have taken no notice and nothing has happened to them [1].

When the Long Parliament met in 1640 and the opposition against Anglican totalitarianism got a chance of becoming vocal, the foreign communities grasped the opportunity with both hands. In April 1641 they sent a petition to the House of Commons with an account of what had happened and with a direct attack on Laud [2]. In the same year it was decided to address a petition to the King [3]. Pressure and danger had by now passed. Kindred spirits were beginning to set the tone in the United Kingdom. Early in October 1641 there was passed the "Act of Parliament for settlinge the free exercise of Religion and Discipline for the reformed Forreine Churches in this Kingdom accordinge to the Order of theire Churches beyond the seas" [4]. We may look upon this Act as being the outcome of the petition which the Colloquium of 1641 had submitted to Parliament. In the meantime the communities had lost a number of members, for which reason it was decided in 1644 that those who wanted to rejoin would not be turned away [5]. It was Laud who came off worse in these developments. His tragic end is well-known to history. Already in 1641 he had been arraigned by Parliament for high treason and arrested, and in 1645 he was beheaded. By his campaign against the foreign communities he had put an additional weapon into the hands of his opponents. Article 12 of the Bill of Indictment reads to the effect that: He has tried in a treacherous way to bring about division and disunity between

---

1) *Ibid.*, pp. 1752 et seq. The quotation is a paraphrase of the original old Dutch wording.

2) *Ibid.*, pp. 1815 et seq. This document bears no date. Hessels places it in 1640, but this is not correct because no Colloquium was held in that year.

3) *Ibid.*, p. 1875. According to Hessels, this petition was never submitted, submission having been postponed according to *Colloquia*, p. 332. This, however, is not correct. The petition referred to went to Parliament. For the rest, it is not improbable that as this petition was postponed, the same thing happened in the case of the petition to the King.

4) *Archivum*, III^II, pp. 1878 et seq.

5) *Colloquia*, p. 324.

the English and the other Reformed Churches. For this purpose
he has attacked the rights and liberties which had been given by
the King and his predecessors to the Dutch and French churches
in this Kingdom. In divers other ways he has demonstrated his
ill-will and his aversion to these churches, so that through such
a split the papists would have a greater chance of over-throwing
and destroying both"[1]. The accusation was unjust. This had never
been Laud's intention. His episcopalian-catholic conception of
the Church had never been Roman-Catholic, but, and this is the
tragic element in these events, it was utterly foreign to his Puri-
tan-Reformed opponents, incidentally his victims, who were quite
incapable of grasping Laud's conception. The summing up of his
character by Guizot: "Fanatique aussi sincère que dure, sa conscience ne lui reprochait rien", is just, and with this we can
conclude our considerations of the troubles experienced under
Laud. Although we have found it necessary to devote much attention to the other communities, this does not mean that the
London Community was not greatly involved. The contrary
is the case, and in fact the story of these events is illustrative of
the strain to which the London Community was exposed time
and again.

From the Long Parliament nothing but good could be expected. A resolution by the House of Lords, passed in January 1643,
determined that the French and the Dutch communities "shall
haue the Libertie and Exercise of their Religion and Discipline,
as it is vsed beyond the Seas, in the Reformed Churches in seuerall Nations, And as by Charter of King Edward the Sixt, they
haue enioyed it in his Raigne, and since, in the seuerall Raignes of
Queene Elizabeth, and King James; as likewise in the raigne of
his Maiesty that now is" [2]. The Restoration of 1660 did bring the
re-instatement of the episcopal State Church, but the changed
times and circumstances now left little room for troubles like
those experienced before the Commonwealth. True, Charles II
and presently James II, the latter in particular, steered a Roman
Catholic course, but they found too little support in this amongst
their people for it to have been a possible cause of hostile measures against the foreign churches. The "glorious revolution"
exorcised any danger that might have existed, and the Act of

---

[1] De Schickler, Les égl. du refuge, T. II, p. 162.
[2] Archivum, III[II], p. 1905.

Toleration of 1689 guaranteed to the Dissenters complete freedom, once for all. On yet one more occasion did danger threaten.
In 1702, after the death of William III, a "Bill for preventing
occationall Conformity" was introduced in Parliament. The London Coetus protested and secured the support of the Bishop of
London, Henry Compton, who wanted to introduce a petition
from the Coetus in the House of Lords. Several members of the
Upper House co-operated and an amendment was passed which
made an exception in the case of the French and of the Dutch.
However, the amendment was defeated in the Lower House on
the second reading of the Bill. All the same, both parties maintained their standpoint. The Bill was not passed, and thus the
danger was averted, and this time for good [1].

---

1) *Acta*, VIII f° 148 r°.

CHAPTER VI

THE COMMUNITY IN THE
17TH AND 18TH CENTURIES

After the somewhat systematic treatment of our material in the last two chapters, we now propose to return to a more chronological method of relating the fortunes of the London Community. It is no longer the agitated events of the first decades which claim our attention. The pace at which events are moving has slowed down, has become somewhat sluggish, and at times even sleepy. There were actually periods of stagnation and of decline. Yet the history of this independent, isolated Community exhibits a sufficient number of remarkable incidents and developments to repay closer attention to them. Besides, recovery has followed threatening decay. Moreover, there was as yet no question of decline in the beginning of the 17th century. Listen to what the Reverend Calandrinus, continuing Ruytinck's "History" in 1625, writes about the condition of the Community: "in the same way as the church building in those days was in a splendid state of preservation, so the Community flourished and continued to grow ..... The membership was large, and so were the congregations, the sermons learned, powerful and insistent. The religious instruction of the young was carried out in real earnestness, Church discipline was practised and applied in moderation. Several promising young men were enabled to study from the purses of the brethren, in order that in due course they may serve the Church as ministers, so that its reputation grew daily, and its report reached all Reformed churches abroad, which greatly honoured and respected this Community ..... As transpires clearly from the thread of the preceding History, many other churches of the Reformed Religion have from time to time, when in distress and difficulty, taken refuge to ours as to a true Asylum" [1].

---

[1] Ruytinck, *Gheschiedenissen*, p. 490.

After the threat in the days of Laud, there are no further events of such a character as to shake the Community to its foundations. Yet, when we bear in mind the anxiety which the unrest and the confusion in the spiritual and in the political domain, during the Commonwealth and in the years immediately preceding it, have caused the Community, we do link up to a certain extent with the history of the trials due to Laud. The puritanical spirit of the Nonconformists was, on the whole, favourable to the Community, but now danger threatened from the side of rigorous Puritanism which, for instance, took offence at the strolling of young men of the Community in front of the Exchange on Sundays after the service, as happened, when in 1645 a Lord Mayor took office who was an advocate of the strict observance of Sunday [1]. Moreover, similar complaints had already been voiced in 1611 and two years before that the elaborate and costly repasts of the Dutch had given offence. On that occasion the Consistory decided to issue a warning, and if need be, to take appropriate action [2]. In the degree in which the presbyterial-synodal course set by succeeding parliaments adjusted itself under the influence of independent Nonconformity, Dutch communities had cause for concern about another extreme. The Bishops had been relieved of their typically episcopal function, and the High Church festivals were no longer observed by many English people, as lying under a ban of superstition. What attitude should the Dutch adopt in the face of this? Continue with the celebration of Christmas, Easter and Whitsun, decreed the Colloquium of 1646 [3]. In the background of this Puritanism, there loomed the threatening shapes of Independentism, of Ranterism and fanaticism, tendencies to which the evil sounding names of Baptists and Anabaptists were very quickly attached, and with which the London Church, founded as it was on sound continental principles, did not want to have anything to do. The Reverend Calandrinus thought it worth while to have a public debate with a Baptist minister, the object, of course, being to guard his own sheep from straying. There actually were members who showed signs of wanting to secede

---

[1] *Acta* VIII, f° 148 r°.
[2] *Acta* VII, f° 65 v°, 51 v°.
[3] *Colloquia*, pp. 336 et seq.

on account of the question of baptism [1], and there were complaints about Independent Anabaptists who tried to persuade
members to leave the Community, which actually caused the
Consistory to consider submitting a complaint to Parliament [2].
Yet it was deemed wise for the Community to keep its dislike
of such movements in the background and to show some consideration for Puritanism in its extreme manifestations. There
was a case in which some sectarians, evidently followers of
Ranters or Levellers, who were something midway between
undisciplined "Saints" and gangsters, exercised a kind of terror
on those whom they could make suspect of being papists or tra-
ditionalists [3]. But even if there were no serious developments,
there was every reason for treading warily in the face of the
new dispensation with its radical extremes. How much trouble
Cromwell himself has experienced at the hands of the extremists!
A warning received in those days from a well-disposed Englishman goes to show how careful one had to be and how necessary
it was to avoid the appearance of ritualism. It concerned the
space reserved for the Communion table as being "railes", which
had been prohibited by Parliament, and which he thought might
be the cause of disturbances by the mob, with all their attendant
evil consequences. There was no reaction, because the criticised
custom dated from before the analagous custom in the Anglican
Church [4]. In 1648 the question of whether or not to celebrate
Christmas, which might be regarded as a Saint's day, was argued again. In the end Christmas was celebrated [5]. Great efforts
were made to remain Reformed in the strict presbyterian tradition. There was, therefore, no liking for that minister of the
French Community who preached exclusively in the spirit of
the "Saints", and who urged that the King should be executed [6].
In 1644 the Community even arranged for the publication of
the work by Wilh. Apollonius "Consideratio quarundam con-
troversarium quae in Angliae regno hodie agitantur", which
he had compiled on the invitation of the "Classis" Walcheren,

[1] *Acta* VIII, f° 133 v°. Compare with what has been said about Fromenteel see p.
56.
[2] *Ibid.*, f° 158 v°.
[3] A telling example in *Archivum*, III[11], p. 1936.
[4] *Acta* VIII, f° 103 v°.
[5] *Ibid.*, f° 189 r°.
[6] *Archivum*, III[11], p. 2004.

with the object of warning the Westminster Synod of Divines of the threatening dangers of radicalism [1]. In December 1647 the Colloquium submitted a petition to the House of Commons, in which the value of the true Reformed church order was stressed, and the lawlessness on the part of the turbulent spirits, who had been disturbing order in the church, was condemned. The petition called on Parliament to help in maintaining the presbyterial church order of the foreign churches [2]. Confession of faith, catechism, liturgy and church order were all translated into English about that time, partly as a source of reference and partly to serve by way of "letters of credential". We know that all these efforts have not succeeded in diverting the radical course and that Cromwell's "Saints" have for a time held the leadership. These were evil times. The London Community managed to get through without harm, but the one in Colchester uttered a cry of anguish in 1648: situated between the rival armies it had been a close witness of the fighting and the victorious Parliamentary troops had caused great harm to the Community [3]. Of course, London came once again to the rescue; a collection for Colchester brought in more than £ 200 [4]. Three years later Colchester reported that the population of the town consisted mostly of Independents, Anabaptists and Separatists, all very ill disposed towards the Presbyterians, for which reason it was considered inadvisable to hold the planned Colloquium there [5].

These difficulties were the last which the Community had to experience as a result of these external political and ecclesiastical happenings. It is a remarkable fact that the Community has, for all practical purposes, hardly been affected by the stirring events in the political life both of England and of the Republic and in the Napoleonic times. When Charles II made his entry into London, the Dutch Community erected a costly "Arcus triumphalis" for the King. It was decided straightaway to include in the prayers, a prayer for the King and for his cousin the Prince of Orange. The latter was not exactly *persona grata*

---

[1] *Ibid.*, p. 2022. Concerning Apollonius and his book see *Biogr. Woordenboek*, v. *prot. godgel. in Ned.*, part I, i.v.

[2] *Archivum*, III[II], p. 2083.

[3] *Ibid.*, pp. 2129 et seq.

[4] *Acta* VIII, f° 191 r°; *Archivum*, III[II], p. 2136.

[5] *Archivum*, III[II], p. 2201.

in the Netherlands, but family relationships had to be considered[1]!
We have seen that the wars between England and the Republic
have not harmed the London Community. The Roman Catholic
course, on which Charles II embarked towards the end of his
reign and which James II followed very openly, brought no
change in the life of the church of Austin Friars. Actually it
had practically no following in the country. Worthy of mention,
as being a solitary case, is the complaint by the Norwich Community, which the London Church Council told the Ambassador,
Van Citters, had its full concurrence, that trouble was being
experienced from the papists[2]. There are no references in the
minutes, nor in the correspondence, to the "glorious revolution",
nor to the reign of the Stadtholder-King. From its very nature,
the kingship of William III has been favourable to the foreign
residents, even to such a degree as to excite the envy of many
of the English. The utterance by Defoe in his "The True-born
Englishman" is well-kwown:
"We blame the King that he relies too much
   on strangers, Germans, Hugenots and Dutch, etc."
Yet there does not seem to have been any contact between the
Court and the Dutch Church Community. There is an explanation for this, namely that the Court had for its Court Chapel,
established in 1689, its own Dutch chaplains. This arrangement
lasted until 1809[3]. No relations of any sort were entertained
between the Court preachers and Austin Friars. This follows
clearly from an incident in 1742. There was at that time a vacancy
in St. James' and it was suggested that the post should be offered
to the minister of the Dutch community, so as to combine the
two posts. The Bishop of London was prepared to give his support, but the Consistory of Austin Friars considered this solution to be undesirable[4].

From the English side we have a favourable picture dating
from this time, i.e., 1720. John Stow, who was a contemporary,
relates in his "Survey of London": "They have two ministers.
These preach every Lord's Day, and once in the week besides;
and they administer the holy sacrament monthly, the last Sunday

---

[1] *Acta* VIII, f° 262 v°.
[2] *Archivum*, III[II], p. 2680.
[3] Moens, *The Dutch Church Registers*, p. XLI; Burn, *History of the refugees*, pp. 222
et seq., where a list of the chaplains is given.
[4] *Acta* VIII, f° 175 v°.

in the month. The ministers have allowed them a good yearly
salary, and houses to dwell in, conveniently situate neer the
said Church: and competent subsistance allowed also to their
widows. M. Vander Mersch, a merchant and one of their Elders,
at his own cost built a good house for one of their ministers,
which cost £ 400, and after, finished it within at a considerable
further expense; very much to his commendation, and the lasting memory of his charity and good will to this Church. They
maintain their poor at their own charge, which stands them
in neer £ 1,200 per ann., part of which they collect every Sunday,
and week day customarily whensoever there is a sermon, at the
Church door, by Deacons of the Church, who stand there with
basins to receive what the people are pleased to throw in. They
have a fair Almeshouse, built by themselves, standing in Moor-
fields, to contain 26 poor: together with a very handsome room
for their Elders and Overseers to meet in, to consult together
for the good estate and ordering of these poor, as occasion
may require" [1]. Naturally there were also internal difficulties.
We will meet them presently. However, there is one class of
difficulties, anything but rare in church communities, from
which the London Community has been practically free, namely
internal dissensions, partisanship, doctrinal differences, whether
or not connected with the attitude of one of the ministers. The
very rare exceptions, which were in any case of only small importance, prove the rule. In 1640 the Reverend John Ruytinck,
most probably a son of the author of the "History" (see page 87)
was appointed to one of the vacancies. He was an *alumnus* of
the London Community and was minister of one of the other
foreign churches in England. Immediately after he had been called
there arose opposition amongst the members, and there even
appeared a defamatory pamphlet, a most unusal occurrence
in the Community of Austin Friars. It was claimed that his
voice was too weak for the church. It ended with the appointment being revoked and with Philippus op den Beke being appointed. He had acted for a year as assistant to the minister
and had thereby quite possibly obtained a certain following
among the congregation. There had been some unpleasant incidents connected with his election, and this caused the Consistory on the occasion of the house visits which preceded the ce-

---

[1] Quoted in Moens, *The Dutch Church Registers*, p. XLII.

lebration of Communion, to point once more to the unseemliness
of such behaviour. A small difficulty presented itself in connection with the call of Op den Beke. He had only passed his intermediate examination and had, therefore, still to pass his final
examination. The question then arose as to who would examine
him. Should the aid of the French pastors or of the ministers
who were members of the Colloquium be called in? It was decided
that the two other ministers of the London Church would act
as examiners. They questioned Op den Beke for two half days,
after which they pronounced him to be "orthodox, able and
learned" [1]. He has served the Community during 42 years, until
1682, to the mutual satisfaction of the Community and of himself. An incident connected with this same Op den Beke goes
to show that the Community kept a close watch on its ministers.
In 1564 he was on leave in Holland, where he stayed for several
months. The Consistory expressed its displeasure, not so much
on account of his prolonged absence, but because it was said
that he did not preach once during all that time [2].

The difficulties surrounding the person of the Reverend Aemilius van Cuilemborgh were of a somewhat more serious nature.
A rather able and willing, but unbalanced man, possessed of a
violent and impulsive temper, he had come to London from
Heusden in Holland in 1692. There soon developed friction between him and the Consistory. In 1702 the differences of outlook
became so great that it became advisable to part company. The
Consistory accused him of keeping undesirable company, of
slander, and of undignified conduct, and gave him the opportunity of offering his resignation. He asked for respite, but made
matters worse by writing an abusive letter. This caused the
Consistory to dismiss him on the spot, although he had a certain
following among the congregation. Van Cuilemborgh appealed
to the Bishop of London, who summoned the Consistory to
appear before him. The brethren sought the support of the Bishop's Attorney General, which resulted in the Bishop's deciding
to keep out of the dispute as much as possible, though he did
condemn the behaviour of the minister. However, a few days
later both parties were once more asked to appear before the
Bishop, who, on this occasion, was represented by his Chancellor.

---

1) *Acta* VIII, f° 94 v°–96 r°.
2) *Ibid.*, f° 219 r°.

At this interview, Van Cuilemborgh appealed to the Bishop in his capacity as Superintendent, certain members of the Consistory countering this argument by saying that they were ignorant of any such office. For the time being the Bishop kept in the background. Van Cuilemborgh remained obstinate. One morning he mounted the pulpit before a casually collected gathering. It became a real church scandal. Now the Consistory appealed to the Bishop, who declared his willingness to come to the church in person, to compose the dispute. For this occasion Van Cuilemborgh had brought with him a scratch collection of "rabble" which nearly filled the vestry. The Bishop gave his judgment, which put Van Cuilemborgh in the wrong [1]. It was a heavy blow for Van Cuilemborgh, who had clearly not expected this result. He wrote a letter to the Consistory, in which he admitted having been altogether confused, both as regards head and heart, which had even totally incapacitated him from putting up a proper defence of his good right. He maintained that he was innocent; if in matters of small import he had done wrong, he being advanced in years, but never having been in conflict with the Church's censorship, asked for pardon. A few days later, on February 7th, 1703, he sent in his resignation with a claim for a pension [2]. From a few quarters, petitions in his support were addressed to the Bishop, whilst he himself went into hiding, leaving only an address to which communications could be sent. There runs a strain of persecution mania through it all, not at all impossible, considering his unmistakable querulousness. From the aforementioned address he wrote a short letter to his wife which begins: "Dearest child and most worthy angel", the note sounded being in any case a good deal more human than so many formalistic writings dating from that period. The letter gives a clue to the nature and the extent of his misbehaviour of which he had been accused. It concerned mainly his intimate contacts with women and girls — the letter mentions a good many names — but he denies having been guilty of serious misconduct [3]. He got his pension of £ 55 (the Bishop had also put in a good word for him) and went into retirement on the lonely Canvey Island, where he died a few

---

1) *Archivum*, IIIᴵᴵ, p. 2729–2736.
2) *Ibid.*, p. 2743.
3) *Ibid.*, p. 2754.

years later. Also his widow was awarded a small pension of £ 20.
She communicated the news of his death to the Church Council
in a pathetic letter, sending at the same time some of his writings. Amongst them was the (second) supplement of Ruytinck's
"History", which has served to preserve his name [1]. The Bishop's advice to the Consistory that the account of the case
should now be deleted from the records, was superfluous. The
minutes contain no reference to the case apart from a statement,
after it was all over, that a summary will be drawn up. It is
this summary which has been printed in Hessel's "Archivum"
and which relates the sad story.

A century later the Community was once more disturbed by
a difficulty connected with one of the ministers. It concerned
Dr. J. Werninck. He had come from Kalslagen in Holland in
1803 and since 1805 had been the only appointed minister in
London, his former colleague, L. H. Schippers Paal, having two
years previously, for personal reasons, gone to the West Indies
where he subsequently decided to make his home. It may be
mentioned in passing that cases of emigration to the West Indies
were not unknown at that time. Dr Werninck's predecessor, Dr.
Conradus Schwiers, who had been a minister in the Netherlands
East Indies, had, in 1800, gone to Surinam on leave of absence
and had not returned. He had accepted a call as minister to
Berbice on a stipend of fls. 7,000, and had been assisted in the
purchase of a plantation for fls. 162,000, of which fls. 40,000
were to be paid as a first instalment. The minister was permitted to live on the plantation instead of in the town. Had the
church's minister become an owner of slaves? For the rest, his
letters do not lack edifying commonplaces [2]. — To return to Dr.
Werninck. In 1814, when also the place of precentor had become vacant, it was decided to appoint an assistant minister
to take one service a month. When one minister preached the
other would act as precentor. The assistant minister would also
have to take upon himself the pastoral care of the Almshouses,
where he would live rent free. He would receive an annual stipend
of £ 100 plus £ 15 for the service in Norwich (Dr. Werninck
had £ 350) [3]. It was anything but an elegant solution and it

1) *Ibid.*, p. 2765.
2) *Acta IX*, f° 271 v°.
3) *Ibid.*, f° 298 v°.

must be admitted that the status of the assistant was decidedly inferior, but economic considerations weighed heavily. Following enquiries in Leyden, the Reverend R. S. ten Harmsen, who was still studying there, came to London to act as assistant-minister-cum-precentor. Very soon after his arrival he pressed for full status of minister to be given him, saying that otherwise he would leave. After some hesitation the Council decided on fixing the stipend of the two ministers at £ 300 and £ 200 respectively, with rent-free living accommodation and a nominal allowance for the activities attached to the post of precentor. Ten Harmsen accepted. He went back to Holland for his final examination, but when he returned he objected to living in the Almshouses. The sexton thereupon went to live in the Almshouses against payment of rent, which was to be paid by way of indemnity to Ten Harmsen, who, however, never saw a penny of the money. The allowance for the precentorship, £ 25 to each minister, was not paid out until seven years later, but Ten Harmsen declined to accept the money and at the same time resigned his precentorship. This post was thereafter filled by an inmate of the Almshouses [1]. Meanwhile so violent a quarrel had broken out between the two ministers that the elders and deacons found it necessary to write to them telling them to compose their quarrel [2]. It was not until 1820 that there was a reconciliation through the mediation of the Bishop of London and of the clergy of the German Church. Each one of the latter was presented by the Church Council with half an anker (4 imperial gallons) of wine in recognition of their services! But a few months later the quarrel broke out again. After many efforts the Bishop at last managed to effect a peace which proved to be lasting. However, when in 1829 we see the Reverend Ten Harmsen leaving the Community, we cannot rid ourselves of the impression that he was more or less dismissed for fear of worse to come. He received an annual pension of £ 60, which he continued to enjoy in Holland for the next 30 years [3]. It cannot be said that he has brought much joy to the Community or has been of much help to it. The minutes also maintain a charitable silence regarding this affair,

---

[1]) See the *Acta* of those years, *Acta* X.
[2]) *Archivum*, III[11], p. 2862.
[3]) *Ibid.*, pp. 2867–2872.

which is only referred to in a few words after it was all over.

These quarrels fortunately never went very deep. It does not seem ever to have been a case of "odium theologicum". Moreover, if we assess their number by comparison with the long line of ministers, who during the centuries have co-operated. in harmony with each other and the Consistory, the shadow which these quarrels throw on the relations within the Community during all this time, is a very faint one. For these relations have in actual fact been very good. In the first place we can state that cases of friction between the ministers, the elders and the deacons have been extremely rare. When in 1671 the college of deacons raised objections against officiating at the Communion Service a friendly discussion, in which the Scriptural basis of their functioning in this capacity was demonstrated, put the matter right [1]. In 1702 the elders decided on dining together in the "Sun Taverne" every three months, after the meeting [2]. This joint repast after the agenda had been dealt with, later extended to include the entire Consistory, has been kept up to this day, and the notice of the meeting is still worded in the old style [3]. The treasuries of church and deacons have assisted each other repeatedly. For instance, in 1739, it was decided that the pension paid to the widow of the Reverend Bolten would temporarily be a charge on the deacons [4]. In later years, in the 19th century, when the income from the property owned by the Church, increased considerably, it was decided that every three months £ 250 from the accounts of the Church would be transferred to the deacons. In 1890 the amount was increased to £ 100 monthly. In 1908 the sum was fixed at £ 1800 [5]. We have seen that from the very start the material interests of the ministers were well cared for. Utenhove, who was only an elder, though for that matter three parts a minister as far as labour and disposition were concerned, was given an annuity of £ 26 because of his straitened circumstances [6].

---

1) *Acta* IX, f° 1 r°.
2) *Archivum*, III II, p. 2726.
3) It runs thus: "May it be known to Your Worship that the Friendly Gathering of the brethren Elders and Deacons, will be Holden coming .... the .... in the evening at .... o'clock, in the ..... Taverne .... where the presence of Your Worship is requested. Be pleased to express your Worship's consent to the sexton".
4) *Acta* IX, f° 171 r°.
5) *Acta*, of those years.
6) *Kerkeraads-protocollen 1560–1563*, p. 95.

This care also extended to the dependents of the ministers after their death. As early as 1576 there was talk of a pension for widows . The widow of the Reverend Van Vleteren received a pension of £ 30, a not inconsiderable amount for those days, in addition to which she continued to live rent-free [2]. Although the Reverend Van Royen only occupied his post for a short time, just over a year, his widow was, in 1689, awarded a pension for ten years of £ 40 and finally a lump sum of £ 100 [3]. The difficult times through which the Church was then passing, made it necessary in 1739 for the payment to widows to be fixed at a lump sum of £ 100 [4]. Needy or mentally deficient children of deceased ministers were also cared for. As time went on the stipends of ministers were increased. In 1708 the stipend amounted to £ 120 plus an allowance of £ 30 for rent. We need not go into the various increases, but will limit ourselves to a few examples, partly in order to show how appreciation of the minister's work found expression in the stipend. When in 1873 the Reverend Gehle, to whom the Community owed much, resigned, he was awarded a pension equal to his salary of £ 550. His successor, the Reverend Adama van Scheltema, started on £ 450 which, however, was soon increased. In 1883 the stipend was £ 600, and it certainly did not stop at that, also for his successors.

We have seen that for a long time, down to the 17th century, the minister came from within the Community, although even then it was generally accepted that ministers must have studied abroad. The majority of the ministers remained connected with the Church until the time of their death. When in 1685 the Reverend Gerard van der Port received a call to the ministry in Amsterdam, it was the first call for 100 years received by a London minister [5]. The original number of ministers, four, has not been maintained. In 1833 the Reverend Gehle became the first sole minister, and so it has remained after him. Already in 1797 the Reverend Schwiers, in a letter to Holland asking for names to fill a vacancy, wrote that the Community was very small, and that he could easily do the work by himself. All the same he considered it desirable to have a colleague, as

---

1) *Ibid.*, p. 121.
2) *Acta* VIII, f° 113 v°.
3) *Archivum*, III[II], p. 2722.
4) *Acta* IX, f° 171 r°.
5) *Archivum*, III[II], p. 2664.

no assistance can be obtained in case of illness [1]. There was not much zest for coming to London. Two years went by before a candidate offered his services, but the Consistory considered his demands excessive, and so Schwiers remained alone until 1801. In 1722 there had been a curious reversal to the old number of four ministers. Difficulties had arisen concerning the property rights of the Church. It was decided to go to law. For this it was necessary to submit the Charter. Not only was a Superintendent once more appointed (see above page 131) but also, entirely as a matter of form, two additional ministers, namely the minister of the sister community in Colchester and the French pastor in London [2]. After a few years this camouflage was no longer considered necessary. It is perhaps in connection with these measures that permission was given to the ministers in the year mentioned to wear the English clerical dress.

The persons and the activity of the ministers during the centuries following the turbulent early years, do not really call for comment. Though certainly faithful shepherds and teachers they are not remarkable for their outstanding learning or ecclesiastical achievements. An exception was the man whose name has already been mentioned several times, the Reverend Simeon Ruytinck, the author of the "Gheschiedenissen en Handelingen". He was born about 1575, probably in Norwich, whither his parents had fled from Ghent, had studied in Leyden and Geneva as *alumnus* of the London Community, became minister in London in 1601 and died there in 1621. He was a man of many learned interests, especially history and numismatology. He has written a great deal, amongst other works the biography of his friend, the historian Emanuel van Meteren, which is printed at the back of the latter's well-known History. The library of the Community owes its existence to him [3]. His work on the "Gheschiedenissen" (History) was continued by the Reverend Calandrinus, and after him, by the unhappy Van Cuilemborgh. Calandrinus, it should be observed in passing, was serving in an Anglican parish at the time of his call to the ministry of the London Community in 1639. On that occasion a testimonial from 14 clergy of the Anglican Church, testifying

---

1) *Acta* IX, f° 263 v°.
2) *Ibid.*, f° 138 r°.
3) Concerning him see *Nieuw Nederl. Biogr. Woordenboek*, part IV.

to his sound Reformed principles, was obtained [1]. In addition he was asked to sign a declaration to the effect that, if at any time cases of tension in Church matters should arise, he would side with the Community, and would not allow himself to be used as an instrument for introducing foreign ceremonies [2]. About the same time a similar declaration was demanded from the Reverend Proost, who was minister in Colchester, when he received the call to London. Although he was serving the Dutch Community in Colchester, he had previously served in the Church of England, having been ordained by the Bishop of London. He had to declare that he would not consider himself bound to the Anglican Church on the strength of his episcopal ordination or previous canonical obedience to that Church, nor that he would endeavour to introduce its customs into the Dutch Community [3]. In this connection we must bear in mind that these were times of dangerous tensions in Church matters.

Next to the ministers, mention should be made of the schoolmasters, whose appointment and supervision was a continuous care of the Consistory. We meet with them up to the latter part of the 18th century. Some of the members of the Community made special money contributions towards defraying their cost. There were also the private schools [4]. In 1697 two "German" (actually Dutch!) schoolmistresses, who kept a private school, asked for a subsidy for their school and got it [5].

We must also remember the comforters of the sick. They were appointed at irregular intervals i.e. whenever a dangerous epidemic broke out. An instance is the appointment, in May 1636, on the approach of the plague, of Jan Schram as "pest-sicknesscomforter" for a period of six months at a weekly wage of 3 shillings. Many members of the Community went to live in the country, so that there was actually a doubt as to whether it would be worth while holding an extra collection. However, the collection was held and brought in £ 143. It was not until December that the epidemic abated [6].

---

1) *Archivum*, III[II], p. 1804.
2) *Acta* VIII, f° 76 r° et seq.
3) *Ibid.*, f° 134 r°.
4) *Ibid.*, f° 22 r°.
5) *Acta*, IX, f° 92 r°.
6) *Acta* VIII, f° 42 v° et seq.

We have referred above to the small role which, apart perhaps from the very early years, the "odium theologicum" has played in the life of the Community. We find confirmation of this in the favourable opinion which the well-known churchman and pacifist, John Dury, entertained of the Dutch Community. This remarkable man, whom one can best typify by calling him a 17th century advocate of the oecumenical idea, devoted his turbulent life entirely to the ideal of the reunion of the churches, that is within the framework of Protestantism. He pursued this ideal with great persistency and with an indestructible optimism, but, at the same time, with a certain superficiality and under-estimation of the real and fundamental objections to his views. He travelled extensively for the purpose of gaining support for his ideas alike from churches and from governments. On these travels he established connections, collected written evidence of agreement with his ideas, and, in short, moved about as an international figure, propagating the idea of reli-gious tolerance at a time when the word, as well as the concep-tion, were scarcely known, or at least, found but little accept-ance. In his endeavours he had the support of such men as Cromwell and of enlightened minds on the Continent. It is the same Duraeus who, in 1664, wrote to the Dutch Church Council that he regarded the London Community as "the most faithfull and the fittest of any Societie of Christians which I know in England". His duties and his life's work, he wrote, oblige him to live outside England (he was an Anglican cleric). Wherefore he asks the Council whether he might deposit into it's keeping "such public Acts as concern the work which I haue had in hand so many years ago, and which haue with you been given unto me by all the Churches and Uniuersities with which I haue dealt hitherto". He also asked the Council whether it would supervise the education of his daughter and her estate. Should she die a spinster, then her estate would pass to the Dutch Church. The Council accepted these obligations. It ap-pears that at that time the daughter was still in the care of the wife of Mr. Oldenburg, who was the secretary of the recently founded Royal Society [1]. In 1665 Mrs. Oldenburg died and Ol-denburg asked the Counncil whether it would stand by its promise to Duraeus, jointly with himself. However, three years

1) *Archivum*, III[II], pp. 2506 et seq.; *Acta*, VIII, f° 272 v°.

later he married his ward [1]. The Community, therefore, received no material benefits from this arrangement. The relations in which it stood with men of the stamp of Dury, Oldenburg and others, shows the enlightened and tolerant sphere in which the leaders of the Church then moved.

Moreover, we have seen earlier that the dogmatic inflexibility of ideas and way of life had gradually disappeared during the 17th century. The time had gone for resolutions, such as the one taken in 1572, for holding a general censorship in the Church every six months. In the course of the next century cases of censorship disappear entirely from the minutes, where at one time they occupied such a preponderating place that they filled them almost entirely [2]. There is no longer any insistence on applications in every case for permission to get married and of the minute consideration given to each case, which so often led to admonition and postponement. In the 18th century marriages were contracted practically without reference to the Church, and marriages solemnized in the church were the exception where once they were the rule. In 1573, when the French Community proposed a joint petition to Parliament asking for exemption in common with Jews and Quakers from the "Act to prevent clandestine marriages", the Dutch Community did not respond, giving as its reason that marriages in the Church were in any case so very rare [3]. Formally there was adherence to Reformed doctrine. When a young man, who was a Lutheran, wanted to join the Reformed Church, his Lutheran religion was referred to as his "deflection" [4], but in actual practice the attitude taken became more and more broadminded. In 1651 there was a German widow, who, on the point of death, desired to be baptized (in her youth she had been brought up amongst the Mennonites). It was decided that a deputation from the Consistory would point out to her that God's mercy does not depend on "outward and visible signs", but they would tell her that in case she particularly desired it, and it could be done without "superstition", she would be baptized in her home [5]. A sign

---

[1]) G. H. Turnbull, *Hartlib, Dury and Comenius*, Liverpool-London 1947, p. 299.

[2]) In 1707 a case of disciplinary action against a member on account of stealing is mentioned as a rarity. She was denied admission to Communion; *Acta* IX, f° 118 r°.

[3]) *Ibid.*, f° 210 r°.

[4]) *Acta* VIII, f° 2 v°.

[5]) *Ibid.*, f° 205 r°.

that the old interest in questions of dogma had not entirely disappeared, was the request, in 1679, by some young men for the re-instatement of the public Bible Class. The request was granted, but this was no longer the old public, polemical Bible Class held in the Church. It was held for one hour in one of the two vestries, and a set of rules provided all sorts of safeguards against the class deteriorating into a dogmatic tournament [1]. One is inclined to doubt whether it had a long life, because in 1718 it was decided to form a Bible Class for young persons, therefore, rather like the Confirmation classes of today, the remark being added that the young people should understand and speak the language adequately [2]. The following case shows that the Community adhered to the Dutch language as a rampart in defence of its individuality. An English clergyman, in 1756, asked to be allowed to preach in Austin Friars once a week in English. He was probably a Methodist preacher, who wanted to have a pulpit of his own. He offered to pay handsomely. The request was turned down [3]. In 1815 it was once more decided to hold a Bible Class in public on Sunday afternoons, provided sufficient interest was shown. However, by the following year, the interest had evaporated [4]. At about the same time the week-day services appear to have been abolished. Towards the end of the 18th century there are signs that the liberal ideas and the tolerance practised by the London Community were going too far in the opinion of some in the home country. It is possible to conclude this from a remark, made in 1792, by the Consistory of the Reformed Church Community of Rotterdam, to the effect that a letter of commendation issued by the London Community is addressed "to all members of the Community." This, it is observed, might easily include Remonstrants and Socinians. The Rotterdam Consistory accordingly tenders the advice that letters of commendation should in future be addressed to: "Christian Reformed Communities". The letter was read out in the Consistory but the minutes do not reveal what was decided. We need have no doubt on the point [5].

---

1) *Acta* IX, f° 22 v° et seq.
2) *Ibid.*, f° 134 r°.
3) *Ibid.*, f° 209 r°.
4) *Acta* X of those years.
5) *Acta* IX, f° 261 r°.

We could but rejoice in the loosening of the dogmatic confessional ties, and in the weakening of clericalism and its related exclusively ecclesiastical consciousness, if at the same time, the life of the Community had maintained itself in its full strength and intensity. It was not so during this period. This is not the place to enquire into the causal connection between these two developments, though, for a sound conclusion, it is well to remember that they may well have been the result, each in its own way, of a changed mentality, of a new attitude of mind in a process of growing secularization and of criticism which cut deeper as time went on. It is also quite likely that the Great Fire of London, in 1666, had had a serious effect on the material well-being of many members and, in consequence, of the Community as a whole. What is certain is that "la crise de la conscience européenne" set in early, finding its expression in the life of the church in a spirit of moral lassitude and in an abandonment of the old unifying values. In 1646, there are already complaints within the Consistory about "great laxity", even amongst the ministers, elders and deacons, which may cause the Community to backslide. It was decided to call on the brethren to attend the services with greater earnestness and diligence [1]. Two years later the complaint is voiced once more [2]. The minutes show that towards 1670 the meetings of the Council became less important, and that they took less time than they had done before. Also, the Council met less frequently. Where were the days when the Consistory met several times during the week and the spiritual and mundane activities of all members were examined as through a magnifying glass? Between July 1st and October 6th, 1697, only two meetings were called, and these could not be held because of insufficient attendance. This happened again and again in the following years. On October 1st, 1700, only the minister, Van Cuilemborgh, was present. This may have been due to conflicts of personality. One gets the strong impression that the events connected with this minister played havoc with the life of the Church. Often no meetings of the Consistory were held, because, let us admit it, there was nothing to discuss. In 1730 it was decided that the minister should in future call on the members

---

[1] *Acta* VII, f° 165 v°.
[2] *Ibid.*, f° 184 r°, 186 v°.

only once a year instead of twice. Yet, two week-day services,
one in the morning and one in the evening, were still being
held [1]. When in 1739 the Reverend Bolten died, the question
was actually discussed seriously as to whether the financial
resources allowed of a successor being appointed. These business-
like considerations, understandable as they are, reveal a very
different spirit from that existing in 1627, when the Reverend
Carolus Dematius was about to be invited to the ministry and
the Community first devoted a day to fasting and prayer [2].
There were many changes in the personnel of the Consistory
in these years, and the filling of the vacancies was indeed no
simple matter. It was not until 1771 that one person was found
for vacancies amongst the elders dating from 1762 and 1766 [3].
In 1774 there were five vacancies amongst the elders. In 1772
it was decided, on the example of Leyden, that elders should
henceforth no longer accompany the minister on his annual
visits to the members [4]. The minutes for the years 1792–1799
are missing from the minute book of the Consistory meetings.
Must we conclude that no meetings were held, or that any meetings held were so unimportant that there was no occasion for
any minutes? On the arrival of the Reverend Werninck in 1803,
the number of elders and deacons was reduced to six each [5].
This was rather a sensible innovation as the number of places
had been too great. During the course of the 19th century there
have, as a rule, been two elders and two deacons.

The tale of woe, concerning the efforts to acquire an organ,
is symptomatic of the depressing conditions which obtained
during a good part of the 18th century. It was not until 1720
that the Reformed dislike of organ accompaniment to the singing
had been overcome so far, as to make it possible for a group of
members, who favoured organ accompaniment, to collect among
themselves £ 1,000 for the purchase of an organ. It was, therefore, decided to proceed with the purchase, but seven years
later there was still no organ. By that time the wall of the church

---

[1] *Acta* IX, f° 186 r°. But compare p. 154.
[2] *Archivum*, III[1], p. 1341. A picture of all that was connected with the calling
of a minister, is to be found in the same volume on pp. 1343–1350; the day of fasting
and prayer preceding the calling of a minister has not been observed since 1718;
Archivum, III[11], p. 2785.
[3] *Acta* IX, f° 236 v°.
[4] *Ibid.*, f° 239 r°.
[5] *Ibid.*, f° 275 v°.

needed early attention and it was resolved, with the consent
of the contributors, to devote part of this money to that purpose.
In 1742 an elder left a legacy to the Church of £ 100 towards
the cost of an organ, provided that within a year the total sum
required had been collected. Also this effort came to nought.
Twenty five years later an anonymous would-be donor was
prepared to present the Church with a complete organ. He
stipulated that he would have the appointment of the organist
during his lifetime, and that the instrument would be solemnly
dedicated, with "voices and instruments". The organist and
the blower would have to be paid by the Church and this caused
the matter to be dropped. There was no money; the houses
adjoining the church were old and greatly in need of repair.
It was not until 1799 that an organ was purchased, thanks to
an improvement in the finances of the Church [1].

If the story of the organ does not shine in the annals of the
London Community, a very different story can be told of the
library. It was the Reverend Ruytinck, with his gift for learning,
who, in 1605, gave the first impulse towards the formation of
a library for which there was, understandably, great need in
the isolated Community, especially on the part of the ministers,
although also many lay members were interested in theology,
this being a time of theological disputes. From the very beginning great interest was taken in the library. Each year a couple
of members of the Consistory were designated to take charge
of the library. Later, the library Committee consisted of a minister and two elders [2]. As early as 1628 additional bookcases
were needed and provided, and five years later there was question of putting aside special space for the library [3]. However,
in 1647 the bookcases apparently still stood in the vestry of
the deacons at the west end of the Church, close to the entrance [4].
In 1658 it was decided to build a special room to house the library.
The necessary sum of money, £ 250, had been given by a female
member of the congregation. The space above the two vestries (at
either side of the west entrance) and in front of the large west
window was designated for the purpose[5]. Much care and attention
continued to be bestowed on the library. For instance, in 1692, it

---

1) *Ibid.*, f° 136 r°, 146 r°, 176 v°, 177 v°, 229 r°, 266 v°.
2) *Acta* VIII, f° 173 r°, VIII, f° 102 v°.
3) *Ibid.*, f° 18 r°.
4) *Ibid.*, f° 182 v°.
5) *Ibid.*, f° 246 r°.

was decided to remove to a safer place, namely one of the vestries, three folios containing "rare and weighty Letters and
Relics" of Prince William I (William the Silent), Beza and
others, a Turkish Alkoran and a Latin Bible in manuscript,
none of which, by the way, could be borrowed [1]. For the rest,
the conditions attached to the use of the library were very liberal.
There were no restrictions for the ministers. Other users had to
sign their names in a register. The period for borrowing was fixed
at one month [2]. The library continued to grow considerably
during the course of the years. It contained precious old works,
manuscripts, letters, etc. In 1862 the Consistory, therefore,
decided to ask the Committee of the City of London Library,
whether it would be prepared to take into safe custody "the
interesting and valuable and original papers, which have been so
long buried in our library". The bookcases in oak, dating from
1650, a gift from a certain Marie Dupuis [3], would be placed at their
disposal. The negotiations were still in progress when the big
fire in November largely destroyed the church. Fortunately the
damage to the library was found to be comparatively small. It
was estimated at £ 450, and the greater part could be made good [4].
Meanwhile the negotiations with the Committee of the Guildhall
were continued. In 1863 the Council contracted for the entire library
to be taken from Dowgate Hill, where it had been temporarily
stored, to the Guildhall, where it came under the care of the
Corporation of the City of London. When in 1894 a fireproof strongroom was constructed in the church for the purpose of housing
the archives, the manuscripts, which had in the meantime received
expert attention and been arranged in their proper order, were
stored there.

The rich contents of the library have been catalogued many
times. There are in manuscript: two consecutive catalogues
in folio, a third in quarto, one in two parts of 1650 in folio and
a list of donors in quarto. The last printed catalogue dates from
1879 [5]. The works cover for the greater part theological and
philosophical subjects, mostly in Dutch, Latin and English.

---

[1]) *Acta* IX, f° 83 r°.
[2]) *Acta* VIII, f° 278 r°.
[3]) *Index to vol. XXVIII and XXIX*, no. 4448.
[4]) *Ibid.*, nos. 4482, 4491.
[5]) *A catalogue of books, manuscripts, letters, etc. belonging to the Dutch Church,
Austin Friars, London, deposited in the library of the Corporation of the City of London,*
1879.

Some of the volumes are rare and of great importance. Apart
from the printed volumes exceeding 1500 in number, there are
a score or two in manuscript. The collection of letters contains
some important documents. It also includes the correspondence
relating to the Community, amongst which some very curious
specimens are to be found, especially in the correspondence
relating to the first decades. Of particular interest are the
Ortelius letters etc., which, though their substance has no direct
connection with the Church, have contributed not a little to
the value of the collection. These are letters from and to Abraham Ortelius, the Antwerp geographer (1528–1598), letters to
his nephew, Jac. Colius, sometimes called Ortelius, merchant in
London (1563–1628), and a few collected documents, the entire
collection totalling 376 items, covering the years between 1524 and
1628. They were all the gift from Jac. Colius, who was an elder
of the Church. Among them are letters from Erasmus, Dürer,
Budaeus, Arrius Montanus, Marnix van St. Aldegonde, Grapheus,
Coornhert, Donellus, Bonaventura Vulcanius, Clusius, Lipsius
and others. The catalogue of 1879 contains an alphabetical list.
Hessels gives a chronological list in his edition of the Archivum.

This is the right place to refer with a few words to Hessels
and his work. It is largely due to him that the Dutch Church
Community in London has maintained its place in history, and
we may say that Hessels, through his devoted labours, has himself
become a part of that history. Convinced as it was of the significance of its treasured possession, and wishing to make it as
accessible as possible, the Consistory got into communication,
in 1884, with J. H. Hessels, M. A., an erudite Dutch scholar
living in Cambridge, with a view to his arranging the archives
of the Community and editing the entire collection of letters
for publication. It was not suspected at that time that such a
vast amount of work would be involved as ultimately transpired
to be the case. In 1887 the first volume, containing the Ortelius
collection, appeared. In 1889 the second volume (the first one
of the Church's own correspondence) issued from the press.
When Mr. Hessels was getting ready for compiling the third
volume for the press (it has appeared in two parts), he came across
a large number of letters and documents which should have
been included in the second volume. This explains why the earlier parts of the second and third volumes run parallel. The third

part appeared in 1897, completing the work which contains 4,413 items. It is a treasure house for historians, and it will stand as a witness to the historical sense, the industry and the accuracy of the learned compiler [1]. It may be considered something of a rarity that this material has been preserved in so excellent and complete a state, even though in certain periods during the last two centuries fewer documents were preserved than in other periods. The riches of the archives are not exhausted by this publication. Several scores of bindings contain, in addition, the carefully preserved accounts, registers, letters of commendation, etc., not to speak of the minute (Acta) books of the Consistory, Colloquium and Coetus. All is proof of the devotion with which the dignitaries of the Church, ministers, elders and deacons, have, throughout the centuries, fulfilled their task. Mention should finally be made of the fact that a provisional supplement in the form of a calendar of the correspondence covering the years 1874–1900 (including some items unaccountably omitted by Hessels) has been compiled by Mr. J. Rus, Jr. [2]

We can but make a guess as to the use which has been made throughout the centuries of this large library and of the treasures in the archives. The former will undoubtedly have been a source of instruction and of inspiration to the ministers, who, far removed from their native centres of culture and standing more or less isolated from their colleagues, who differed from them in language, habit of thought and culture, no doubt found it difficult to maintain their mental level or raise themselves above it. In later years the documents, whether published or not, have been of service to Dutch and other scholars in their work. Whereas no useful purpose would be served by mentioning names, we should like to make an exception in the case of two such scholars. The first is Prof. Daniel Gerdes, Professor of Theology at Groningen, who, in 1747, was granted the loan, at his request, of important documents from the archives in connection with his work. They were sent over with full precautions for their safety, an inventory of the documents being sealed and signed by Prof. Gerdes [3]. He has made good use of them for the com-

---

[1]) For the complete titles of the volumes see above, page XIII. Although the last two volumes are similar in appearance to the first two, the execution, though excellent, is a little less luxurious because of the growing extent of the work.

[2]) For the title, see above, page 83. For particulars relating to the archives of the Community, see the preface by Hessels for volume III of the *Archivum*.

[3]) *Archivum*, III[II], p. 2838; *Acta* IX, f° 184 r° et seq.

pilation of his "Historia Reformationis" in four volumes, of which on its publication he offered a copy to the library. The well-known Dr. Abraham Kuyper obtained in 1867, through the intervention of the Dutch Foreign Office, the loan of documents belonging to the London Community for the purpose of editing the Church Council minutes.

We have emphasized the streak of light represented by the library in much that was grey in the picture of the life of the Church in the admittedly somewhat sleepy 18th century. By what right, we must ask ourselves, could we expect the London Community to have been an exception to the general spirit in the domain of theology and church life which characterized that century? In times of stress people turn to prayer. Momentous and shattering events cause both tensions and violent discharges, and this applies also to church and religion — but there was no stress nor did chattering events occur. How one misses all fervour in the spiritless sermon in which the Reverend Van Haemstede commemorates in 1750 the second centenary of the Community! [1] No longer did tales of straitened circumstances in the sister communities stir the heart of the London Community. Was there perhaps too great a preoccupation with questions relating to the Church's investments? We read of shares in the South Sea Company which the Church owned in 1729, of the sale in 1744 of £ 1,000 shares in the East India Company at 198% and of their subsequent re-purchase at 176%, the profit of £ 200 to be invested in debentures of the East India Company [2]. Do these transactions reveal, we ask ourselves, that earning interest and making profit was beginning to dull the readiness to make sacrifices for others? However, we must be fair. A special collection for the Community held in 1740 yielded £ 1,100 [3], which does not compare badly with a collection of £ 600 in 1634 (two years later, in 1636, another special collection for the poor yielded £ 800) [4]. In fairness we must also take into account that the ageing church edifice, with its mounting cost of upkeep, imposed heavy burdens on the Community.

---

[1] *Gedachtenis van Gods Wonderen of Jubel-Preek op het Tweede Eeuwgetij der Hervorminge des Godsdienst van Engeland: in het bijzonder der Gifte van de Augustijner Monnikken-Kerke enz. over P.III: 4a*, door Hendrik van Haemstede, Amsterdam 1750. After the service, the day of commemoration was further celebrated together with the French Community by a dinner party in the "Kings' Arms"; *Acta* IX, f° 194 v°.

[2] *Acta* IX, f° 148 v°, 186 r°.

[3] *Ibid.*, f° 171 v°.

[4] *Acta* VIII, f° 33 v°, 54 v°.

CHAPTER VII

THE ADVENTURES OF THE CHURCH BUILDING
THE COMMUNITY IN THE 19TH AND 20TH
CENTURIES

The church building with its adjacent buildings now claims our attention. It is not under-estimation of the significance of the building which had caused its consideration to be postponed to the last chapter. Throughout the centuries Austin Friars has been the fixed centre of the life of the Community, a centre which constituted an asset of great material and spiritual value, though it also brought its responsibilities. We know very little of the appearance of the interior of the old church. A few old representations, they are not contemporary but were made later, do not tell us much. It is only possible to gather a few scattered details from minutes and correspondence. The edifice had a leaden roof, it was whitewashed inside and the ceiling was boarded in. On either side of the west entrance were the two vestries, for the ministers and the elders, and for the deacons respectively. Above these was the library, as we saw in the last chapter, later replaced by the organ. The pulpit stood against one of the pillars of the north aisle, and this has been the position of the pulpit until the thirties of the nineteenth century. In 1661 Prince Joan Maurice of Nassau, "the Brazilian", on the occasion of his stay in London, presented a black velvet cloth to the church, which was to be hung over the pulpit [1]. The Communion table stood against the east wall. In the 17th century there was a question of providing galleried benches for the men. The Ambassador had his own pew. It was an imposing structure, in keeping with the times when formal manners and outward signs of homage were the custom. It was stylishly upholstered and in front of it lay a carpet which at first had been

---

[1] *Archivum*, III[11], p. 2455.

lent by the Reverend Calandrinus [1]. There was also a pew for the graduates. In 1652 the Swedish Ambassador, Spierinck, was given a seat in this pew. An "elegant carpet", for which a hire of ten shillings was paid, was laid in front of it. It appears that the Ambassador was not entirely satisfied with this seat and he asked for it to be made a bit wider [2]. It is unlikely that the church was heated in the early years. In 1844 we read of the purchase of two stoves with underground smoke ducts. The boards which hung above the Communion table and on which were painted the Ten Commandments, the Lord's Prayer and the Apostles' Creed, dated from 1780. They were the gift of Mr. P. van Notten and cost £ 155. As already mentioned, the structure was continually in need of repair. The year 1605 saw extensive repairs, whilst major repairs were executed in 1615, on which occasion the interior of the church was redecorated throughout. The work took a long time and cost a total of £ 1,500 [3]. In 1640 further expenditure had to be incurred. On this occasion the vestries of the ministers and elders were renovated and a new green tablecloth provided. The Communion table got a new cloth and the old one was given to the sexton [4]. A few years later there was once more need of a special collection for necessary repairs. It took the usual form of a circulating list and brought in over £ 630 [5]. In those days the Community was ever ready to make sacrifices for its church. The structure escaped in the Great Fire of London, probably because it was surrounded by open spaces. As from 1718 the church and the surrounding properties have been insured against fire [6].

The reader will remember that the structure which became the property of the Community, comprised the nave with the two aisles, but that the transepts and the chancel, as well as the beautiful tower above the crossing, with its spire, had passed into the ownership of the Marquis of Winchester. It appears that he neglected the upkeep of the tower, so that in course of time the spire threatened to collapse. When in 1609 the Privy

---

[1]) Actually the Ambassador, Joachimi, was badly in arrears with his contributions to the Community.
[2]) *Acta* VIII, f° 207 v°.
[3]) Ruytinck, *Gheschiedenissen*, pp. 201, 313.
[4]) *Acta* VIII, f° 100 v°.
[5]) *Ibid.*, f° 171 r°.
[6]) *Acta* IX, f° 132 r°.

Council drew his attention to the matter, he announced his intention to pull down the tower in its entirety. The Privy Council thereupon pointed out to the Church Council the importance of this monument and asked it to contribute towards the repairs. The Council expressed its agreement, but the matter dragged on, and meanwhile the marquis sold his part of the church to a certain Robinson, who in his turn wanted to proceed with the demolition of the tower. An expert report by the "Viewers" of the City of London, made at the bidding of the Lord Mayor, showed that the foundations and the substructure of the tower were in good condition. Both the Lord Mayor and the Community appealed to the Privy Council on the strength of this report, whilst the Reverend Ruytinck asked the Bishop of London for his intervention. However, in the midst of these deliberations, Robinson, in 1613, had made a beginning with the demolition. It looked as if the demolition was going to be carried out so thoroughly, that also the main piers which supported the tower, as well as the adjacent buttresses which formed part of the east wall of the church, would be affected, resulting in a weakening of the entire east wall. Robinson was ordered by the Privy Council to suspend operations and so this danger to the Community was averted. But Austin Friars had for ever lost its tower, "a special ornament to the city", as the Lord Mayor had expressed it [1].

The transaction in connection with the churchyard to the south of the church, which was to be of such great importance to the material well-being of the Community, dates from about this time. The approach to the entrance of the church led across this churchyard. The ground on either side of the path to the church did not belong to the Community, but was held to be the property of the Marquis of Winchester. Nevertheless, the Community claimed ownership of this ground on the strength of the wording of the Charter of 1550: "concedimus totum templum ac totam terram, fundum et solum ecclesiae" and of a declaration made in 1578 by a past deacon of the Community, Jac. Jansen, the Reverend Saravia, and Em. van Meteren, as well as others, to the effect that the churchyard was the property of the Community, as were also the small houses between the buttresses (which was said to account for their chimneys having

---

1) *Archivum*, III[II], pp. 1216 et seq., 1243–1250.

been built inside the walls of the church, with the consent of
the Consistory. The declaration also stated that it had actually
been the intention to build a house for à Lasco on this very piece
of ground. At that time there had even been a question of sending a petition to Queen Elizabeth on the strength of these
facts, asking for the restitution of the churchyard. — In 1609 the
matter was taken seriously in hand and it was decided to place
it before the Ambassador of the States General, Noël de Caron [1].
The immediate occasion was the annoyance caused by the tenants of the dwelling houses in the churchyard and the use they
made of the spaces between the buttresses. A carpenter piled up
his timber against the wall to a height which caused it to inter-
cept the light, further he disturbed the services with his sawing
and carpentering and prevented the drainage of the ground,
causing the walls to perish, and the church floor, which was
at a lower level, to be affected by the water. Another tenant
had intercepted the light by growing plants against the wall,
and had also caused the wall to be damaged by water, and so
forth. All this had been described already in 1607, in a report
submitted to the Lord Mayor by the sworn "Viewers" of the
City [2], in which report the free disposal by the Church, of at
least the spaces between the buttresses, was claimed on behalf
of the Church. The afore-mentioned carpenter in particular proved
adamant. It was, therefore, decided to pursue the matter to
its end. A lawyer, who had been consulted, had discovered that
the churchyard was not mentioned in the deeds of the marquis,
and that in consequence it had to be regarded as "concealed land",
from which it followed, that it was at the disposal of the King.
The marquis and his highly placed, influential relatives were
found to be open to argument and prepared to consider the good
right of the Dutch Community. A settlement was proposed, under
which the Community would get a lease for a period of 60 years
of a part of the churchyard on the west side, on which a dwelling
house for one of the ministers could be built, as also a strip of
ground alongside the remaining more eastern section of the
south wall of the church, all against a consideration of two Dutch
cheeses and two Westphalian hams to be paid on the feast of
the Annunciation. The Community was grateful but not satis-

---

1) *Acta* VII, f° 3 r°.
2) *Archivum*, III¹, pp. 1202 et seq.

fied. The negotiations were continued with the help of Noël de Caron. On behalf of the marquis they were conducted by his wife. An offer was made by the marquis for the sale of the larger part of the churchyard for £ 500. Was the marquis possibly in need of funds? Whatever the position, an agreement was arrived at. For the sum of £ 600 the Community became the owner of the entire churchyard including the lean-to buildings, let to the two tenants. The agreement was made on September 23rd, 1610, and the following year the transfer, which was confirmed by the King, took place [1]. "In this year, 1611", Ruytinck wrote in his "History", "our Community after great pains mostly taken by Pieter van Laar and Jacques Wittewrongel, elders, and myself (he might also have mentioned Noël de Caron), has for the sum of £ 600 bought and paid the Churchyard situated next to the church, as also the houses built thereon by the Marquis of Winchester" [2].

This transaction proved to be of great benefit to the Church, at that time and more especially so in later years. Two dwelling houses for ministers stood in the churchyard in the early days, the rental value of each house apparently being £ 20 per annum, this being the allowance for living accommodation which those ministers received who did not live in one of these houses. The drying and bleaching of clothes in the churchyard was prohibited, except by permission of the ministers living there [3]. Rather inconsistently, small houses were later on erected between the buttresses of the south wall of the church. After the middle of the 18th century, however, all the small lean-to shops against the wall of the church were demolished [4]. While they were there, these small erections gave rise to many disputes, whenever the tenants encroached on the church wall or, as did happen, constructed smoke ducts or chimneys in the wall or in the buttresses. One can easily imagine that the buttresses, which projected five feet, offered ample scope for this. One tenant, a certain Mr. Hardcastle, gave much trouble in this

---

[1] *Archivum*, III[II], pp. 2900–2905.
[2] Ruytinck, *Gheschiedenissen*, p. 271; compare *Archivum*, III[I], pp. 1209–1223 and pass.; *Acta*, VII, f° 24 et seq. Moens, *The Dutch Church Registers*, p. XXIX states mistakenly that "the church bought from the Marquis of Winchester for the sum of £ 600 a house called the 'kerckof'", an error, which subsequently has been copied by others.
[3] *Acta* VII, f° 182 r°.
[4] *Acta* IX, f° 79 r°, 209 r°.

respect, about the middle of the 17th century, and his widow after him. She even had a privy dug below one of the buttresses! It was a relief for the Church when Mrs. Hardcastle surrendered her rent agreement. The new tenant was not granted any rights to the ground between the buttresses [1]. A more fundamental question arose in connection with tenements erected against the eastern part of the north wall. This wall was not supported by buttresses, but by a section of the old cloister. On top of this section wooden dwellings had been constructed, and even in the cloister itself dwelling accommodation had been provided. People did live on top of one another in the old London! In the beginning of the 18th century these constructions were converted into stables, coach-houses and warehouses, to which end the colonnade of the cloister was removed and the church wall dug into, with a view to enlarging the space for coaches. This gradually caused a considerable weakening of the church wall and forced the Church Council to take steps to protect its rights. It was on this occasion that the Church took recourse to re-instating the office of Superintendent, so that it might with absolute security appeal to the Charter (see above page 133). Expert investigation into the whole matter confirmed the claim of the Church but, at the same time, maintained the rights established through lapse of time, of those who had caused the "encroachments", though on condition that they agreed to the Church's having the wall properly repaired, on payment by them of a lump sum and in addition a small annual rent for a period of 200 years. These repairs were executed in 1722 [2].

Being thus well cared for, the church building continued in existence. In 1862, consideration was given to the removal of the wooden ceiling with the object of re-exposing the oak roofing to view. There was also a question of constructing a memorial window in the west façade, at an estimated cost of between £ 200 and £ 300 [3]. But, in the early morning of November 22nd of that year the Community experienced an overwhelming disaster,

---

[1] *Acta* VIII, f° 192 v°, 195 r°, 216 r°, 235 v°, 247 r°, 252 r°, 257 r°. Apparently this applied to erections against the western part of the north wall.

[2] *Archivum*, III[II], pp. 2793 et seq., 2796–2803, 2807. Twentyfive years later the question threatened to crop up once more, but on this occasion it was promptly solved; *Acta* IX, f° 231 r°. In 1899 a letter from the legal adviser and proxy Tweedie drew attention to the fact that the contract would expire in 1922, whereupon a new contract was made; *Index to vol. XXVIII and XXIX*, nos. 5215, 5217.

[3] *Ibid.*, nos. 4460, 4462.

in that the church was for the greater part destroyed by a fire
caused by a defective chimney. The walls and the pillars withstood the fire, but the roof and the interior were destroyed. However, the library, though damaged, was saved, as were also
the floor monuments. The damage was covered by a £ 9000
insurance.

The question now was, should the church be rebuilt by making
use of the undamaged parts, or should an entirely new edifice
be erected? Some were in favour of the latter solution. They
proposed that a new church should be built in the north west
corner of the old church, after demolition, but fortunately
strong protests were voiced against this suggestion. The Committee of Consulting Architects of the Incorporated Society for
Building and Enlarging Churches, drew the attention of the
trustees to the historic value of the church and to the responsibilities of the trustees arising therefrom. Demolition would mean
"lasting discredit on those who should sanction it" [1]. Also the
minister, Dr. Gehle, pleaded powerfully for restoration, and so
it was decided. At the end of October 1863 a beginning was
made with the restoration. The architects were Edward I'Anson
and William Lightly, the latter a specialist in church building.
On October 1st, 1863, the first service was held, with an entirely
new organ. A central heating plant had been installed. The total
cost amounted to £ 13,097 of which £ 12,250 was covered by
insurance, sales of assets, etc. The style of the interior was neo-
Gothic, which style was greatly in vogue at that time. Fortunately, it did not harmonize too badly with the original style
of the building. The part reserved for the service certainly had
atmosphere. It occupied the eastern part of the nave. The western part of the nave as well as the aisles, had been left free.
The pulpit remained in its old place at the northern side of the
nave against one of the columns; it was the least beautiful piece
of the otherwise handsome church furniture. At a later date,
in the year 1938, the pulpit was removed and a rostrum
constructed against the eastern wall, below the organ, which
had been moved to that position in 1885. Electric lighting was
installed in 1895. During the process of rebuilding, the congregation had been meeting for worship in the chapel of the Mercers'
Company, who were presented afterwards with a piece of silver

---

1) *Ibid.*, No. 4527.

Plate V

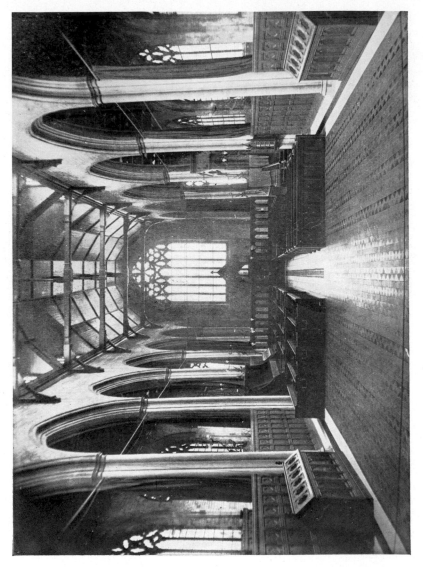

The interior of the restored old church

plate to the value of £ 25. The treasurer of the Board of Trustees, the elder Wijnen, who had been very active in the matter of the rebuilding, received a similar gift. During nearly 75 years the restored church served as the place of worship for the Dutch Community. On three occasions, in 1898, 1899 and 1919, offers were made for the purchase of the church and the valuable site which belonged to it. For obvious reasons these offers were not considered; it is even questionable whether the Trustees would have had a free hand in the matter. In 1901 there was a question of the construction under the church of a tunnel for the underground railway. The plan did not materialize, but considerable expense was incurred in connection with the counter measures which its execution would have necessitated.

Time and again the management of the church and the property owned by the Community, has imposed heavy burdens on the Consistory. The Community has never had a separate council for property management, as have the Reformed churches in Holland, though in the early days two elders were charged with the care of the immovable assets. In 1670 the two ministers, six elders and six deacons were appointed to act as trustees for the properties owned by the Community [1]. In 1799 the entire Consistory, without qualification, was so appointed [2]. In 1901 the minister ceased to be a member of the Board of Trustees, though he continued to attend its meetings [3]. In this connection mention should be made of two gentlemen by the name of Tweedie, who acted as legal advisers and proxies to the Consistory during the second half of the last century. Since 1901 it is the firm of A. F. and R. W. Tweedie which is acting in this capacity. Let no one think lightly of what is involved in the management of the assets of the Community. During the early centuries it has often been a laborious effort to make both ends meet. Gradually the cares became less oppressive, consequent upon the increase in the value of the assets, but to the same degree the administration claimed more time and attention. The assets of the deacons had gradually accumulated since the middle of

---

[1] *Acta* VIII, f° 278 v°.
[2] *Acta* IX, f° 265 v°.
[3] Since 1919 the entire Consistory is acting as trustees for the properties of the former Dutch Reformed Community at Norwich. They do not amount to much. For a time certain payments were made from the income for pensions etc., but this is no longer the case.

the 18th century. By the end of the 19th century they amounted
to £ 11,600, invested in consols. The deacons also owned immovable property in the form of a farm at Barnet. It was acquired
in 1793 by exchange for a piece of land in Huntingdon, which
had been left to the Church in 1738. Whereas its value as grazing
land went down, its value for building sites increased. The question of the disposal of the farm had been under consideration
since the beginning of the 20th century, but it was not until
1924 that it was sold. However, notwithstanding increasing
assets, the means at the disposal of the deacons gradually became
inadequate in the face of the growing needs. The metropolis
continued to attract increasing numbers of people, many of
Dutch nationality. Unavoidably there were among the new
arrivals, persons who had suffered social shipwreck in their own
country. There were also those who went under in the maelstrom
of the great metropolis. In the case of such people of Dutch
nationality the Church Community was the only or the last
refuge. The Community gave unstinted help, be it to individuals
direct, or to philanthropic institutions, such as the Netherland
Benevolent Society (Koning Willem Fonds). Since 1886, the treasury of the Church has assisted the deacons financially by
means of regular payments. It has already been mentioned that
the annual sum so paid amounted in 1908 to £ 1800. The buildings
on the Austin Friars site (the former churchyard had gradually
been almost entirely built over [1]), had increased manifold in
value. The rents had increased considerably in amount. By way
of example we may mention that the building known as Austin
Friars 6, yielded after 1874 an annual rental of £ 750, against
£ 350 previously. In 1880 an expert estimate of the annual rental value of the various buildings amounted to £ 3,725 and in
1882 the rents were accordingly fixed at this amount. After
demolition of these houses, a modern office building, Austin
Friars House, was erected on the site in 1911, by the London
Offices Company Limited, which Company had taken a long
lease of the site. The new building was to be considerably higher
than the old houses had been, and due provision was therefore
made in the lease for the protection of the "ancient lights"
rights of the Church. This has not prevented the church being

---

[1] Burials in the churchyard had been discontinued; interments in the church
took place until 1853.

filled at times with a mysterious, dim light. Living accommodation for the sexton was provided in the new building.

We herewith take leave of the "pars materialis" of our subject in order to devote our attention to the more spiritual aspect. Reference has already been made to the period of stagnation and decline in the 18th century. This decline was not permanent. Despite unfavourable external conditions, the Community has maintained itself as a centre of spiritual life. We may even say that it has actually grown in significance as a centre of spiritual life, be it on a different level from that obtaining during the first centuries of its existence. The esteem in which the church was held has grown with the years, not least because the leaders have known how to preserve its Dutch character, whilst at the same time adapting the church to English conditions and circumstances. It is fitting, at this point, to recall the resolution passed by the Consistory in 1898, on the occasion of the marriage of the daughter of one of its members with an Englishman, that henceforth the use in the services of the Dutch language would be compulsory. The significance of Austin Friars as a national centre, in the past as in the present, has been demonstrated on numerous occasions in its attachment to the House of Orange, which, on its side, has given evidence, in increasing measure, of its interest in the Dutch Church Community. When the Prince of Orange, who, at that time, was Stadtholder of the province of Friesland only, came to England, in 1733, for his marriage to Princess Anna, daughter of King George II, he was ceremoniously greeted by a procession which wound its way from the church to Somerset House. It had been organized by the Consistory, though anyone who felt so inclined could take part in it. It was a stately procession, consisting of 38 coaches, "no hired or common coaches, only private coaches". The Reverend Van Bracht delivered a gracious and dignified address. The Prince subsequently visited the church. He also partook of Communion, though in his private apartments, he himself being seated at a separate table and taking the Communion by himself, after the minister and the elders. Everything, including the details of the departure of their Highnesses from England, was documented in great detail "in futuram rei memoriam" [1]. On the arrival of the hereditary

---

[1] *Acta* IX, f° 155 r° et seq.

Prince of Orange in May 1813, he was welcomed by a deputation from the Consistory [1]. On August 3rd, 1845, King William II visited the church. On April 30th, 1882, King William III and his consort, Queen Emma, who were staying in London in connection with the marriage of the Duke of Albany with the Queen's sister, Princess Helena of Waldeck-Pyrmont, were to have attended divine service at the church, but the sudden death of Princess Wilhelm of Württemberg, the younger sister of the King, prevented them from attending the service. The visit to the church took place a year later. A most solemn memorial service was held in November 1890, on the occasion of the death of King William III. The special mission which subsequently came over to announce the accession of Queen Wilhelmina, attended a service in the church. On April 28th, 1895, Queen Wilhelmina and the Queen Mother, attended a service in the church, which service, at their express wish, bore an informal character. Mention should also be made of the memorial service held on September 28th, 1893, in honour of the deceased Ambassador, Count van Bylandt, to whom the Community owed much, because of his interest and help on many occasions. Of recent memory is the interest in the Church and its gatherings for worship, shown by Queen Wilhelmina in her days of exile in London during the second World War. This interest was shared by the exiled Netherlands Government.

It is due in no small measure to two men that the prestige of the Community has increased considerably during the 19th century. They are Dr. Hendrik Gehle, who was the Church's minister from 1830 to 1874, and the Reverend Dirk Adama van Scheltema, who occupied the pulpit from 1874 to 1901. Reading through the minutes one gets the impression that these two men, by virtue of their gift for organization and their personal qualities, have been of great value to the Community. If, notwithstanding this, the treasurer, Wijnen, could write to deacon Overzee in 1876: "the expectation of any revival here has been frustrated by the loss of so many among the few Dutch, taking any interest in the Church", the cause might be sought, though it is no more than a guess, in the ecclesiastical and theological radicalism of the views held by the Reverend Dirk Adama van Scheltema, with whom, as we saw earlier, modernism made its

[1) *Ibid.*, f° 295 r°.

entry into the Church. In the same year the custom of opening the meetings of the Consistory with prayer, was discontinued. Communion, formerly celebrated four times a year, was now celebrated only twice a year. Another symptom of a new orientation was the substitution, in 1891, of the "Reformed Psalms and Hymns", by the collection published by the Netherlands Union of Protestant Churches [1]. On the publication of the new synodal hymn book a return was made to the Reformed tradition.

If, in some respects, the new orientation might be regarded as a set-back, we must not lose sight of the positive spiritual gain which resulted from it. The Dutch Church Community in London has steadily developed during the last 80 years into a Community, which is characterized by tolerance, and in which there is no insistence on a definite creed. In reality, it was the logical development of a course, which had been set from the start. Even in the early years of the Community's existence we meet with an attitude of caution and moderation, whenever the Church was being confronted with sectarian elements. It was thus in the case of the Van Winghen disputes, and in the position taken up when the Baptists were being persecuted by the Government, all proofs of a broadminded and tolerant outlook. The prosecution to the bitter end of dogmatic differences did not fit in with this attitude, rather the application of the old saying on religious tolerance: unity in essentials, liberty in non-essentials, charity in all things. A church community, like the Reformed Community of London, can only continue to justify its existence by keeping an open door to all those of good will, who, as Christian men and women, are filled with a simple and sincere longing for God, without any trace of exclusivism or narrowness of outlook. This is one of the reasons why the Church receives within its community, Baptists, Lutherans, Remonstrants, even those having no definite connection with any church or denomination, accepts all letters of commendation by whomsoever issued, and gives a letter of commendation on departure [2]. It does this, whilst adhering fully to its basic and

---

[1] In the beginning the change over to the new melodies with their unfamiliar rhythms caused some difficulty; a small kernel of regular worshippers was formed, who, properly trained, could lead the singing.

[2] The letters of commendation are worded as follows: "X, being a member of the Netherlands Reformed Church in London, and as far as known to us not having been guilty of offensive conduct, the members of the honourable Consistory to whom this,

original principle of being a Reformed Community. Whilst in all this a link with the Netherlands Reformed Church is taken for granted, there is no organizational tie with that Church [1].

Exclusivism and intolerance would not have benefited the Church. This becomes fully evident when we consider the position of the Church in the light of the changes, particularly in the second half of the 19th century, in the character and in the composition of the group of Dutch nationals in London. The time had gone when the Church constituted the sole "corpus corporatum et politicum." The Dutch group had grown in numbers, its character now partaking more of that of a floating population, and the Church no longer formed the sole bond between the Dutch nationals. Next to the Church, around it as it were, there had come into existence the Dutch "colony," having its own structure and its own organizations, though the Church continues to this day to fulfil a leading function in the colony. In 1873 the "Nederlandsche Vereeniging" (Dutch Club) was founded, and in 1874 the "Koning Willem Fonds" (Netherland Benevolent Society) was instituted for the purpose of assisting co-nationals in need of help. The officials and the members of the Church have at all times taken a big share in the activities of this and other Dutch philantrropic institutions. All the same, the members of the Church were now also members of the colony. To a great many Dutch people living in London the colony was more important than the Church. It was the

---

our testimonial, will be handed, are requested to recognize the aforementioned X as such, to extend to him their pastoral care and to admit him to the Holy Communion of our Lord Jesus Christ".

[1]) As a typical example of how in the 19th century the Church desired in the one hand to maintain and strengthen the tie with the Netherlands Reformed Church, and on the other hand wanted to preserve its individuality, may be cited the "proposal for simplifying the government of the Church and for a friendly connection with the Reformed Church in Holland", in the archives of the Community, probably from the hand of elder Wijnen, dated April 25, 1866 (*Index to vol. XXVIII and XXIX*, no. 4653) in which the following appears: "without attemping to shackle our successors we might for *their* Government (and our own in the meantime) agree upon Rules for simplifying and better working the machinery of the Church. If it is considered best to have but *one* minister as at present, the "Kerkbestuuren" of one or more of the principal cities and universities might be requested annually (and alternately) to appoint one of their body to visit London (say for *two* months) to officiate during the proposed vacations of the Pastor—with a liberal compensation from the Church. This would keep up a friendly connexion with the reformed church in Holland and interest influential ministers there in ours. No doubt the ministers so chosen by their colleagues would consider it a mark of respect. It will I think much depend on the Interest taken by the Dutch themselves in the church whether it will exist beyond the present generation".

natural outcome of a process of secularization, which in itself
was as irresistable as it was unavoidable. If the Church were
to remain a living force, and if it were to retain its appeal to
the colony, this could only be ensured by the exercise of tolerance
and by keeping an open door. Intolerance and exclusivism would
have done incalculable harm. Successive ministers and members
of the Consistory have understood this and they have acted
accordingly.

Before we take leave of the 19th century, we should call to
mind the celebration, in 1850, of the 300 years' existence of the
Church. This is particularly appropriate, seeing that the present
year, 1950, will witness the celebration of the fourth centenary
Although some irritation had been caused by a circular which
the French Church had sent out in 1848, and which contained
the statement that "the French Congregation retains its normal
occupation of the Church in Austin Friars", it was all the same
decided to commemorate the event jointly with the French.
Amongst other events there was a dinner in the Albion Tavern
in Aldersgate Street at which 80 guests sat down. The inmates
of the Almshouses were given a festive repast in the hall of these
houses. The French Consistory, which at that time still included
two ministers, proposed that the occasion of the jubilee be taken
to issue a joint manifesto. The Dutch Consistory, however, opposed the idea on the ground that it was unnecessary to underline
once more the principles of Reformed Protestantism, moreover
it judged the document to be lacking in tact towards the English and their Church. In 1862 the Consistory of Austin Friars
made an effort for a joint address of condolence on the occasion
of the death of Prince Albert. The French, however, declined
to participate, because of a quarrel which was just then going
on between the two ministers. The Dutch Consistory then sent
an address on its own.

In the beginning of 1901 the Reverend Adama van Scheltema
found himself obliged to resign after a long illness. In his place
the Consistory appointed Dr. S. Baart de la Faille, who was
Netherlands Reformed minister at Krommenie, in Holland.
His ministry in London lasted 28 years. In some ways his spiritual attitude and his leadership differed from those of his immediate predecessors. He belonged to a generation of theologians,

then young, which was inspired by social ideals and which saw in social work the logical consequence, as well as the first condition, of the preaching of the Gospel. To this task the Reverend Baart de la Faille devoted himself with zeal and devotion, supported and inspired by his wife (née Wichers Hoeth). This new course (because that is what it can be called), has undoubtedly been of great benefit to the Community in many ways. The social work of the Church, viewed in connection with the altered structure of the colony as described above, served to strengthen the function it performed within the larger whole, and was a fresh justification of its existence and a recommendation of the Christian message of brotherly love and devotion which it was its task to proclaim. It is obvious that there were drawbacks to this development and they did not fail to reveal themselves. In the first place, there was the danger, to use a biblical image, of a tower being built before the cost had first been counted, as sometimes happened. Plans might be made which exceeded the available resources, both material and human, and this inevitably led to disappointment. Another danger, one not to be under-estimated, was that the attention might be focussed too much on things of this world, and that the activity, or what passed for it, threatened to take the place of the proclamation of the Word, of the bringing of the message of consolation and redemption. Both the gains and the losses have become apparent in the Netherlands, where the social orientation of the first decades of the present century has left clear and broad, though shallow tracks.

We should like to mention a few of the organizations for social well-being. Some were formed by the Church Council itself, or the Council might provide the financial backing, or give indirect financial support [1]. In the very early years of the present century a "Friendship Union" for assisting women, was formed. In 1903 the Commission for Winter-evening Lectures came into existence. The original intention was that the lectures should deal with religious subjects only, but later, the subjects were more general and the meetings no longer took place in the Church, as they did in the beginning. In the same year a district nurse

---

[1] See for the period 1901–1928: H. Baart de la Faille-Wichers Hoeth, *Herinneringen, 28 jaar in de pastorie te Londen*, Assen 1933.

was appointed. At first she worked for a Commission for District Nursing, but later on her activities were controlled by the Church Council. In 1905 a household school was started on a modest scale in the Homes at Charlton. A scheme for giving employment at home, principally needlework for women, was started in 1907. In the same year a beginning was made with the organizing of social evening gatherings in the church for Dutch girls living in or near London. In 1920 the Dutch Home for Women (Neerlandia House for Lady Residents Ltd). was opened. In 1921 a holiday home, "Hollandia", was opened in Southend-on-Sea, for the children who were formerly sent to the Homes at Charlton for a holiday. These institutions have not all survived. Much energy, time and money was spent on them, and often it all ended in disappointment. These activities have at times overshadowed the spiritual side of the activities of the Church, but they have nevertheless contributed to the good name of Austin Friars. Among the factors which operated to the disadvantage of the Church's activities in the social domain, must be mentioned, in the first place, the First World War, when both colony and church were completely isolated, and the very name Dutch was suspect, a suspicion from which even the minister, going about his lawful business, was not free.

Dr. Baart de la Faille found himself compelled, for reasons of health, to resign from the ministry in 1928. The Church Council nominated as his successor, the Reverend J. van Dorp, who was Netherlands Reformed minister in Enschede, in Holland. Both in his person and in his activities this pastor was representative of the theological and general spiritual currents then running in the Netherlands, where in the circles professing unorthodox Protestantism, a deeper consciousness of the eternal values of Christianity, coupled with a closer attachment to the traditions of the Church, had broken through. The Reverend Van Dorp, who was possessed of artistic talent, was a gifted preacher, who used to attract large congregations in the Netherlands. Also in the London church his eloquent preaching touched the hearts of his hearers, and called up the deeper religious feelings of the congregation, thereby bringing many to a closer attachment to Scripture and to the Church. Also during his ministry there occurred events and disasters which have had a profound effect on the life of the Dutch Church: the Second

World War, in which both the Church and its minister were so closely involved [1].

Even before the actual declaration of war on September 3rd, 1939, the Almshouses at Charlton had been evacuated on account of their exposed situation. The inmates were transferred to Libury Hall, Ware, Hertfordshire. They did not return to Charlton after the war. The number of those in need of this kind of help has greatly decreased and no longer warrants the upkeep of a large and costly institution, such as Charlton. The London Community came into direct contact with the miseries of war, when on November 18th, 1939, the Dutch vessel, the "Simon Bolivar", struck a mine in the North Sea. Both the colony and the Church Community have borne a large share in the relief measures for the survivors of this disaster. However, it was not until after May 1940, with the arrival of the Royal House, the Netherlands Government and the big stream of fugitives from the Netherlands, that both Church and colony became thoroughly involved in the work of organizing help and relief. The Church Council was represented on an Emergency Committee for fugitives from the Netherlands and gave active help. In many ways it was as if the days of the struggle for liberty of the 16th century had returned, and London had once more become the safe refuge for all those, in the home country and outside it, who had been hit by the disasters of war. Once again the London Church became a centre for the dispensing of help, spiritual as well as material. In connection with the former, mention should be made in the first place of the addresses which were broadcast by the Reverend Van Dorp, initially for the British Broadcasting Corporation and subsequently for Radio Oranje [2], addresses to which people in the home country listened with avidity and by which so many have been cheered and strengthened. There was the christening by the Reverend Van Dorp on May 31st, 1940, in the private chapel of Buckingham Palace of Princess Irene of the Netherlands, in the presence of our Royal House and of the English Royal Family, an event of equal importance to the Dutch Church Community as to the home country. The elder, who attended the baptism service, was Mr. J. T. C. van Dulken,

---

[1] For a full account see the book by J. van Dorp, *Het licht achter den muur*, Amsterdam 1946.

[2] The Dutch war-time broadcasting centre in London.

Plate VI

The interior of the church of St. Mary

who had been a member of the Consistory during 60 years. Princess Irene was registered as a baptized member of the Netherlands Reformed Church.

The Church in Austin Friars became an important factor for the spiritual care of the members of the Netherlands forces in England (Army, Navy and Air Force) on the appointment of the Reverend Van Dorp, by decree of June 6th, 1940, as chaplain of the Army and of the Navy with the rank of Colonel and Captain respectively. The appointment laid an enormous burden on the shoulders of the minister. In the beginning he faced the task, which had to be executed under the most difficult circumstances, by himself. It was not until some time later that other Dutch ministers came to assist him, under his general guidance. These arrangements continued in existence for some time after the end of the war. After September, 1944, contacts could again be made with that part of the Netherlands which had been liberated. This led to an increase in the activities of the ministers. After 1945 the Reverend Van Dorp continued for a couple of years to act as chaplain for those members of the forces, who had not yet been repatriated, or who were undergoing training in England. There is no need to give a detailed account of his activities as chaplain of the Army and of the Fleet. They only touched the Community indirectly and are moreover fully dealt with in his book "Het Licht achter den Muur" (The Light behind the Wall). Mention should, however, be made of the fact that the spiritual care exercised by the minister also extended to the sailors of the Netherlands Mercantile Marine (the minister of the Dutch Church was a member of the Committee of the Christian Seamen's Union).

Let us now return to the church building. In the night of the 15th to the 16th October, 1940, during one of the heavy air bombardments of London, a landmine attached to a parachute, sucked into the space enclosed by the higher office buildings surrounding the church, fell on Austin Friars. The explosion completely destroyed the church. A few pages from the Bible which was in the pulpit, some fragments of the walls and of the monuments, were all that remained of the edifice, which was reduced to a mountainous heap of rubble and dust. Also the strongroom containing the archives and the beautiful silver christening bowl had been destroyed, though the precious contents were fortunately found to have sustained practically no damage (the valuable antique silver Communion vessels and salvers had been deposited in the safe of one of the City banks). The disaster happened in the early morning of Tuesday, October 16th, but already on the following Sunday the Community met for worship, now in the air-raid shelter of the bank building of the firma B. W. Blydenstein & Co. in Threadneedle Street, where it gathered consolation and strength from the sermon on the text taken from Daniel IX : 17.

Expressions of sympathy, as well as offers of help, poured in from all sides. The British and Foreign Bible Society provided Dutch Bibles. Financial help on a considerable scale came from an unexpected private donor. It was greatly needed, because owing to the damage sustained by the office building which, as mentioned above, stands on ground belonging to the Church, making it impossible of occupation, ground-rent payments had stopped. But the most touching help came in the form of an offer, for the use during an indefinite period, of a church building. When on February 15th, 1939, the Hugo Grotius Society for International Law caused a memorial tablet commemorating Grotius to be un-veiled in the church, one of the invited guests was the Venerable, the Honourable S. H. Phillimore, Archdeacon of Middlesex, son of the founder of the Society, Lord Phillimore. Immediately after the disaster, the Reverend S. H. Phillimore communicated with the minister of the Dutch Church and drew his attention to a vacant church building in the West End of London belong-ing to the Church of England where he, the Reverend Philli-more, had at one time occupied the pulpit. He undertook to obtain the consent of the Bishop of London for the temporary use of this church by the Dutch Community. And so it was decid-ed. The church of St. Mary, Bourdon Street, Berkeley Square — a fine and friendly church building of moderate size built in the neo-Gothic style of the middle of the last century — was temporarily placed at the disposal of the Dutch Church Com-munity, rent-free, the only condition being that of upkeep. Also in this respect the 16th century had returned, in this case not with its distress and struggle, but in the unstinted help and brotherly hospitality with which England and its Church came to the rescue of those who had been hard hit and were in deep affliction. On October 27th, 1940, the first service could already be held in St. Mary's. The congregation has worshipped there ever since [1], and will continue to do so until the new church in Austin Friars is built. In 1950 a start will be made with the building of the new church. When the congregation moves into the new church, St. Mary's will go down under the hammers of the demolishers, because it will not revert to its former use as a Chapel of Ease of St. George's, Hanover Square. The church of St. Mary, a most attractive building will, however, continue to live in the memory of the present generation of church goers. May future generations continue to treasure the memory of the help and support thus given, a help and support worthy of the benefactors of 1550.

Many years had to pass and much had to happen, before those of Dutch nationality who had remained behind in London, could join the congregation of the Church on May 6th, 1945, in a solemn Service of Thanksgiving for the liberation of the Netherlands. During these years the Church Community was a centre which radiated activity, a source of encouragement for Dutch men and women in London and all over the world, and a central point where contacts in diverse departments of life were made and maintained. As an instance we may cite the day of prayer on October 22nd, 1944, at which time the distress in Holland was nearing its peak, the service from the church, which was filled to capacity, being broadcast to the Netherlands. These difficult years have contributed greatly to the good name of the Dutch Church in London and to the esteem in which it is held. Its existence had tended to be forgotten in the home country, whereas now the Church is an actuality to many. The composition of the Community has changed in certain respects from what it was before the war. Of the old members only a few remain; many are dead or have moved. The preponderant part of the host of Dutch nationals, who came to swell the congregation in and after 1940, has either returned to the Netherlands or has emigrated. A practically new congregation will have to come into existence, with the help of the old nucleus. The greater part of the old members of the Consistory are still at their posts, tried and experienced men, who have steered the ship through

---

[1] Whenever Queen Wilhelmina was in London during the war years she attended Divine Service in this house of prayer of the Netherlands Community. Also many connected with the Government, and soldiers and sailors went to church in St. Mary's.

Lindeboom   13

the difficult years. The Reverend Van Dorp felt that the responsibility for the rebuilding of the Community, also of its church, should be vested in younger hands than his. He was succeeded in 1946 by the Reverend R. H. van Apeldoorn, who had been active under his direction as chaplain of the armed forces, and who, prior to this, had been minister in Witmarsum. In February 1949 the Reverend Van Dorp died in England.

The Reverend Van Apeldoorn has devoted himself to his task with ability and energy. It is a task which makes great demands on the capacity for organization and on the physical stamina of the minister. The consideration of the future prospects of the Church does not come within the scope of this book. However, there is one aspect to which reference must be made, and that is the contacts with other Dutch-speaking parts of the world, particularly with South Africa. The contact with South Africa is of long standing. As far back as 1818 the Consistory of the Dutch Reformed Church in Cape Town approached the London Consistory with the request for the regular exchange of information, with the object of maintaining contact with the Church in the Netherlands with possible benefit to the organization of the Cape Church. Prior to this, that is during the Republic, the contact with the Reformed Church in the Netherlands had been maintained via the "Classis" Amsterdam. As a result of the transfer of the Cape to England, this contact had been broken, and this is the reason why this endeavour was made to re-establish contact through the medium of the kindred community in England [1]. The Church Council, in a letter written on its behalf by the Reverend Werninck, declined the request on the ground that at no time in the existence of the Church since 1550, "had there been any connection with the churches in Holland or in the Dutch possessions in other parts of the world" [2]. The letter from the Reverend Werninck then continues to the effect that the affairs of the Church, during the recent Napoleonic war, have not been dealt with by the Consistory, but by him in his private capacity, and he readily offers his services in this capacity to the Cape Church Council [3]. It is obvious that this is not what the men in South

---

[1] *Archivum*, III[II], pp. 2864 et seq.
[2] This was not entirely correct, but it does once more show the extent to which the Community valued its autonomy.
[3] *Archivum*, III[II], p. 2866.

Africa had had in mind. They wanted official contacts, and so this effort came to nought, though it is not excluded that personal contacts were made and that these persisted for a time. There would anyhow have been an important precedent for such contacts. In 1806 the Evangelical Hymnal had been introduced into the Reformed Church in the Netherlands. London wished to follow this example, but copies could not be sent from Holland because of the war. The London Community, therefore, arranged in 1813 to have the hymnal printed in London. Spare copies of this edition were made available for other churches outside the Netherlands. The churches in South Africa made use of this opportunity. By way of guarantee of the authenticity of the text, the hymn books were marked as follows: "This Evangelical Hymn Book has been printed and published under the supervision of J. Werninck, S. S. Theol. Doctor, Minister of the Netherlands Reformed Community in London and member of the Zeeland Society for Learning in Middelburg". The hymnal was introduced into the churches in South Africa on the second Sunday in January, 1814 [1].

The contact with Austin Friars continued to exist, though in an unofficial way. The Dutch Church in London has always been the spiritual centre of contact for the Dutch from South Africa, who have never had a church building of their own in London. Their marriages have been solemnized in the church and they have had their children baptized there. The wedding, in 1908, of Miss M. M. Botha, the sister of the South African prime Minister, Louis Botha, was an important event. In 1928, on the occasion of the unfurling of the flag of the Union of South Africa in Trafalgar Square, the minister of the Dutch Church in London, in the company of the Bishop of St. Albans, asked, in a prayer pronounced in the Dutch language, a blessing on the new standard. On December 16th, 1938, the centenary of Dingaan's Day was commemorated in the church of Austin Friars. During the second World War, the Reverend Van Dorp was on many occasions invited by the British Broadcasting Corporation to broadcast to South Africa. It was in one of these broadcasts that he communicated to the Dutch in South Africa

---

[1] Statement by Prof. Dr. S. P. Engelbrecht in *Almanak van die Nederduitsch Hervormde Kerk van Afrika*, 1941, 35e jaargang, p. 74.

the news of the calamity which had befallen the London Community. The sermon delivered by the Reverend Van Dorp on the occasion of the service of intercession on October 22nd, 1944, for the Netherlands, had to be repeated for broadcast to South Africa.

The endeavour on the part of the Church Council to renew the contact with the numerous Dutch population in South Africa, and to broaden the basis of such contact at a time when, after 400 years, the Community is entering upon a new phase in its existence, not only constitutes an act of foresight, but it links up with a past which goes back nearly 150 years. In the Autumn of 1949 the Reverend Van Apeldoorn undertook a tour of the churches in South Africa, where he found, not only great appreciation of what the Church had done for their members in the past, but also warm approval of suggestions for closer co-operation in the future. The gratifying result of this visit has caused the Church Council to decide, that every two months, beginning with 1950, a minister from South Africa, who is completing his studies in Holland, shall be invited to preach in the London Church and to work for a few days amongst his compatriots in London. To this end the assistance will be sought of someone in the South African Community in London, who will act as the connecting link [1].

We like to end this book on this hopeful note. The South African plan is only one indication among others, which goes to show that the Dutch Community of Austin Friars, which has its roots in so rich a past, and which but recently has sustained great trial in adversity, still has a future before it. The extent to which the past, which it has been our endeavour to bring to life, can have significance for the present, is brought home to us by the following quotation from J. Huizinga's "Man and Multitude in America": "Once transferred to the new country of his choice, the emigrant has now little contact with the historical past which colours the life in the mother country". This is so. Many an emigrant finds himself in the new country

---

[1] This co-operation will be expressed symbolically in the new church, the pews for which will be made of South African wood, the gift of the Protestant (Nederduitsch Hervormde and (Nederduitsch) Gereformeerde) churches of South Africa.

During a visit to the United States of America by the Reverend Van Apeldoorn in the latter part of 1949, the Reformed Churches there of Dutch origin, offered to present the organ to the new church.

without a historical background to his surroundings, and this spells impoverishment of the inner life. Not so in London, where the Church of Austin Friars provides Dutch nationals, be their stay long or short, with a link with the old, rich past, with the old, dear mother country, and with the old, tried Faith.

CHARTER OF KING EDWARD VI, GRANTING THE CHURCH OF THE
AUGUSTINE FRIARS, LONDON TO FOREIGN PROTESTANT REFUGERS

EDWARDUS SEXTUS DEI GRACIA ANGLIE FRANCIE / et hibernie Rex
fidei defensor et in terra ecclesie Anglicane et hibernice supremum
caput Omnibus ad quos presentes littere peruenerint, salutem. Cum
magne quedam et graues consideraciones / nos ad presens specialiter
impulerunt Tum etiam cogitantes illud quanto studio et charitate,
Christianos Principes in sacrosanctum Dei Euangelium et religionem
apostolicam ab ipso Christo inchoatam / institutam et traditam ani-
matos et propensos esse conueniat sine qua haud dubie politia et
ciuile Regimen neque consistere diu neque nomen suum tueri potest
nisi principes ceterique praepotentes viri / quos deus ad regnorum
gubernacula sedere voluit, Id in primis operam dent vt per totum rei
publice corpus casta sinceraque religio diffundatur et ecclesia in uere
christianis et apostolicis opinionibus / et ritibus instituta et adulta per
sanctos ac carni et mundo mortuos ministros conseruetur, pro eo quod
christiani Principis officium esse statuimus inter alias grauissimas de
regno suo bene / splendideque administrando cogitaciones etiam religioni
et religionis causa calamitate fractis et afflictis exulibus consulere
Sciatis quod non solum premissa contemplantes et ecclesiam a / papatus
tirannide per nos vindicatam in pristina libertate conseruare cupientes,
uerumetiam exulum et peregrinorum condicionem miserantes qui iam
bonis temporibus in regno nostro Anglie / commorati sunt voluntario
exilio Religionis et ecclesie causa mulctati quia hospites et exteros
homines propter Christi Evangelium ex patria profligatos et eiectos et
in regnum nostrum profugos / praesidijs ad vitam degendam necessarijs
in regno nostro egere non dignum esse, negue Christiano homine neque
Principis Magnificentia dignum esse, duximus cuius liberalitas nullo
modo in tali / rerum statu restricta clausaue esse debet ac quoniam
multi germane nacionis homines ac alij peregrini qui confluxerunt et
innies singulas confluunt is regcum nostoum Anglie ex germania et
alijs / remotioribus partibus in quibus papatu dominatu Euangelij
libertas labefactari et premi cepta est, non habent certam sedem &
locum in Regno nostro vbi conuentos suos celebrare ualeant vbi inter
sue / gentis et moderni Idiomatis homines Religionis negocia et res
ecclesiasticas pro patria ritu et more intelligenter obire et tractare
possint Idcirco de gracia nostra speciali ac ex certa sciencia et mero
motu / nostris Necnon de auisamento Consilij nostri volumus concedimus
et ordinamus quod de cetero sit et erit unum templum siue sacra edes

Ciuitate nostra Londoniensi quod vel que vocabitur Templum Domini Iesu vbi / congregacio et conuentus Germanorum et aliorum peregrinorum fieri & celebrari possit eo intencione et proposito vt a ministris ecclesie Germanorum aliorumque peregrinorum Sacrosancti Euangelij incorrupta interpretacio sacramentorum / iuxta verbum Dei et apostolicam observacionem administracio fiat de templum illud siue sacram edem illam de vno superintendente et quatuor verbi Ministris erigimus creamus ordinamus et fundamus per proesentes / Et quod idem Superintendens et Ministri in re et nomine sint et erunt vnum corpus corporatum et politicum de se per nomen Superintendentis et Ministrorum ecclesie Germanorum et aliorum peregrinorum ex fundacione Regis Edwardi / sexti in Ciuitate Londoniensi per presentes incorporamus ac corpus corporatum et politicum per idem nomen realiter et ad plenum creamus erigimus ordinamus facimus et constituimus per presentes et quod successionem / habeant Et ULTERIUS de gracia nostra speciali ac ex certa sciencia et mero motu nostris necnon de auisamento Consilij nostri dedimus et concessimus ac per presentes damus et concedimus prefato Superintendenti / et Ministris ecclesie Germanorum et aliorum peregrinorum in Ciuitate Londoniensi totum illud templum siue ecclesiam nuper fratrum Augustinencium in Ciuitate nostra Londoniensi, Ae totam terram fundum et solum ecclesie predicte exceptis / toto Choro dicte ecclesie terris fundo et solo eiusdem HABENDUM et gaudendum dictum templum siue ecclesiam ac cetera premissa, exceptis preexceptis, prefatis Superintendenti et Ministris et Successoribus suis TENENDUM / de nobis heredibus et successoribus nostris in puram et liberam elemosinam DAMUS vlterius de auisamento predicto ac ex certa sciencia et mero motu nostris predictis per presentes concedimus prefatis Superintendenti / et Ministris et Successoribus suis plenam facultatem potestatem et aucthoritatem ampliandi et maiorem faciendi numerum Ministrorum et nominandi ac appunctuandi de tempore in tempus tales et huiusmodi subministros / ad seruiendum in templo predicto quales prefatis Superintendenti et Ministris necessarium visum fuerit Et quidem hec omnia iuxta bene placitum Regium volumus preterea quod Johannes A Lasco nacione Polonus homo propter / integritatem et innocentiam vite ae morum et singularem erudicionem valde celebris sit primus et modernus Superintendens dicte ecclesie et quod Gualterus de Loenus Martinus Flandrus Franciscus Riuerius / Ricardus Gallus sint quatuor primi et moderni Ministri DAMUS preterea et concedimus prefatis Superintendenti et Ministris et successoribus suis facultatem, aucthoritatem et licenciam post mortem vel / vacacionem alicuius Ministri predictorum de tempore in tempus eligendi nominandi et surrogandi alium personam habilem et idoneum in locum suum Ita tamen quod persona sic nominatus et electus presentatur et sistatur coram nobis / heredibus vel successoribus nostris et per nos heredes vel successores nostras instituatur in ministerium predictum. DAMUS eciam et concedimus prefatis Superintendenti Ministris et successoribus suis facultatem / aucthoritatem et licenciam post mortem seu vacacionem Superintendentis de tempore in tempus eligendi nomi-

nandi et surrogandi alium personam doctum et grauem in locum suum
Ita tamen quod persona sic nominatus et electus / presentetur et sistatur
coram nobis heredibus vel successoribus nostris et per nos heredes vel
successores nostros instituatur in officium Superintendentis predictum
MANDAMUS et firmiter iniungendum precipimus tam / Maiori Vicecomi-
tibus et Aldermannis Ciuitatis nostre Londoniensis Episcopo Londiniensi
et successoribus suis cum omnibus aliis Archiepiscopis Episcopis Iusti-
ciarijs Officiarijs et Ministris nostris quibuscumque quod permittant
prefatis Superintendenti / et Ministris et sua suos libere et quiete frui
gaudere vti et exercere ritus et ceremonias suas proprias et disciplinam
ecclesiasticam propriam et peculiarem non obstante quod non conueni-
ant cum ritibus et ceremonijs in Regno nostro / vsitatis absque impetici-
one perturbacione aut inquietacione eorum vel eorum alicuius Aliquo
statuto actu proclamacione iniuncione restriccione seu vsu incontrarium
inde antehac habitis factiseditis seu promulgatis incontrarium non
obstantibus Eo / QUOD expressa mentio de vero valore annuo aut de
certitudine premissorum siue eorum alicuius aut de alijs donis siue
concessionibus per nos prefatis Superintendenti Ministris et successoribus suis ante hec tempora factis in / presentibus minime facta existit,
Aut aliquo statuto actu ordinacione prouisione siue restriccione inde
incontrarium factis editis ordinatis seu prouisis, Aut aliqua alia re
causa vel materia quacumque in aliquo non obstante IN / CUIUS rei
testimonium has litteras nostras fieri fecimus patentes, TESTE me ipso
apud Leighes vicesimo quarto die Iulij Anno regni nostri quarto. .per
breve de priuato sigillo & de datis praedicta auctoritate parliamenti.

P. SOUTHWELL.

[*Large Wax Seal*]

FULL TRANSLATION OF EXTENDED TRANSCRIPT

Edward the sixth by the grace of God, King of England, France and
Ireland, Defender of the Faith, and on earth the Supreme Head of the
Church of England and Ireland, To all to whom these present letters
may come, Greeting, Whereas certain great and grave considerations
now have especially moved us, We, also bearing in mind with how
great zeal and charity it behoves Christian princes to be animated and
inclined towards the most holy Gospel of God and to the apostolic
religion, commenced, instituted, and delivered by Christ himself, without which doubtless, politics and civil government can neither long
subsist nor preserve their name, except princes and others in great
authority, whom God has willed to sit at the helm of kingdoms, make
it their first care that pure and undefiled religion may be spread abroad
throughout the whole body of the commonwealth and that a church
founded and brought to maturity in truly Christian and apostolic
doctrines and rites, may be served by holy ministers, dead to the flesh

and the world: And Because we account it to be the duty of a Christian Prince, among other most weighty cogitations respecting the wise and glorious government of his realm, to take thought also for religion and for exiles who for the sake of religion are broken with calamity and afflicted:

Know Ye therefore that we — not only having regard to the aforesaid premises and desiring to preserve in her pristine liberty, the Church which we have delivered from the tyranny of the Papacy, but also having compassion for the state of the exiles and foreigners who, for some time past, have resided in our realm of England, having submitted to voluntary banishment for the sake of religion and the Church, because we thought it neither worthy for a Christian man or for the manificance of a prince, whose liberality ought in no way to be restricted or niggardly in such a state of affairs, that strangers and foreigners, banished and cast out from their own country for the sake of the Gospel of Christ, and taking refuge in our realm, should stand in need of necessary subsistence: And Whereas many men of the German nation and other foreigners who have poured in and every day continue to pour in to our realm of England from Germany and other more distant parts in which the liberty of the Gospel had begun to be weakened and hard-pressed by the domination of the Papacy, have no fixed seat (sedem) and place in our realm where they may hold their assemblies, where, among men of their own race and their present speech, they can intelligently discuss and treat of their religious affairs and ecclesiastical business according to the rite and custom of their country — of our special grace, certain knowledge, and mere motion, and also with the advice of our Council, will, grant and ordain that from henceforth there may be and shall be one temple or holy church in our city of London, which shall be called the Temple of the Lord Jesus, where a congregation and meeting of Germans and other foreigners may be held and celebrated, to the intent and purpose that there may be, by ministers of the Church of the Germans and of other foreigners, an incorrupt interpretation of the most Holy Gospel and administration of the sacraments according to the word of God and Apostolic Observance; and such temple or sacred building of one superintendent and four ministers of the Word, we, by these presents, erect, create, ordain and found, and, that the superintendent and ministers may and shall be, in fact and name, one body corporate and politic of themselves, by the name of the Superintendent and Ministers of the Church of the Germans and other Foreigners of the foundation of King Edward VI in the City of London, we, by these presents, incorporate, create, erect, ordain, make and constitute them, really and to the full, by the same name, a body corporate and politic and (grant) that they may have succession.

And Further of our special grace, certain knowledge, and mere motion, and also with the advice of our Council, we have given and granted and by these presents do give and grant to the said superintendent and ministers of the Church of the Germans and other foreigners in the City of London all that temple or church lately belonging to the Augustinian

Friars in our City of London, and all the land, ground and soil of the aforesaid Church, except the whole choir of the said church (and) the land, ground and soil of the same.

To have and enjoy the said temple or church and other the premises, except before excepted, to the aforesaid superintendent and ministers an their successors; to hold of us, our heirs and successors in pure and free alms.

Moreover we give, by the advice aforesaid, and of our certain knowledge and mere motion aforesaid, and by these presents do grant to the aforesaid superintendent and ministers and their successors, full faculty, power and authority to amplify and make greater the number of ministers, and from time to time to nominate and appoint such and the like under-ministers to serve in the aforesaid temple as to the aforesaid superintendent and ministers may seem necessary; and, that all these things may be at the royal pleasure, we will that John à Lasco, a Pole by race, a man very famous on account of the integrity and innocency of life and manners and singular learning, to be the first and present superintendent of the said church; and that Walter Loenus (sic), Martin Flandrus, Francis Riverius and Richard Gallus, be the four first and present ministers.

Further we give and grant to the aforesaid Superintendent and Ministers and their successors faculty, authority and licence, after the death or voidance of any of the aforesaid ministers, from time to time, to elect nominate and depute another able and fit person in his place; so nevertheless that the person so nominated and elected shall be presented and brought before us, our heirs or successors, and by us, our heirs or successors instituted into the ministry aforesaid.

We give also and grant to the said superintendent ministers and their successors faculty, authority and licence, after the death or voidance of the superintendent, from time to time to elect, nominate and depute another learned and grave person in his place; so nevertheless that the person so nominated and elected be presented and brought before us our heirs or successors, and by us, our heirs or successors instituted into the office of superintendent aforesaid.

We order, and firmly enjoining, command as well the Mayor, Sheriffs and Aldermen of our City of London, the Bishop of London and his successors, with all other our Archbishops, Bishops, Judges, Officers and Ministers whomsoever, that they permit the aforesaid superintendent and ministers and their successors freely and quietly to practise, enjoy, use and exercise their own rites, and ceremonies and their own peculiar ecclesiastical discipline, notwithstanding that they do not conform with the rites and ceremonies used in our Kingdom, without impeachment, disturbance or vexation of them or any of them; any statute, act, proclamation, injunction, restriction or use to the contrary thereof, heretofore had, made, published or promulgated, to the contrary notwithstanding. Albeit express mention of the true annual value or of the description of the premises or any of them, or of any of the gifts or grants by us, before this time made to the aforenamed superintendent, ministers and their successors, be, in the presents made too little; or any statute, act, ordinance, provision or restriction thereof to the contrary made, issued, ordained or provided, or any other reason cause or matter whatsoever in anyway notwithstanding.

In Witness whereof we have caused these our letters to be made patent,

Witness myself at Leighes the 24th day of July, in the fourth year of our Reign, by writ of Privy Seal, and of date aforesaid, by authority of Parliament.

P. SOUTHWELL.

[*Large Wax Seal*]

LIST OF MINISTERS OF THE NETHERLANDS
REFORMED CHURCH IN LONDON
1550–1950

1. 1550. Marten Micron, born in Ghent, left for Norden 1554.
2. 1550. Wouter Delenus, born in Alkmaar (?), died in London 1563.
3. 1559. Petrus Delenus, born in Alkmaar (?), died in London 1563.
4. 1559. Adriaan van Haemstede, born in Zierikzee, excommunicated 1560.
5. 1562. Nicolaas Carinaeus, arrived from Jennelt (East Friesland), died in London 1563.
6. 1563. Godfried van Winghen, arrived from Sandwich, died in London 1590.
7. 1569. Bartholdus Wilhelmi, born in Naarden (?), left for Dordrecht 1572.
8. 1569. Joris Wybo (Georgius Sylvanus) arrived from Emden, died in London 1576.
9. 1572. Joh. Cubus, of London, left for Antwerp 1577.
10. 1572. Jac. Regius, arrived from Coventry, died in London 1601
11. 1580. Joh. Soillot, of London, died in London 1598.
12. 1580. Joh. van Roo, of London, died in London 1583.
13. 1581. Assuerus Regemorter, born in Antwerp, died in London 1603.
14. 1585. Lucas van Peenen, arrived from Ghent, died in London 1586.
15. 1592. Jac. Wibo, of London, died in London 1593.
16. 1594. Joh. Marquinus, of London, died in London 1599.
17. 1601. Joh. Regius, arrived from Biggekerke, died in London 1627.
18. 1601. Simeon Ruytinck, born in Norwich, died in London 1621.
19. 1604. Leon. Moyart, arrived from Domburg, died in London 1606.
20. 1608. Ambrosius Regemorter, arrived from Wezel (?), died in London 1640.
21. 1624. Wilh. Thilenus, arrived from Grijpskerke (Zeeland), died in London 1638.
22. 1628. Timoth. van Vleteren, arrived from Zoutelande, died in London 1641.
23. 1632. Jeremias van Laren, arrived from Arnemuiden, died in London 1638..
24. 1639. Caes. Calandrinus, arrived from Stapleford Abbots, died in London 1665.
25. 1641. Phil. op den Beke, of London (assistant preacher), died in London 1682.
26. 1644. Jonas Proost, arrived from Colchester, died in London 1667.

27. 1668. Sam. Biscop, arrived from Colchester, died in London 1700.
28. 1680. Ger. van der Port, arrived from Vrouwepolder, left for Amsterdam 1691.
29. 1686. Joh. van Royen, arrived from W. Souburg, died in Londen 1687.
30. 1687. Adr. van Oostrum, arrived from Zwijndrecht, left for Amsterdam 1716.
31. 1692. Aem. van Cuilemborgh, arrived from Heusden, resigned 1703.
32. 1702. Will. Biscop, arrived from Serooskerke, left 1712 for Middelburg.
33. 1711. Theod. Bolten, arrived from Breda, died in London 1739.
34. 1714. Ludolfus de With, arrived from Wijk bij Duurstede, left for Utrecht 1717.
35. 1718. Paulus Colignon, arrived from Haaften, died in London 1728.
36. 1728. Herm. van Bracht, arrived from Hardinksveld, died in London 1735.
37. 1735. Fred. Dan. Bongardt, arrived from Sluis, died in London 1737.
38. 1737. Marten Adr. de Jongh, arrived from Nederhorst den Berg, left for Maastricht 1749.
39. 1740. Henricus van Haemstede, arrived from Ouwerkerk, died in London 1765.
40. 1751. Henricus Putman, of Amsterdam (candidate), died in London 1797.
41. 1765. Melchior Justus van Effen, of Utrecht (candidate), died in London 1797.
42. 1784. Dr. Conradus Schwiers, previously minister in the Dutch East Indies, resigned 1802.
43. 1801. Dr. Lamb. Henricus Schippers Paal, arrived from Ouderkerk a.d. Amstel, resigned 1804.
44. 1802. Dr. Jan. Werninck, arrived from Kalslagen, resigned 1833.
45. 1815. Rutger Seyen ten Harmsen, active from 1814 as candidate-assistant preacher, resigned 1829.
46. 1830. Dr. Hendrik Gehle, arrived as candidate, resigned 1873.
47. 1874. Abraham Dirk Adama van Scheltema, arrived from Purmer, resigned 1901.
48. 1901. Dr. Samuel Baart de la Faille, arrived from Krommenie, resigned 1928.
49. 1929. Johan van Dorp, arrived from Enschede, resigned 1940.
50. 1946. Rudolf Herman van Apeldoorn, arrived from Witmarsum, army chaplain.

INDEX

Abbott, archbish., 129, 136
Adama v. Scheltema, the Rev., 82,
   161, 184, 187, 205
Acontius, 43, 45
Albert, prince-cons., 84
Anna v. East-Friesland, 4, 22
Anson, Edw. I', 180
Apeldoorn, the Rev. Van, 194, 196,
   205
Apollonius, the Rev., 152
Arminius, 54
Arundel, Rich. of, 12
Asche, Ant., 30
Assonleville, d', 40
Ayton, the Rev., 106

Baart de la Faille, the Rev., 187,
   189, 195, 205
Baart d. l. F.-Wichers Hoeth, H.,
   188
Baerle, Joh. van, 109
Balck, Ysbr., 92, 93, 106
Beke, the Rev. Op den, 156, 204
Beke, Van, der, 35
Bert, Petr. de, 52
Bert, Pieter de, 52
Berti, Franc., 6
Beuningen, Coenr. v., 75
Beverningk, Van, 76
Beza, 169
Blakers, Amele, 66
Bohun, Humphrey de, 11
Boisot, 36
Bolten, the Rev., 160, 168, 205
Botha, L., 195
Bracht, the Rev. Van, 183, 205
Brent, Sir Nath., 140, 143, 144
Browne, Rob., 70, 97, 144
Brune, Pieter de, 64
Bucer, 3
Buckingham, 137
Bullinger, 4, 7
Bulteel, the Rev., 139, 140
Bylandt, count of, 184

Cabelliau, Liv., 86
Calandrinus, the Rev., 100, 151,
   162, 174, 204
Calvin, 7, 19, 25, 27, 48, 144

Carinaeus, the Rev., 40, 46, 204
Caron, Noël de, 95, 122, 125, 178
Cats, Jac., 109
Cheeke, 6
Christian II, 21
Cecil, Will., 30
Charles I, 78, 125, 128, 136–142
Charles II, 108, 149, 154
Citters, Van, 154
Colius, Jac., 171
Comenius, 81
Compton, bish., 149
Cooltuyn, the Rev., 48
Cooke, Dr., 6
Cornelis, N., 74
Corput, the Rev. v.d., 58
Coverdale, 12
Crane, Sir Francis, 109
Cranmer, archbish., 3, 4, 7
Cromwell, Ol., 57, 81, 126, 127, 152
   153
Cromwell, Rich., 109
Cromwell, Thom., 12
Cubus, the Rev., 34, 59, 204
Cuilemborgh, the Rev. Van, 132,
   133, 156, 158, 162, 167, 205

Damselius, the Rev., 106
Datheen, 17, 18, 90, 93
Delenus, Petr., 15, 23, 30, 40, 43,
   46, 67, 204
Delenus, Wout., 6, 8, 15, 19, 22,
   23, 25, 199, 202, 204
Dematius, the Rev., 168
Dorp, the Rev. Van, 189–191, 194,
   195, 205
Drake, Sir Francis, 36
Dulken, J. T. C. v., 190.
Dumasius, 30
Dupuis, Mary, 170
Duraeus, Joh., 143, 164, 165
Dyrkinus, 28

Edward VI, 3, 6, 8–11, 20, 30. 128
Elizabeth, Queen, 29, 30, 36, 37,
   119, 127, 128, 148, 176
Emma, Queen, 183
Engelram, Joh., 50
Erasmus, 3, 12

Fontanus, Joh., 83
Franck, Seb., 53
Frederick IV, Elect. Palatine, 80
Frederick V, Elect. Palatine, 78
Fromenteel, Ahasv., 56, 151

Gehle, the Rev., 161, 180, 184, 205
Gerdes, Dan., 172
Gogh, Mich. v., 76
Gomarus, 86, 97
Grindal, archbish., 31, 57, 138
Gustav Adolph, 80

Harboe, 20
Have, Ten, 73
Hawley, bish., 133
Henry VIII, 3, 29
Haemstede, Adr. v., 30, 41–46, 67
Haemstede, the Rev. H. v., 172
Hardcastle, 178
Harmsen, the Rev. Ten, 159
Hessels, J. H., 171, 172
Hieronymus, Godfr., 44
Holbroeck, L. v., 53
Hommius, the Rev. F., 89, 94–96
Hoper, 15, 20
Horenbeek, Joh., 98
Hulsius, 68
Hunnings, 6
Huygens, Const., 109

Irene, Princess, 190

James I, 101, 114, 121, 124, 134,
   135, 148
James II, 148, 154
Jansen, Jac., 176
Joachimi, 141
Joan Maurice of Nassau, 174

Kinderen, Abr. der, 52
Knox, 6, 29
Korton, elder, 168
Kuenen, Abr., 83
Kuyper, Abr., IX, XI, 51, 173

Laar, Pieter v., 178
Lambregts, Pieter, 86
Lamotte, elder, 83
Laren, Arn. v., 87
Laren, the Rev. Jer. v., 87, 204
Lasco, J. à, 3, 4–8, 10, 15–17, 19–
   27, 31, 46, 52, 90, 117, 199, 202
Latimer, 3
Laud, archbish., 71, 80, 102, 107,
   110, 136–148
Liebaert, Corn., 95, 96
Lightley, Will., 180
Louise of Orange, 80
Loyseleur de Villiers, 60, 118

Luck, Cath., 44, 67
Luther, 2

Manchester, earl of, 80
Margaretha of Parma, 40
Marnet, the Rev., 142
Mary Tudor, 20, 29, 30
Menno Simonsz, 22
Mersch, Van der, 155
Meteren, Em. v., 44, 67, 84, 162,
   176.
Micron, Maart., 4, 5, 6–8, 14–17,
   20–25, 33, 90, 91, 199, 202, 204
Middleton, Sir Thom., 126

Niclaesz, Hendr., 53
Nieren, the Rev. Van, 146
Norris, Sir John, 36
Notten, P. v., 175

Obry, the Rev., 106
Ochino, 3
Oldenburg, 164, 165
Ortelius, 171
Over, Roland, 41
Overall, 94
Overzee, deacon Van, 184

Parker, archbish., 138
Paulus IV, 29
Peenen, the Rev. Van, 97, 204
Phillimore, S. H., 192
Plancius, 120
Plockhoy, 57
Port, the Rev. Van der, 161, 205
Poujade, the Rev., 102
Poulett, Sir Will., 13
Primerose, the Rev., 141
Proost, the Rev., 95, 141, 163, 204
Pijper, F., IX.

Radermaker, Joh., 100
Raet, Aeg., 129
Rauweel, 72
Regemorter, the Rev., 86, 141, 204
Regius, the Rev. Jac., 34, 36, 59, 97
   204
Regius, the Rev. Joh., 54, 100, 204
Regius, Tob., 10
Reynolds, Conr., 130
Richardson, 95
Richardus Gallus, see Vauvilius
Riche, Sir Rich., 13
Ridley, bish., 10
Riverius, see Rivius
Rivius, Franc., 8, 199, 202
Robinson, bish., 133
Robinson, 176
Roo, Jac, de. 86
Roo, elder Van, 93

Royen, the Rev. Van, 161, 205
Rus Sr., J., XII
Rus Jr., J., 172
Ruytinck, Joh., 85
Ruytinck, the Rev. Joh., 87, 155
Ruytinck Sr., the Rev. Sim., 54,
    83, 86, 94–96, 123, 131, 162, 169,
    176, 204
Ruytinck Jr., the Rev. Sim., 87

Saravia, 176
Satler, Jann., 44
Saudys, archbish., 138
Schelven, A. A. v., IX, XII
Schippers Paal, the Rev., 158
Schoonenberg, Hendr., 48
Schorstick, George, 68
Schram, Jan, 163
Schultens, 82
Schwiers, the Rev., 158, 162
Selnavus, the Rev., 49, 59
Somerset, 3, 7
Soubise, 142
Spierinck, 175
Stel, Hans, 67
Stouppe, J. B., 103
Stow, John, 154
Stretes, Will., 6
Suffolk, duchess of, 6
Sylvanus, see Wybo

Taffin, 34, 97
Tay, Mart., 52
Textor, Will., 68
Tilly, 78
Trabius, see Balck
Turquet de Mayerne, 141
Tweedie, 179, 181
Tyler, Wat, 12
Tyndale, Will., 2

Utenhove, 5–8, 14–25, 28, 30,
    33, 40, 52, 160

Vauvilius, Rich., 8, 197, 202
Velsius, Just., 39–41, 52
Verbeke, Jan, 68
Verhaeghe, Math., 66
Vermiglio, 3
Vermuyden, Corn., 55, 56, 83, 109
Vleteren, the Rev. Van, 139, 161,
    204
Voetius, 97
Vorstius, 94

Walsingham, 36
Warninck, Eliz., 65
Watkines, J., 74
Wayd, Armigall, 6
Werninck, the Rev., 158, 168, 194,
    195, 205
Westphal, Joach., 20, 22
Wilhelmi, the Rev. Barth., 34, 49,
    59, 204
Wilhelmina, Queen, 184, 192
William I, King (o.t. Netherl.), 184
William II, King (o.t. Netherl.),
    184
William III, King (o.t. Netherl.),
    184
William III, King Stadth., 149,
    154
William IV, Stadth., 183
William Louis, Stadth. o. Fries-
    land, 97
William of Orange, 33, 36, 51, 92,
    118, 168
Winghen, the Rev. Van. 34, 46–
    51, 59, 97, 204
Wittewrongel, Jacq., 178
Wittewrongel, 65
Wybo, Jor., 49, 204
Wijnen, elder, 181, 186.

Zuylen van Nijevelt, Van, 17
Zwingli, 26